# "I'm Not a Giver-Upper"

The Story of Juliana Irina Carver – A Little Girl Who Waged War Against Cancer 8 Times

Written by

John W. Carver, III

(Juliana's Dad)

Edited by Tamara Carver

(Juliana's Mom)

A Portion of the proceeds, from this book, will be donated to The Children's Cancer Foundation
They provide a grant, to a Pediatric Cancer Researcher, in Juliana's name each year.
https://childrenscancerfoundation.org/

My wife, Tammy, and I would like to thank:

Our parents and siblings.

Our surviving children (Rebecca, Matthew, Lindsay, Timothy and Kristina) for their amazing patience and love as Juliana fought cancer for so many years.

Current and former members of Faith Outreach Chapel

Our extended family members and friends.

Iryna (Juliana and Kristina's birth mother)

The country of Belarus

The Cohen, Bromley and Thompson Families

Juliana's fans from around the world that said so many prayers for her and sent cards and gifts to cheer her up.

Emily Kolenda – Juliana's hospital buddy

Believe in Tomorrow
(https://believeintomorrow.org/)

Casey Cares (http://caseycares.org/)

Children's Cancer Foundation (http://www.childrenscancerfoundation.org/)

Cool Kids Campaign (https://www.coolkidscampaign.org/)

Children's Roads to Recovery (http://www.childrensroadstorecovery.org/)

Giant Food (giantfood.com)

Make a Wish (www.wish.org)

Give Kids the World (http://www.gktw.org/)

Chef Robert Irvine and Robert Irvine Foundation (http://www.robertirvinefoundation.org/)

Strong Hope Foundation (http://stronghopefoundation.org/)

America Red Cross (http://www.redcross.org/)

Lighthouse Family Retreat (https://www.lighthousefamilyretreat.org/)

Amy Baldwin (for creating "Angels for Juliana" on Facebook)

Gauge Digital Media
https://gaugedigitalmedia.com/

"Juliana was memorable in many ways. I will always be reminded of her lovely smile, her unwavering resolve (no matter the adversity), her ever so kind affect and way (Juliana was always polite; she never hesitated to put down her iPad when spoken to, she would look me in the eye, and pleasantly address my litany of questions). Juliana's spirit and her inner strength were uplifting. She clearly loved both you and Tammy; bearing witness to the family interactions was reaffirming. Needless to say, although she is missed by many, her impact remains meaningful and indelible."
Yoram Unguru, M.D., MS, MA

## Chapter 1

Our story goes back to 1987 when I was working at Caldor Department Store in Westminster Maryland. By that time, in my life, I came to believe that I would have to remain single for the rest of my life because I couldn't imagine any woman loving me. When May 1987 rolled around I thought it would be like any other month. Then, one day, the personnel manager introduced me to my new part time employee who was going to work in my photography department which I was in charge.

WOW! She was blond, had a beautiful tan and her name was Tammy. I had a secret desire that, one day, I would marry a girl named Tammy. Within a few weeks I had the courage to ask her out but it came out all wrong. I said, "Do you think anyone would mind if we went out for dinner one evening?" That sounded so stupid but she agreed to have dinner with me.

Months passed and we began to fall in love. On April 16, 1988 Tammy and I were married. We were both introverts and didn't mind just staying home and enjoying each other's company. After we got married we moved into an apartment in Reisterstown Maryland. Within six months we bought our first home in Baltimore Maryland.

In 1989 Tammy and I talked and decided to start trying to have children. Tammy and I were, both, working full time but having children was a priority. Months passed and no pregnancy. Year one, year two, year three and no children would come into our lives. We would see relatives, friends, co workers and neighbors have children and we were not conceiving.

Year four, year five, year six came and went and we, always, came home to a quiet house void of little feet running around and playing with their toys. One day, I saw a news program on Romanian orphans and how desperate the lives of these children were as they were starving and lived in horrible conditions.

I had a conversation, with Tammy, about adopting internationally but she decided to keep trying to conceive. Year seven, year eight passed with no children. Finally, Tammy agreed that we should look into adopting a child.

One day, one of my insurance clients called me and asked me to come see her. I drove to her apartment and she told me that she was pregnant (again) and did not want her child. She knew that Tammy and I were trying to start a family so she asked if we would be interested in adopting her child. I asked her to give me a couple days to talk to Tammy and I would get back to her.

A couple days passed and I went back to see my client and I was devastated. My client decided to have an abortion instead of waiting for me to come back and tell her we would love to adopt her baby. The agony and guild, I carried, lasted for many years.

A few weeks later, I contacted Catholic Charities (I am not Catholic) and proceeded to ask to start the process of them helping us adopt a child. I was shocked to find out that they would not help us because we are not Catholic.

Next, I contacted the Baltimore Maryland Department of Social Services in order to go through the process of adopting a child. The color of the child did not matter to us and, at the time, there were a lot of black children who needed permanent parents. My client, I mentioned earlier, was black and it didn't matter to me because a child is a child is a child. I was told, by Social Services, that they would not allow us to adopt a black child because we are not black. I was disgusted.

That was the last straw. We were going to adopt internationally because, from our limited experience, the system in America was screwed up. In late 1997 I started contacting adoption agencies around the country. They sent me packets of information to review. One day in 1997 I received a phone call from a woman named Terry. Terry is an adoptive mom who used one of the adoption agencies we received information in the mail.

She said Ron Stoddart who was the Director of Nightlight Christian Adoptions was flying into the area to hold a seminar about international adoptions and we were invited to attend. Tammy and drove to Gaithersburg Maryland, where the seminar was held, and was amazed.

At the end of the seminar several families walked up to the front with their adopted children. We found the adoption agency we wanted to help us adopt children. It was Nightlight Christian Adoptions out of California. We started the process of applying to adopt a boy and a girl from Russia.

We moved from Baltimore Maryland to a house in Catonsville Maryland where there was a back year and the house was not attached to other houses like our house in Baltimore.

Tammy quit her job to be a stay-at-home mom. In February 1998 we flew to St. Petersburg Russia to adopt a little girl name Ksenia (who was almost five years old) who we renamed Rebecca and a little boy (who was two and a half) named Ivan we renamed Matthew. Our family was complete. Everyone welcomed our new children.

In early 1999, Tammy received a lump sum from her retirement account where she used to work. I remember the day when she asked why don't we use this money to adopt a baby? Of course, I agreed. We contacted Nightlight Christian Adoptions and on December 1, 1999, while in St. Petersburg Russia we adopted a six month old little girl named Alina who we renamed Lindsay.

Our house was starting to get a little cramped. It was a three bedroom ranch style house. Rebecca and Lindsay shared a room and Matthew had his own room.

We were done adopting children. In the year 2000 I had this "bright idea" to take my parents on a humanitarian trip back to Russia and bring a lot of clothes, medicines, shoes, toys and other things children might need to live in orphanages. Our church, Faith Outreach Chapel, jumped at the chance to help.

One day, I was shopping for the humanitarian trip at a Wal-Mart in Ellicott City Maryland. I had two shopping carts full of items for several orphanages. I was pulling one cart and pushing the other. I was half-way to the front of the store, to pay to the merchandise, when my cell phone rang. It was Ron Stoddart, Director of Nightlight Christian Adoptions, to say that he heard we were going back overseas to help some orphanages.

Remember, I was half-way from the back of the store heading to the front of the store which happens to be where the intimate apparel is displayed. Ron and I began to talk and he mentioned that he knows of a little boy, in the same orphanage where Matthew and Lindsay lived, who needs a home but a few families have turned him down because he had some minor health issues.

I said, "Ron, we are broke…we just adopted Lindsay less than a year earlier." He said, "Okay." Before he hung up I asked Ron the age of this little boy he was talking about. He looked up the file and said his birthday is May 4, 1999. I started yelling, "WOW…WOW…WOW." Chills were going down my arms. Remember where I am standing…across from the intimate apparel section. I noticed that people started to stare at me, I am sure, thinking I was some pervert.

I asked him to check the birthday again. He did and confirmed it was May 4, 1999. I said, "Ron, that's Lindsay's birthday." This could not be a coincidence. Weeks later, while my parents and I were in the orphanage where Matthew and Lindsay lived the orphanage director walked in this little toddler named Sergie. I sat on the floor and played with him and told him, in Russian, my name is John. The orphanage director, across the room, spoke up and said (in Russian) "No No Daddy." It seems Sergie was going to be our fourth child.

In late May 2001 Tammy and I traveled back to Russia, with our other three kids, and adopted Sergie who we renamed Timothy. His eyes were crossed and, in the Russian, culture that seemed to be a sign of some sort of mental delay.

Within a few months of being back in America we had Timothy's eyes corrected.

Our family was complete. Within a few weeks of Timothy joining our family we moved into a larger house in Westminster Maryland.

## Chapter 2

By 2002, our four kids were the center of our lives. After all, we were done adopting and our family was complete. In late 2002 I have another "bright idea." This time, I decided to begin to help other families learn about international adoptions by hearing our adoption story. We did a lot of advertising and marketing with hopes that a lot of people would show up and fill the banquet-size-room we rented at a hotel. I called Ron Stoddart and asked him to mail me a lot of information from his agency.

Ron told me that he was going to fly, from California, to Maryland where we were holding the seminar to help us help families learn about international adoptions. We did more marketing because, if Ron Stoddart, was flying all the way from California we had to have a full banquet room. The day came, for the seminar, and only eight people showed up. Ron brought a photo album of children, who lived in orphanages in Russia and Belarus, who needed moms and dads. No one signed up to adopt. We were devastated and embarrassed.

We held the seminar, told our story and Ron shared the details on what the steps were to get started in the adoption process. Not one person signed up to adopt. Tammy and I were humiliated.

We gathered all the material we brought to help a room full of people become adoptive parents and went up to Ron's hotel room. Tammy and I could not apologize enough times to Ron after he spent all that money flying to Maryland with the understanding that a lot of people were going to show up for our seminar. While we were talking Tammy and I were, casually, flipping through Ron's photo album of orphaned children who were available for adoption.

We kept coming back to this little, tiny girl with crossed eyes. It's as if her eyes were speaking to us. I began to cry and walked out of the hotel room out of embarrassment and confusion why I was crying because we were done adopting kids. Was it because her eyes were crossed like our son Timothy's eyes were crossed or was there something else?

I walked back in the room and found out the little girl lived in Minsk Belarus and her name was Irina. She was born on December 4, 2001 and weighed 2,220 grams and was 47 centimeters in height. Tammy and I agreed that there was something about this tiny little girl that grabbed our hearts and she had to be our third daughter. We began the same procedure as we did with our other children like completing lots of forms, getting another home study done by a social worker and waiting and waiting for the people in Belarus to process everything and schedule a court date in Minsk Belarus to go and adopt this little girl. We decided on renaming her Juliana Irina Carver.

By the Spring and Summer of 2003 our other four children kept us active as Tammy continued to home school all of them. Several of them celebrated their birthdays and adoption anniversaries. Tammy's father, Ray Gettle, came to our house and helped build the kids a swing set. They loved it.

One day in May 2003 we, all, boarded a Southwest Airplane and took a trip to Disney World. Everyone had so much fun. The summer was full of laughter, the kids playing and enjoying the benefits of being a Daddy.

In late August 2003 Tammy and I boarded a plane to adopt Juliana. My parents were kind enough to watch our other children while we went to get Juliana. I don't think Tammy slept, at all, on the long flight. We had a layover in Frankfurt Germany (2:30am United States East Coast Time). We stayed in Frankfurt for several hours, walked around parts of the city and ate a chocolate covered pretzel. Finally, we boarded a Lufthansa flight to Minsk to adopt Juliana. I remember the seats were very narrow and uncomfortable.

We got off the plane, stopped by the hotel for a few minutes, and went right to meet Juliana for the first time along with our driver and translator. Juliana's orphanage was tucked away and surrounded by big apartment buildings. The court yard, of the orphanage, was painted with bright colors, painted animals and cartoon characters. There was a big fence around the orphanage. You can see video of this day at "Falling in Love with Juliana" on YouTube.

Our driver parked the van and all of us began to walk up to the orphanage not saying too much and so excited about meeting this little girl that grabbed our hearts. The orphanage was called "Baby House #32." The, two story, building was made of brick and had large windows. I estimate the ground where the orphanage sat was a couple of acres in size.

Once inside I noticed the walls were painted with bright colors with pretty curtains hanging in the windows. It seemed to be a maze to locate Juliana. Our translator was trying to find which room Juliana was in at the moment. We turned, corner after corner, looking for that tiny little girl. Where could she be? We turned another corner and there were no lights. The walls painted with shiny white paint. We looked to the left, inside, one door and kept walking.

We walked through another door way and made a right turn. The corridors seemed to go on forever. We walked past a staircase and our translator asked an orphanage employee if she was in the right place to find Juliana. She was not so we kept looking for Juliana.

Inside another door way, we walked, which seemed like a children's play room. We turned to the left and found our translator speaking to an orphanage employee. There were several other little orphan children looking up as I peered by video camera toward the doorway.

Within a few minutes we were led into that room after the other children were taken to a different room. Minutes seemed to drag by as we could not wait to see Juliana, face to face, for the first time. We could hear orphanage employees speaking to the other children. Our translator started to explain to us that this, particular, orphanage was a "special needs" because thirty percent of the children, in that "baby house" had "special needs." The translator explained that when many international adoptive parents find out about that particular orphanage and the percentage of "special needs" orphans in it they choose a different orphanage to adopt a child. Minutes continued to drag by and we waited to see Juliana.

I told our other kids that we would be meeting Juliana around a certain time if they wanted to call me on my cell phone. Just as the translator continued updating us on the orphanage my phone rang. It was our son Matthew. We talked for several minutes.

Finally, Juliana walks through the door as Tammy lifted her into her aching arms to hold this precious little girl. Juliana tilted her head, as her eyes were crossed, to get a good look at us and smiled from ear to ear. I laughed, with glee, as the time came that began in a hotel room several months earlier. We could hear the other children, in a distant room, screaming and crying.

Tammy gave Juliana her first kiss, from her new Mommy, on her left cheek. I flipped the video camera screen around so Juliana and Tammy could see them as I continued to video this amazing event. Juliana was wearing a red shirt with a red and white jumpsuit with white tights and dark colored sandles. Juliana reached out to touch the video camera lens and smiled as she saw her own face maybe for the first time. Juliana was twenty months old.

Tammy continued to hold Juliana and speak to her in English (we don't know much Russian) and Juliana continued to smile so big. The translator spoke up and said, "they call her (Juliana) little foxy." We brought her a few toys. Juliana ignored the toys, for a few minutes, and was amazed at seeing herself in the video camera viewer. Tammy tickled Juliana a little bit and Juliana's smile got bigger.

I sat the video camera down, aimed it into the room, and held Juliana for the very first time. She was so light and tiny. Juliana reached out to me as I lifted her into my arms and life (tears are streaming down my face as I write these words). I gave Juliana her first kiss on that same right cheek as Tammy did moments earlier. Tammy reached out a touched Juliana's nose a few times and made a funny noise which Juliana enjoyed. Juliana and I embraced for the first time. She gripped me as I gripped her. It is impossible to describe that feeling. I gave her a kiss on her left temple as I told her "I Love you" in Russian. I gave her another kiss on the back of her head. I looked at Juliana and said, "You're so tiny." Of course, Juliana couldn't understand me because she didn't speak or understand Russian.

I handed Juliana back to Tammy to take some photographs of both of them. Tammy stooped down and put Juliana on the floor as she reached into her purse and took out some more toys and some a bottle to make bubbles for Juliana. Again, I turned the video camera around so Juliana could see herself. She smiled so beautifully. I said, to Juliana, "you're such a happy little girl." Juliana took two steps forward and reached her hands up to me so I would pick her up. We had just met less than fifteen minutes earlier.

Tammy sat Juliana on her lap and began to sing to her the song "Sally the Camel." Tammy put Juliana down and she ran over to "the play room" door and tried to open it. She could not reach the door handle so Juliana looked over her left shoulder as if to ask for help to open it. We could hear other children screaming in that room. One of the orphanage employees, slowly, opened the door and walked into the room and began to talk to Juliana and Tammy. In Russian, the employee told Juliana to give Tammy a hug which she did right away.

Tammy opened a bag of "cheese goldfish" as Juliana sat on her left leg and gave one to Juliana. She loved them. Juliana embraced Tammy, again, for another hug. I said, "she is so huggable." A different orphanage employee walked in the room and brought some sort of chocolate marshmallow cake and something to drink for Juliana. Tammy said, "Chocolate...yum...chocolate." We continued to hear, at least one child, screaming from the next room. Juliana kicked her feet with a big smile as she looked into Tammy's eyes. The translator told us that the orphanage employees prepared Juliana for our visit and to tell her, as much as possible for a twenty month old to understand, about her new family. Tammy said to Juliana, "you're a sweety." Juliana reached up, with her left hand, and touched Tammy's nose then Tammy reached over, with her left hand, and touched Juliana's nose and said (in English) "nose."

Tammy told the translator that our daughter, Lindsay, could not wait to share her room with Juliana. Juliana continued to eat her chocolate marshmallow cake. Tammy cleaned her up from eating so I got on the floor and played with Juliana while Tammy videotaped our time together. I lay back and let Juliana sit on my stomach. I tickled her and she laughed out loud. I handed her a toy that played music from the "Barney" television show. Juliana tried to dance. By this time, we had been in a little room with Juliana for about forty five minutes.

The time came when an orphanage employee/caretaker, who brought her the food, walked back into the room to take Juliana back with the other children. The employee told Juliana to say good bye. Juliana waved and gave us a big smile. The employee, then, told Juliana to say, "Mama." The employee looked at Juliana and showed her how to put her lips together to make the M sound. Juliana said, "Mama." Oh my, it was so precious.

The employee, then, told Juliana to say "Papa." Juliana looked at the orphanage employee's lips to see the P sound and she said, in her tiny little voice, "Papa." I laughed and tears were filling my eyes. Juliana had stolen my heart. I said, "she's adorable." The process was repeated. Juliana said, "Mama" for the second time.

We were taken back to our hotel, which was a beautiful and sunny day, which was on an upper floor so we could see over part of Minsk Belarus. The next day, we went back to the orphanage where the translator was reviewing with us some of the details about Juliana. She said Juliana was "sociable, established emotional contact with people around her, she prefers communication with adults instead of communication with children, she stretches her arms to anyone who smiles to her, her speech is quite developed, she can say give me…yes…no, her favorite occupation is to be on the swings, loves dancing, tries to undress and dress herself, she likes to pay outside in the sunshine, likes active games, likes running, likes playing with the bucket in the sand box, friendly and gentle."

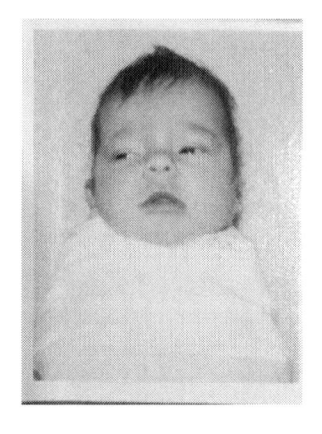

Just then, they handed us a photograph of Juliana that was taken at birth. Next Tammy was Juliana's baptism certificate showing she was baptized in May 2002 in the Russian Orthodox Church. The translator looked over at us and asked, "how do you like her." At that moment I had clicked off the video camera. I am sure we said, "We love her so much!" We, all, rose from our seats and went for a walk on the orphanage grounds to go find Juliana and invest more time with her as we waited for the paperwork to be processed for our court date, in Minsk, to adopt Juliana.

We turned a corner and walked on to a small porch as a door opened up. Juliana took two steps outside the door and raised her arms for Tammy to pick her up. Tammy picked her up and kissed Juliana on her left cheek as Juliana smiled. We stepped back from the open door as the translator closed the door. Juliana was wearing a winter coat and a bonnet even though it was a beautiful and warm day. Once again, Juliana enjoyed seeing herself in my video camera.

The translator coaxed Juliana into saying "Mama" again which she did with a big smile on her face. Her voice was so tiny and petite. The translator, then, coaxed Juliana into saying "Papa" which she did with a big smile on her face. We, all, laughed so loud. Juliana gave Tammy a few more big hugs.

I took Juliana over to the swing and held her as we sat on the swing together. Juliana looked at Tammy and said, "Mama."Tammy held the camera then we switched positions. We played on that swing for several minutes. Tammy looked so happy. Tammy did "patty-cakes" with Juliana as she began to swing some more. Juliana turned to her left and rested her head on Tammy's chest as she continued to swing.

We got up, from the swing, and Tammy showed her some more toys that she brought. We were, now, standing just outside the door where Juliana walked out of moments ago. Tammy started blowing bubbles, for Juliana, again.

Juliana scampered over to the swing and tried climbing up on it. Tammy lifted her up and began to, gently, swing her. After a few minutes Tammy picked her up and took her over to the painted animals that were painted on the perimeter walls of the orphanage. Tammy said, to Juliana in Russian, "I Love you." I looked down the wise walk to see other orphans being taken for a walk by one of the orphanage caregivers. One child, about age three or four, was pushing a stroller with two toddlers in it. Juliana jumped down and ran over to me as I videos Tammy and Juliana. Tammy opened a bag of Cheerios as Juliana ate one at a time. It was getting warm to Tammy took off her jacket as Juliana had to stay in her winter coat and bonnet per the rules of the orphanage.

I could only imagine how many people, from the apartment building surrounding the orphanage, were watching us play with Juliana. I said, on camera, "I'm not sure why God chose us to help all these kids. I'm sure thankful he did." I had walked behind some hedges, close to where Tammy and Juliana were playing, and Juliana noticed I was gone and started looking for me. When she saw me she gave me a big smile. She kept looking for a way to get around or through the hedges. She found the end of the row of hedges, looked to her right, stepped on the sidewalk and started walking toward me. We didn't know, at the time, that her eyesight was pretty bad.

I looked up, toward the apartment buildings surrounding the orphanage and saw laundry hanging on one of the balconies and a woman with a white cap, on her head, painting the edge of another balcony. As I turned the camera around I noticed Tammy had put Juliana on a see-saw. Tammy rocked up, very slowly, up and down. We went back into the orphanage and found out that Juliana had an older sister who lived in another orphanage.

Her name was Svetlana and was five years old. We were shocked. Typically, the adoption agencies know of sibling groups and do their best to keep the siblings together. Our adoption agency was not aware of Svetlana due to circumstances beyond their control.

We said, "let's go meet her" so our driver, translator, Tammy and myself drive a few miles away to meet Svetlana. As we drove to the other orphanage I said, "This sure throws a while new twist in things." We drove up to the other orphanage which had a brown gate with spires on the top. We parked the van and noticed the orphanage was a two story building that was painted a light color. There was a playground just outside the entrance to the building.

We walked up a few steps, with a short blue wall to our right, and turned right. We walked under a brick porch and found Svetlana playing in the yard with other children. As Tammy stooped down to talk to Svetlana the little girl covered her face with her hands. Svetlana was wearing a blue-striped sweater and old blue jeans. Her hair was light brown and cut very short. She continued to cover her eyes. We didn't know, until many years later, that she has 2q23.1 microdeletion syndrome which, among other things, makes her mentally challenged.

A minute or two passed and orphanage caretaker took Svetlana's hand down from her face as Svetlana gave her a hug and would not look at Tammy. Svetlana began to cry as she glanced in Tammy's direction. Svetlana was overwhelmed. Just then, other orphaned children began to surround Tammy and I chatting in Russian. They loved my video camera and wanted to see themselves in it. Svetlana began to melt into the group of other children. Svetlana tried to keep her head down and not attract any attention to her. She was the only one not wearing a little hat.

Svetlana walked behind the other children when our translator took her by the hand and introduced her to us. The translator told the other children they were "playing in the movie" because I was videotaping what was happening. Tammy took some "Tootie Rolls" out of her purse and the children went crazy trying to get some of them. Most of the children were very polite as they said, "thank you" (in Russian) when Tammy handed them a piece of candy.

One of the little girls, wearing a pink and white sweater and grey sweat pants, pulled Svetlana's hair to get her to look up at my camera as I was trying to take a photo of the two girls. I was…stunned that she pulled her hair.

I turned the screen, of the video camera around, and several of the children stood smiling, laughing and waving as they saw themselves. Svetlana stood behind them with little emotion. A blond-haired orphanage caretaker, dressed in dark clothes, picked Svetlana up as she saw over becoming overwhelmed again.

The next day we went back to Juliana's orphanage. We walked in and, as the translator opened the play room door, Juliana saw Tammy and ran to meet her. Juliana was wearing a beautiful knitted dress. Tammy put a coat on Juliana and went back outside for a walk on the orphanage grounds and playing on a sliding board.

While outside, a little boy, who did not have a left arm, ran up to me. He may have been five or six years old. He ran, in circles, around us as we walked around the orphanage yard. Eventually, he made it very clear that he wanted to play soccer with me. I was concerned that, missing one arm, he would fall and get hurt. Juliana just stared at him as he ran and ran and ran.

Eventually, I gave in and played a little soccer with the boy. He dove for the ball, several times, fell on his face, got back up and did it again. I will never forget that little boy.

We walked back into the orphanage as Tammy held the fingers on Juliana's right hand. Juliana ran into the playroom. We said our goodbyes for the day. The orphanage caretakers, genuinely, loved the children. The rest of the day we continued to wait for the rest of the paperwork to be completed so we could go to court and adopt Juliana so we did a little sightseeing.

Tammy and I got dressed up for the court hearing and were driven to the court house. Both of us were nervous as we don't speak much Russian. When it was our turn in the court room our translator stood between Tammy and I translating for us. It was a female judge. Neither, Tammy or me, wanted to say the wrong thing and mess up the chance of adopting Juliana. We told the judge about our family including us adopting four other children and the size of our home.I am sure our translator said all the right things and the adoption was approved. The judge agreed to allow us to take a photograph with her after the court hearing.

Finally, after the court hearing to finalize the adoption we were allowed to take Juliana with us. We went back to the orphanage and Tammy picked Juliana up saying, "We missed you." It was so, incredibly, emotional because the orphanage caretakers had to say their final goodbye to Juliana (then known as Irina). Tears were flowing.

Several of the orphanage caretakers held Juliana and talked with her and played together. We were able to see, before we left, the crib that Juliana slept in every night. The cribs were aligned, from end to end. There were about twenty cribs in that room. She slept next to a little, blond, girl with Down's Syndrome. Tammy gave each of Juliana's, primary, caretakers a gift to show our appreciation for their kindness. I was an emotional wreck (I am the one who cries very easily).

One of the caretakers sat Juliana down at a large table, for children, to give her the last snack she would eat in an orphanage. They said that she had just eaten lunch but never refuses to eat more. When she was finished eating Tammy changed her clothes with some clothes that we brought for

Juliana as the clothes she was wearing had to stay with the orphanage.

I could tell that the caretakers were, already, missing Juliana as they kept playing with her and making her giggle and didn't want her to leave…forever. Juliana was, truly, loved in that orphanage. They, all, played together for about a half hour. Finally, the time came when Juliana was getting ready to leave the orphanage. Tammy put clothes that we brought for Juliana and a little pink jacket and a white bonnet on Juliana. Juliana said, "Bye, bye" (in Russian) to the orphanage caretakers as she turned to walk away with Tammy.

We walked out of the playroom, through the little room where we first met Juliana as Juliana led the way. She thought she knew where she was going. Tammy, gently, picked her up and we walked down the hall toward the waiting van. We climbed in the van and headed toward the hotel. Juliana looked around as if she had never been in a vehicle in her life. She was amazed as the van moved. She looked sleepy. It had been a busy morning.

Juliana walked through the entrance of the hotel. That evening we were going to take a train to

Warsaw Poland in order to be able to take a flight back to the United States. Juliana played with some toys when we got back to the hotel room and acted as if she had been with her for her entire life. Tammy gave Juliana a bath before our train ride and Juliana did not like it. She cried. We are not sure why she was so afraid of the water. She got through the bath, thanks to Tammy's amazing kindness and patience and dressed her in a little outfit. Juliana was making some cute noises while Tammy fixed her hair.

Tammy sat Juliana on her lap and played "patty-cakes" while Juliana smiled from ear to ear. Juliana started getting silly and giving Tammy "raspberries." I gave the video camera to Tammy and got down on the floor and played with Juliana. I got Juliana squealing and laughing so hard. She kept making "raspberry" sounds at me and laughing hysterically.

Our driver and translator came back to the hotel and took us to the train station for our, overnight, journey to Warsaw Poland. The train brought back lots of memories when we took the train from St. Petersburg Russia to Moscow Russia when we adopted Rebecca, Matthew, Lindsay and Timothy. It brought back a rush of memories.

The train cabin, we were assigned had four bunk-beds in it with storage under the two bottom bunks. Before the train started moving Juliana walked up and down the only aisle on our train looking into each cabin. Tammy brought her into our train cabin as she put sheets on the bunks. As the train began to move Juliana, sucking her fingers, drifted off to sleep on one of the lower bunks. She would suck her three middle fingers on her left hand.

The train creaked as it moved down the tracks. We traveled for several hours then came to a stop at the Poland border. Every time the trains traveled to Poland (and Poland to Belarus) they stop the train, for three hours, and change the wheels on the train because the wheels don't match the tracks that are in Poland. They raised each train car and shaking the train cars in the process. I am not joking. I thought, for sure, that it would awaken Juliana but she slept through all of it.

We arrived, in Poland, at 4:05am (Poland Time) but had a few hours to go, on the train, to get to Warsaw. As the sun rose I could see the beautiful landscape of Poland. It looked a lot like where we live in Maryland. We, eventually, pulled into the Warsaw Poland train station as Juliana woke up for a restful night's sleep. She didn't cry one time on the train.

We got off the train to the sounds of someone announcing something in Polish. We were met by a driver and translator. I looked up to see a poster of the movie "Pirates of the Caribbean" written in Polish. We went to a Holiday Inn in Warsaw and put Juliana in a little crib. Juliana wasn't too excited about it. Outside the window there was a high-rise being constructed. The workman worked on the building all day and all night so it got a little loud. We took a little walk around a small part of Warsaw on the beautiful, but breezy, sunny day.

Tammy stopped the stroller and gave Juliana a "sippy-cup" of juice and then we kept walking. I looked to my left and saw a street sign showing an exit to the city of Krakow and Lublin. We walked back to the hotel with Juliana in her stroller. We sat in the hallway and chatted with another American who had traveled to Minsk Belarus to adopt a child. Juliana was getting more vocal and making silly noises.

The next morning we got ready to head to the airport to fly back to America. We took the elevator, at about 6:25am (Poland Time) to the hotel lobby and had breakfast at the "Buffet Brasserie." Juliana acted as if she owned the restaurant and walked all over the place. We ate breakfast and walked back to the elevator to get ready to go to the airport.

We got to the airport and a little girl walked up to Juliana and started to chat with her in Polish. Of course, none of us could understand what she was saying. Once on board the plane we were able to get the front seats, in the coach section, which allowed room to put a little basinet for Juliana to sleep in when she got tired. Tammy sat at the end of the middle row, next to an aisle, with two more people sitting across from her on the other side of the plane. Eventually, Juliana woke up and Tammy gave her some crackers and cheese.

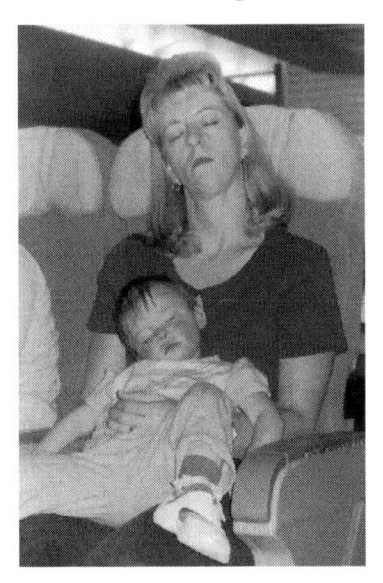

By this time, we had five hours to go on the plane. Juliana was getting a little "stir-crazy" so I played with her in aisle for a few minutes. In time, Juliana started getting sleepy and took a nap on Tammy's lap.

We, finally, got home and put Juliana in a bed next to Lindsay's bed. The next morning I found the rest of the kids playing with Juliana. All the kids loved her. Matthew said, to me, "I missed you." Rebecca loved making Juliana laugh the first morning Juliana woke up in our home. Lindsay was very excited about being a big sister. They all huddled around their new sister. It, still, amazes me how our kids welcome each new child that we adopted. Juliana giggled as Rebecca lifted her up in the air.

The kids got dressed and they started playing in the family room of our house. Juliana found a red balloon that she really enjoyed. Timothy was squealing with happiness. The girls tried to dress her in with "girly" clothes. They got her dressed up like a fairy princess. Everyone moved on to the kitchen for some breakfast.

By this time a couple years earlier, our son Timothy, had his crossed eyes corrected and wore glasses. His white-blond hair and cute demeanor attracted the looks of so many people who wanted to take him home. Juliana and Timothy became extremely close for many years. Timothy loved being a big brother. The other kids continued to love and play with Juliana. Our entire, extended, family welcomed Juliana as well.

There was, still, Svetlana, in Minsk Belarus. How would it be possible for us to adopt her too?

Chapter 3


As the weeks progressed, in late 2003, we tried to figure out a way to finance the adoption of Svetlana. My parents, John and Edna, were friends with the Hall family. The Hall's invested fifty percent of the fees to go back and adopt Svetlana. Our adoption attorney, Ron Stoddard, called Tammy and told her that he heard about a grant and she needs to apply for it. Tammy applied, for the grant, and was accepted. That grant supplied a few more thousand dollars that we needed for the trip to adopt Svetlana.

Juliana continued to meld into our family. We made plans on getting her eyes straightened as soon as possible via an outpatient surgery. Juliana was non-stop and was very active. Timothy took an, extra, amount of time with Juliana and remained that way for years. Juliana had no fear. Tammy continued to home school the rest of the children.

Tammy took Juliana to an eye doctor who recommended that we patch Juliana's right eye, for a few hours a day, to strengthen the left eye before proceeding with surgery to straighten both eyes. The patch didn't bother Juliana at all. Our home, with five children, was very busy and active. Juliana tried to keep up with the rest of the kids.

In late October 2003 the kids were getting excited about Halloween. We purchased pumpkins so they could decorate them. Juliana continued to love seeing herself on my video camera screen. Halloween evening came and Juliana dressed in a care bear outfit. Timothy was Superman, Juliana was an angel, Matthew was a pirate and Rebecca wore a black outfit with a red heart on it.

In early November, 2003, we drove to the Pocono Mountains in Pennsylvania for a few days with all the kids. They had lots of fun with swimming, skating, games, dancing and enjoying the outdoors.

A couple of years, earlier, Tammy had enrolled the kids in a home school gym program which they continued enjoying with other home schooled children. In November 2003 we decided to have our basement finished so the kids would have another place to have fun in our house so we hired a local contractor to make that happen. Tammy and the children started decorating for Christmas, which was Juliana's first Christmas, in America. She was amazed by the lights on the Christmas tree.

All the kids loved to get Juliana to laugh. Her entire body would giggle. In early December we celebrated Lindsay's 4$^{th}$ adoption anniversary with a chocolate cake with purple icing. We adopted Lindsay, from St. Petersburg Russia, when she was six months old. Tammy and I had adoption anniversaries including a cake for each of our children.

On December 4, 2003 we celebrated Juliana's second birthday. The night before, her birthday, she got out of bed and didn't want to go back to sleep for quite a while. Juliana's birthday cake had white icing with pink letters with two hearts on either side of the writing. Tammy baked all the kid's cakes. Juliana wore a pink shirt and blue pants. Tammy held her as Juliana stood on a chair to blow out her birthday candles (Tammy helped her blow them out as Juliana didn't understand about candles). All of us sang Happy Birthday to Juliana.

The day came for Juliana's surgery to straighten her eyes. We had no idea it would be the first of many surgeries (because of cancer) that Juliana would have to endure. Tammy completed the paperwork while Juliana colored in a coloring book and walked around the waiting room. Juliana began to cry as Tammy changed her from her clothes to a hospital gown. I held her to comfort her and get her mind off of what was going on. I put Juliana in a wagon, that was in the waiting room, and pulled her around for a little while.

Tammy got dressed in a hair net and scrubs to go back with Juliana until she was asleep for the surgery. It was so emotional. As Tammy and Juliana went back, for surgery I said to Juliana, "bye bye baby…love you." After the operation Juliana was, of course, groggy from the anesthesia. Juliana began to cry. A nurse carried Juliana to Tammy and placed her in her arms. Juliana and Tammy embraced as Tammy rocked her back and forth. Juliana had just turned two years old a couple of days earlier. Within a few minutes Juliana was sucking her fingers, on her left hand, and went back to sleep.

As Juliana began to wake up Tammy walked her around the recovery area. Tammy found a rocking chair and wrapped Juliana up in a blanket to rock her. When we got home we put Juliana in her bed for a nap. That weekend we had a larger birthday party for Juliana so the extended family could attend. Cousins, aunts, uncles and grandparents joined us for the party.

Christmas Day was a whirlwind of activity. The entire day was full with playing with new toys, sounds of new games and electronic drum sets and lots of laughing. Juliana loved to dance whenever music was played. Every day our home was full of fun and energy as the kids played together.

The day came when Juliana saw her first snowfall at our house. All the kids got their coats on and played outside. Juliana wasn't quite sure about it, at first, but soon copied what the other kids were doing. Juliana wore a purple coat and hat. There was about five inches of snow on the ground. Timothy, as always, stayed close to Juliana. When she stumbled, by her shed, Timothy helped her. He is an amazing big brother.

The time was getting closer to us, hopefully, to fly back to Minsk Belarus and adopt Svetlana (who we renamed Kristina Svetlana). By mid March 2004 we had a travel date which was less than two weeks away. In late March Tammy, Juliana and I boarded a plane to head back to Belarus to bring Svetlana back to America. My parents, graciously, watched the rest of the children for us while we were out of the country.

Once again, we were met by a driver and translator. It felt like we were in a familiar place as we had just been to Belarus back in August 2003 to adopt Juliana. We arrived at Svetlana's orphanage to find no children playing outside. We walked up the same steps that we did when we found out, months earlier, when we met Svetlana for the first time.

We walked down a hall where our translator stopped at a while door with a screen in it. Inside, the room, I could see more than six children standing looking at the strangers peering into the room. The children looked healthy. A few minutes later, I spotted Svetlana in the back looking toward the door way. A little, blond, boy had his left arm around Svetlana's shoulder. Maybe he knew she would be leaving the orphanage very soon. He turned and looked her, in the face and took his right hand and touched her right cheek, and said something to her which I do not know the details.

We walked into the room where the children stood. Svetlana was wearing a jumper outfit with a yellow short. Her brown hair had grown since the last time we were in Belarus. Our driver seemed to tell Svetlana that Juliana was her little sister and Svetlana put her hands behind her head as a sign of being nervous. Tammy stooped down on the right side of Juliana for Svetlana to feel more comfortable. One of the caretakers told Svetlana (in Russian) to say, "Juliana, hello" as she walked the other children out of the room.

Our driver, a bearded man with a red sweatshirt, looked down with a big smile as Svetlana walked toward Juliana. Our driver found a seat, in the room, and continued to smile as he looked at the girls. Our translator, who was the same one we had when we adopted Juliana, stood to the right of our driver. Svetlana looked at Tammy and said something in Russian (which I do know what she said). Svetlana began to chatter at Juliana in a "motherly" kind of way.

We walked a few feet into another room that was about eight feet by eight feet that was full of toys. Juliana jumped on a stuffed lion and began to ride it. Svetlana jumped on behind her. Our translator asked if we brought clothes for Svetlana to wear when she left the orphanage. Tammy said she brought clothes and hope that they fit Svetlana who was five and a half years old.

The girls picked up a red balloon and began to throw it around the room as Svetlana talked in Russian. The sounds of giggles filled the room. That day was the first time, I believe, the girls had ever met even though they are half-sisters. Our translator stooped down and began to give instructions to Svetlana. I heard the words "Mama and Papa" (as of this writing) do not have the translation of what else she told Svetlana. Svetlana acknowledged that she understood by saying "Da" (Yes, in Russian). Juliana continued to play with the red balloon. Our driver joined in the fun with the red balloon which turned the giggles into hysterical laughter by Svetlana as she crawled back on the stuffed lion.

Our translator jumped on a red toy rocking thing that Juliana was sitting on and pretended that they were driving. Svetlana continued to play with the red balloon with our driver. We remained in the room for, at least, a half hour. The room started to get warm with all the activity going on.

It was an amazing sight to see these two girls playing together. Our driver and Svetlana began to throw a stuffed panda bear back and forth. Tammy grabbed Svetlana and began to tickle her which Svetlana did not want her to stop. The tickling went on for several minutes. Eventually, we had to leave the orphanage, for the day, and go back to the hotel with Juliana.

Juliana and I played with a little red ball in the hotel room. The next day we drove to Juliana's orphanage to let the caretakers see how Juliana was doing and that her crossed eyes were straightened after she had surgery. As we turned the corner, into the courtyard, where Juliana lived the emotions of meeting her for the first time came right back at me.

We made a left turn to find the orphanage gates open. Our driver parked closer to the front door than last time. Juliana was the first one to the front door wearing a purple coat and blue pants. Did she remember that place? Juliana leaned over the wooden railing and yelled "Dad" to me. I think she was telling me to hurry up. She motioned, to me, with her left hand to "come here."

Once inside, we walked up the concrete steps with a white metal railing on either side of us.

Tammy held Juliana's right hand as they walked in front of me. The color of the steps turned to brown as we reached the second level. We walked down a long hallway. I could hear the orphanage caretakers saying here comes "Mama and Papa." I walked, into the next room first, and turned my video camera around to see Juliana then Tammy walk in behind me.

The orphanage director began to talk (in Russian) to Juliana. By the sound of her voice she was so happy to see her again. Tammy handed her a gift and received a thank you from the director. Our translator translating a question, by the director, and asked "How is she (Juliana) doing." Tammy and I said (at the same moment) "she's doing great."

    The translator said that the director said Juliana has "beautiful eyes." The orphanage director asked us if we had any problems with Juliana. We said that we had no problems with Juliana. Juliana was sucking the middle fingers on her left hand as we responded to the questions. Juliana was wearing a red jumper with a white long sleeve shirt and blue pants. We told the director that Juliana was very active. Juliana walked across the room and saw a little white stuffed bear sitting on a shelf. A couple of the orphanage caretakers walked in the room and closed the door behind them.

Tammy told the director that Svetlana, the day before, had been calling Juliana "Julianka." Our driver, now dressed in dark clothing, was stooped down with his hands together smiling at Juliana. Juliana was getting sleepy and reached up so Tammy picked her up. Moments later another orphanage caretaker walked in the room. She stooped over, with a big smile on her face, and chatted with Tammy and Juliana. We didn't understand anything they were saying.

One of the caretakers motioned for Juliana to come to her but Juliana turned to Tammy to pick up her again. Tammy walked Juliana over to the caretaker but Juliana wanted nothing to do with the kind woman. Finally, Tammy asked Juliana if she would give the caretaker a hug so Juliana leaned over into the arms of the woman and allowed her to hold Juliana. The caretaker had a huge smile as our driver was watching smiling from ear to ear. Juliana gave the woman a big hug them, without being asked, Juliana gave her a kiss on the right cheek. Immediately, Juliana turned to her left and put her arms out for Tammy to take her back in her arms.

We walked out of that room, through the room where we met Juliana for the first time and approached the play room where we said our goodbyes to the caretakers that helped care for Juliana and so many other children.

We were met by a woman with a white top and a black skirt. Juliana stopped, suddenly, before entering the room. The woman stooped down and motioned for Juliana to come into the room. We had not met that woman in our prior visit. The woman walked into the smaller outer room, where we stood, stooped down and began to talk to Juliana (in Russian). Juliana was nervous.

Tammy picked Juliana up and walked into the playroom. We were met by a couple more caretakers that we did not recognize. There were twelve small children eating a two small round tables as I looked to my left. The caretakers continued to talk to Juliana in Russian. I don't think they understood that Juliana may have forgotten all her Russian language. At that moment, another caretaker walked in from the room that had all the cribs in it that we saw when we adopted Juliana. Juliana clung very close to Tammy. A couple of the, mentally challenged, children at one of the tables began to get loud.

Tammy led Juliana to a very small trampoline which Juliana jumped on several times and smiled. The other children, in the room, looked on at Juliana. Just then, a severely mentally challenged little boy, who was about two or three years old, came up to me to get my attention. I said, "Hi" and tried to engage conversation with him. He reached up and gave me a little kiss on my right cheek. I said, "Ahhh…thank you!" I gave him a kiss also. His empty eyes touched me deeply.

The same caretaker who met us in the doorway of the playroom walked over to the small trampoline, stooped down and tried to get Juliana to come to her. Juliana just shrugged her shoulders a couple times and turned to her left for Tammy to pick her up. A couple of the caretakers said, "Mama, Mama" and shook their heads up and down as if they understood what Juliana was doing.

Tammy put Juliana down and she walked over to me as I was, still, with the little boy. A caretaker picked the boy up and took him to the room with the cribs. I wonder what ever happened to that sweet little boy with empty eyes. I walked over to the table, where the dozen children were eating and wondered how the amazing caretakers could keep up with all the kids in the orphanage.

Juliana followed the caretaker into the room with the cribs without Tammy. I stood up and saw Juliana strut out of the room like she owned the place. Juliana had, always, been so confident and sure of herself even though (at the time) Juliana was two-and-a-half years old. She walked over to Tammy and looked up at her. Juliana turned around and walked over to another caretaker who was spoon feeding one of the children seat at the table closest to Tammy. The little boy who was with me was brought out of the crib room and put in a stroller. Juliana called to me to watch her, once again, jump on the trampoline. I could hear the sounds of spoons, now, banging on the bowls of food that the children were eating.

We were escorted into another room, where babies were kept, as we were getting ready to leave the orphanage. We were told that the caretakers, in that room, were the ones who took care of Juliana when she was a baby. All of them wore, what looked like, white lab coats. They chatted with Juliana (in Russian) but Juliana did not understand what they were saying. We did not see any of the caretakers that we met when we traveled to adopt Juliana. There were two, very, large cribs in the room with a mosaic carpet on the other side of the room.

A caretaker reached in one of the cribs and pulled out the only baby and tried to get Juliana to touch the baby. Juliana reached out her right hand and the baby held her finger for a few seconds. We said our goodbyes and got back in the van to go pick up Svetlana (who we renamed Kristina Svetlana).

We pulled onto the grounds of Kristina's orphanage and made a right hand turn. In front of us was the spot where we first met Kristina after finding out that Juliana had a biological sister in another orphanage in Minsk Belarus. It was March 30, 2004…the day Kristina Svetlana became our six child. It was a beautiful and sunny day as our driver parked the van. The van stopped. I said to Juliana, "Ok…you ready…let's go." Juliana, wearing her purple coat, jumped to her feet with excitement.

We walked into a room, with red carpet and random squares on it, and waited for Kristina to arrive. Juliana climbed up on a chair and leaned, half way, on a table to watch our translator sign some papers. Tammy stood behind Juliana so she wouldn't fall. I think we were in the orphanage director's office. Kristina walked into the room wearing a jumper and green shirt. She had a big smile on her face. Juliana tried to get Kristina to look at me as I was holding my video camera. Juliana kept insisting but I am not sure Kristina understood what Juliana was trying to get her to do.

Juliana motioned for Kristina and her to sit on my left leg. Tammy took the video camera and began to record. I picked Kristina up, gave her a big hug and she started chatting to me in Russian, of course. I had no clue what she was saying. I picked up Juliana and sat her on my right leg. I began to bounce then and make silly noises which got both the girls laughing.

A few minutes later we were taken to where Kristina slept. The, small, wooden beds were lined in neat rows. A caretaker asked Kristina to show us her bed. There were a few children in their beds even though it was daytime. I counted twelve beds in that room. Kristina walked down one of the aisles, between the beds, and stood beside her bed which was against the back wall.

We left the room to find other caretakers that began to shower Kristina with kisses and hugs. One caretaker, wearing gray pants and a pick sleeveless shirt wiped a tear from her eye. She stooped down and called Kristina over to her. She whispered something to Kristina and kissed her left cheek then wiped her lipstick off Kristina's cheek.

Kristina ran across the room and jumped on a sofa to have a group photo taken with several of the caretakers that loved Kristina since she arrived in the orphanage. Two caretakers joined Kristina on the sofa while I took a few photographs. Another caretaker, wearing a white "lab coat" embraced Tammy and told her thank you a couple times.

We left the room as Juliana walked to the left of the orphanage director. Upon entering another room with some tables and chairs and a sofa against a large window Juliana jumped on the back of another stuffed lion that was in front of one of the desks. Tammy began to help Kristina change her clothes because the clothes she had on had to stay with the orphanage. This was a common practice with all the children we adopted. Kristina was, now, wearing a new light green outfit and new tennis shoes. Kristina continued to chatter, in Russian, which we did not understand. One of the caretakers congratulated Tammy for, correctly, guessing the correct show size for Kristina. Juliana picked up a small chair and carried it across the room.

The orphanage director, a tall young woman with short black hair, called Kristina to come to her so she could adjust her new clothes. There was so much conversation going on, in the room, and ninety-five percent of it we had no idea what they were saying as we only know a few words in Russian. We were invited to go have some tea.

After tea, we left the orphanage for the last time. Both of the girls were eating a lollypop as we left the orphanage property. Kristina said (and translated for us), "We're going fast" as we drove down the city road. That evening we were taken to the train. Kristina had never been on a train so she was a bit overwhelmed. We had no idea that Kristina had mental delays as she was diagnosed several years later. We had a different translator who escorted us to the train. She got down on her knee to try to explain to Kristina what was going to be happening. After the conversation, Kristina left our train cabin and started checking out the other train cabins.

Less than an hour later the train began to move so we got the girls ready to go to sleep for the long train ride to Warsaw Poland and then on to America. Kristina didn't want to lay down and go to sleep. Tammy talked to her, in Russian, and told her it was time to sleep. Moments passed and the girls, finally, fell asleep. Several hours later, at 12:45am, we pulled up to the Poland border for the wheels on the train to be changed because they don't match the tracks in Poland. We waited for a few hours for that to happen before we could continue toward Warsaw. Both of the girls slept the entire night.

We arrived in Warsaw and Kristina tried to push Juliana in our, little fold up, stroller as Tammy helped. A porter brought a large cart to put our luggage on instead of trying to carry it. We arrived at the hotel and took a nap as Tammy and I didn't sleep much on the train. The girls slept as well. I brought lunch up to the room as the girls ate together. Tammy gave the girls a bath.

The next morning, before 7am, we went to the airport. Kristina was so excited as the orphanage caretakers told her about going on an airplane. Finally, she got to see a real one for the very first time. Tammy knew so much more Russian than me and tried to tell Kristina more about the airplane. Kristina, clearly, understood we were her new Papa and Mama.

On the plane, Kristina sat on the window side. As the plane took up Juliana said, "weeeee." As the plane left the ground Juliana's face got still for a few seconds then a huge smile appeared on her face. Kristina was chatting away and we had no idea what she was saying.

We had a layover in London so Kristina took a nap on two of the chairs in the terminal. Once awake Juliana and Kristina climbed on a few things and played together. It was interesting that Kristina followed Juliana's lead, in their playing, instead of the other way around.

Hours past and it was time to board British Airways to fly home. We walked up to the desk, at the gate, where we to depart, and we were told the plane was overbooked and could not make the flight. Tammy flipped out. We had to get home. We went back and forth with the airline personnel but there was nothing they could do to get us on our, reserved, flight. We had to wait several more hours for the next flight.

Hours past and to our surprise we were bumped up to first class…all four of us. Tammy and I had never…ever flown in first class. The plane was huge. The seats were so large we could stretch out, completely, to sleep during the flight across the Atlantic Ocean toward home. Juliana insisted that she see herself, in the viewfinder, of my video camera. The girls were able to wear headphones and watch movies using a monitor attached to their seat. In time, they dozed off to sleep for the long flight home.

Finally, the wheels reached America and we drove home. We were met the rest of our children, by Mr. and Mrs. Hall (who contributed a large part of the money it took to adopt Kristina), my parents and sister Michele. Lindsay walked over to Kristina to hand her a wrapped gift in a box. Tammy, Juliana, Timothy and Lindsay surrounded Kristina to show her how to open up a wrapped gift. Inside the box was a baby doll. Our home was full. Six children adopted between 1998 and 2004.

Chapter 4


Before we left to adopt Kristina was put a wall up between the master bedroom and the sitting room that was next to our bedroom. We painted the room yellow and moved Juliana to that bedroom so Kristina could sleep in Lindsay's room.

April 2004 came along and Kristina started melding into the daily routine of our home. Easter was getting close so Tammy helped the kids color Easter eggs. Kristina had never experienced such a tradition. Easter morning came and all the kids were so excited. We started a tradition, years earlier, where the kids would hunt for their Easter baskets around the house. All six kids waited, at the top of the steps, for Tammy to take down the gate (so Juliana wouldn't fall down the steps in the middle of the night). The kids raced down the steps searching for their Easter basket followed by an Easter Egg hunt.

The Spring of 2004 brought fun and laughter. Kristina was picking up English quickly but still chatted in Russian a lot. Tammy continued to home school all the children. In early April we took a trip to Williamsburg Virginia. The kids loved the pool the best. Kristina loved to give Tammy and I kisses…a lot of kisses every day.

Spring lead to Summer. We were able to take the kids to Hilton Head South Carolina. On the day of our arrival we went to the beach. Kristina had never seen an ocean or a beach before. She wasn't sure, exactly, what to do so she followed the other kid's example. Lindsay ran, from the waves to the beach and grabbed Kristina's hand and said, "Come on, Kristina." Juliana was excited about the bubbles, in the water, as the waves hit the beach. Lindsay took Kristina's left hand and led her, into the ocean, as Kristina looked at the water covering her feet. Tammy is an incredible mother to all our children.

We invested a few days at Hilton Head South Carolina and packed up to head home. All the kids were, in our twelve passenger van and we were about to head north toward Maryland where we live, when I said (to all of them), "I need your advice about something. Down the road, here, the road is going to split. Part of the road is going to go north to home and the other part of the road is going to go south and south of us, right now, is a state called Florida. Would you rather go home or would you rather go to Florida?" All the kids screamed, "FLORIDA!" I asked again, "would you rather go home or would you rather to go Disney World?" The eyes got big and Timothy yelled, "DISNEY WORLD!" I said, "Are you sure?" They screamed "YES!" Of course, Tammy and I had that planned before we left for Hilton Head.

We met my parents, sister and my Dad's mother Mary Ellen McKinney. We stayed there for several days having lots of fun. In July we celebrated America's Independence Day and Matthew's birthday. Every week the kids played outside and enjoyed being kids. The summer, of

2004, continued with more fun and lots of activity in our home. By now, we had a pool in our back yard which the kids enjoyed so much. The Autumn was full of more fun, Kristina's birthday, playing outside and Juliana getting eye glasses. Tammy's father was getting sick. In late October, after her Dad was admitted to the hospital, around 4am Tammy's mom called and said he had passed away It was late October 2004. I remember holding Tammy, in my arms, as she sobbed on my shoulder after we hung up the phone. Tammy kept going.

In early December Juliana's third birthday came. Her cake was white with a picture of Barney on it. On the day of her party she was so excited. Her little eye glasses and her pony tails were so cute.

It was getting close to Christmas and the kids were getting more excited. We took the kids to see Santa Clause. Juliana ran through the mall looking for him. Our house was very busy, full of laughter and energy. Christmas morning was a whirlwind of activity with screams of happiness. Christmas was, always, a special time of year for our family.

As 2005 came in Kristina's English skills were getting much better. One day, I was training a new employee in Washington DC when Tammy called me. She said something like, "everything is okay. I'm in the Emergency Room with Juliana." She told me that Juliana had jumped the entire length of the basement steps and landed on her face. Supposedly, Matthew was to catch her and did not do it. I never got the, whole, story. I have to admit that I panicked as Tammy told me Juliana was in the Emergency Room. I got my employee back into my car and raced up the highway to drop him off at his car so I could go to the Emergency Room. The fall caused one of Juliana's front teeth to come out which, under normal circumstances, was not supposed to come up for a few more years. As a result, she had a gap in her teeth for a few years.

We continued our tradition of celebrating our kid's adoption days with a cake and ice cream as well as their birthdays. Another Easter came and went with the kids loving all their candy. It was never a dull moment in our home. We took day trips and lots of fun outdoors. In early December 2005 we celebrated Juliana's fourth birthday. She wore a purple shirt. She was so excited. She blew and blew and blew until the candles were out.

By mid December my employer, at the time, was able to offer us a trip to Florida. As always, the kids loved the beach. We were there for several days and had loads of fun. Christmas time was upon us before we knew it. One day, I heard someone on our piano. Juliana, then age four, climbed up on the piano and started to hit the keys and sing "Bells are Ringing." Of course, I grabbed my video camera and recorded most of it. The excitement, on Christmas morning, was intense. The kids waiting at the top of the steps, as was our custom, so everyone could come downstairs at the same time. The energy, of the morning, was amazing to see as a set of parents who desperately wanted children could watch six happy faces open their gifts.

Tammy and I, soon, started to realize that with six small children our house began to "shrink." There was no way, we thought, that we could afford a larger house so the kids would not have to share bedrooms. It didn't seem possible. Earlier in the year we had new windows, siding and a back porch put on our house. One of the contractors, Bob Thomas, approached us about building a house. We didn't think it was possible much less affordable. He said that we would be surprised how much house we can get if we built it ourselves. After several weeks of thinking Tammy and I started looking for raw land to build a house. By that time, I had been working in the financial services industry since 1988 and my income was increasing.

2006 rolled in just like any other day. The kids continued to get bigger and keep our house very busy. In late January we met my parents at Olive Garden to celebrate my mother's birthday. Juliana, and all the kids, was healthy and Tammy and I were so thankful that our family life was stable.

We enrolled the kids in Martial Arts class as part of their home school gym schedule. Their instructor was Wil Lerp. He is a "biker dude" with a heart of pure gold. He was patient, but firm, with each of the kids as they learned their new skills. Rebecca had a kick that gave grown men a little hesitation in going up against her in matches. Juliana was one of the smallest ones in the group.. Wil not only taught about martial arts but he included lessons about living a life of integrity.

We continued to celebrate each of our children's birthdays and adoption anniversaries. We received several inches of snow in February so the kids went outside and enjoyed the snow. One day, in late March, I came down to the basement (that we have finished so the kids could have more space to play) and found that Juliana had opened the closet. We placed a small chalk board inside it among other things. She was wearing a multi-color striped shirt, pink pants and Elmo slippers and sitting on a plastic container and writing her name on the chalkboard. I asked her, "How did you get so smart?" She said, "Because I want to." I, then, asked her, "Who made you so beautiful." She said, "God." When she finished answering my question she drew a circle on the chalkboard.

      She walked over to the table that was outside the closet and pulled out a chair to drive the pretend car that was on top of the table. She said that she was going to drive to the store so I played along. She invited me to sit next to her in the "passenger seat." The "drive" lasted about thirty seconds. When we were done at the "store" we drove over a few big bumps on our way to "Pizza Hut." We pretended to get out of the car and walk inside to order some drinks and food from "Pizza Hut." Juliana said, "I would like to order some pizza and ketchup and French fries." We pretended to eat our food while sitting at the table in our basement.

Tammy used all kinds of science experiments, over the years, when she did home school with the kids. The same day Juliana showed me a jumping bean that Tammy had ordered for one of her classes with all the kids. She held it in her right hand and squealed as the bean, literally, started moving her tiny hand. Kristina walked up to us, wearing a blue and pink Pink Panther shirt, and told me the bean she was holding in her left hand was alive. Kristina said, "if it's moving it likes me."

A few days later I walked into the kitchen where Tammy was sewing a patch on Matthew's martial arts shirt. Juliana started, looking at her fingers, counting from one to ten for me....in Korean. She learned it in Wil Lerp's martial arts class as part of her training.

There were many nights, due to me traveling for work, I would get home late at night. One evening I heated up my dinner. Juliana came down the steps, from her bedroom which was within eye shot of the kitchen, and helped me finish my dinner. Another night I got home, when the kids were in bed, and couldn't find Timothy. I found him, asleep, on the floor underneath Lindsay's bed. It was so cute. The kids continued martial arts through the balance of 2006.

We continued our search for land to build a large house for our family. We found some land, north of Manchester Maryland, and bought it. It was six-and-a-half acres in the woods. The kids were very excited as we walked around the property imagining living in the woods instead of a neighborhood development.

We were, all, invited to the Russian Embassy in Washington DC, for a musical performance. Our kids wore their best clothes. The wife of the Russian Ambassador told us, and a room full of other families with Russian children and their American families, how special the children and families are in America. The children of the Embassy employees put on a play for all of us. Thankfully, it was in English except for the last few songs. It was a wonderful experience.

Easter came, again, so the kids colored Easter Eggs and found their Easter baskets on Easter morning. The kids continued doing their Martial Arts and were getting better and better. One day, after their Martial Arts class, while still wearing their uniforms we took them to visit my Grandmother (Mary Ellen McKinney) at her assisted living home. They showed some of their martial arts techniques while my Grandmother tried to copy them even though she was eighty-eight years old. In May 2006 we celebrated Timothy and Lindsay's seventh birthday. July fourth came and, as always, we had a cook out and lit sparklers and ground based fireworks.

A few days later we drove back to the land we purchased and walked through and around it. The kids loved the woods. The stakes were in the ground on the four corners of where the house would stand. Tammy, wearing a black shirt and pink pants, began to walk and describe where the house would be built. She could "see it" long before I could "see it." Her ability to see the house, before the ground was dug up, was incredible to me. At one point she said, "We're in our house right now…walking through the dining room." Tammy was very excited about having our house built the way we designed it. Each child would have their own bedroom. We built it for them.

By July 2006 the foundation, of our new home, was dug up. We took the kids, there, many times while it was being built. They were so excited. The kids ran around the woods having so much fun. July 27, 2006 the footers, of the new house, were poured. I, still, could not "see" the house completed. I said, on video, that the house didn't look wide enough. I was, so, wrong. Months passed as construction continued on our home. The kids would play around the construction site when Tammy and I would go check on the progress of the house.

One day, in October 2006, we were back at the new house. It was under roof and the inside was getting finished. Juliana had just run down the sidewalk. In my silly way I asked her (like it was interviewing her for the news), "How did you get so fast maam?" She said, "I'm not a maam…I'm a kid." She hopped up and walked over to me and said, "Dad, I'm Juliana Irina Carver."

December arrived and we celebrated Juliana's fifth birthday. Juliana's birthday cake was white and yellow with a mermaid on it. We invited some other families over to the house to celebrate her birthday. Juliana climbed up on one of the kitchen chairs. Juliana wore a red-striped shirt and blue pants. Her hair was getting so long. Juliana giggled as all of us sang Happy Birthday to her. She was so excited. She leaned forward and blew out the candles on her cake. It took about nine blows to get all the candles out. We clapped as she blew out her last candle and she smiled from ear to ear. Once we ate some cake we, all, walked into the family room where Juliana opened her gifts. Timothy sat a few feet away watching with great delight. Juliana said, "I love this day."

Christmas was coming up fast. The excitement, in our home, was growing by the day. All the kids helped decorate the Christmas Tree. A few days later we went back to our new house as they were putting siding on the house. The kids ran around the inside of the house imagining living in their new home. Less than a week later Tammy started baking Christmas cookies as Juliana, wearing a pink striped shirt, helped her bake them. Juliana said, "I love doing this." Juliana and Tammy would bake Christmas cookies, together, for several more years during the month of December.

A few days later we went up to the new house. The windows were in and the siding was still being put on. I heard, hysterical laughing, in what would be the master bedroom. I walked in and several of the kids are pointing out the window, almost, falling on the floor laughing so hard. They were pointing out one of the windows. The pointed to one of the workmen, on a scaffold, inches from the window hanging siding and his butt-crack was showing. The kids screamed with laughter.

Christmas morning was full of excitement. There was screaming when I told them Santa came to our house the night before. They walked down stairs and Timothy was screaming and jumping up and down. It was an amazing morning.

2006 came to an end. Our lives were about to be changed forever.

Chapter 5

January 2007 came and went. In early February, we were about to get some horrible news about Juliana. In January 2015, Tammy looked back and described it this way:

"Juliana had just turned five in December (2006). In February she came into our bedroom, one morning, and was complaining about a bump under her right arm. We felt it and thought that's really odd because she's not been sick and we don't know why there's this bump under her arm. The next day we took her to the pediatrician and she (the pediatrician) was stumped too. The pediatrician wanted to get some blood work (on Juliana) to see if there was some kind of infection that we couldn't see. We went to pull her sleeve up to drawl blood and that's when I noticed that she had this swollen area underneath her (right) arm. It was hard to see unless you looked at it at the right angle. I showed that to the pediatrician (Dr. Sara Spinner-Block) and she was pretty sure that it had something to do with the (swollen) lymph node and it didn't sound good so she sent her (Juliana) for an X-Ray. That showed nothing wrong with the bones so she decided she needed an MRI and, somehow, talked them into letting her have an MRI that very afternoon. So, we took her to the MRI, brought her (Juliana) home, had dinner and an hour or two after dinner the pediatrician called. That was the worst days of our lives. She told us that Juliana had cancer in her arm and metastasized to her lymph nodes."

I remember when we hung up the phone, talking to the pediatrician, as we stood in the foyer of our home. I embraced Tammy as she sobbed and sobbed on my shoulder. Her Dad, back in October 2004, had passed away from lung cancer and, now, our five year old daughter had cancer.

Tammy continued the story from looking back on it in 2015, "That started a whirlwind of events over the next few weeks. We took her to Sinai Hospital (In Baltimore Maryland) and met her pediatric oncologist for the first time. They talked to us and talked to the surgeon who was going to do a biopsy that day. We scheduled more appointment to get scans finished over the next week…pretty much over the next two weeks (Tammy described the variety of scans and biopsies Juliana received). We found out Juliana had Stage three Group 3 Alveolar Rhabdomysarcoma. Trying to explain to your five year old that she has cancer is really hard to do because they really don't understand it that much. Three weeks after we found out she had cancer she started treatment. The first treatment we had in-patient because they wanted to make sure there were no reactions to any of the chemotherapy drugs they were giving her. Juliana thought it was going to be fun. I told her it was going to be a sleep-over but she found out it wasn't so fun when she started throwing up in the middle of the night. Fortunately, the rest of the treatments were done out-patient. She had fourteen rounds of chemotherapy. There were some weeks we had to skip because her counts weren't high enough. She had six weeks of radiation every day which was back and forth and got really really bad radiation burns especially under her (right) arm."

Let me go back and give you more details from 2007. In February 2007 we celebrated Rebecca and Matthew's ninth adoption anniversary with cake and ice cream. A few days later we took Juliana to the hospital for a biopsy. An amazing nurse, Tracy, was so gentle with Juliana. One of the kids called my cell phone and Juliana was telling them that all she had to do to get the medicine was breathe. She was talking about putting put to sleep for a biopsy of her arm. While she was, still on the phone, she said, "Can I talk to Timmy?" Tim got on the phone and a smile lit up Juliana's face. She said, "Hi Tim…I'm at the, um….Tim?...I'm at the hospital right now. I'm having my test right now…not right now…later."

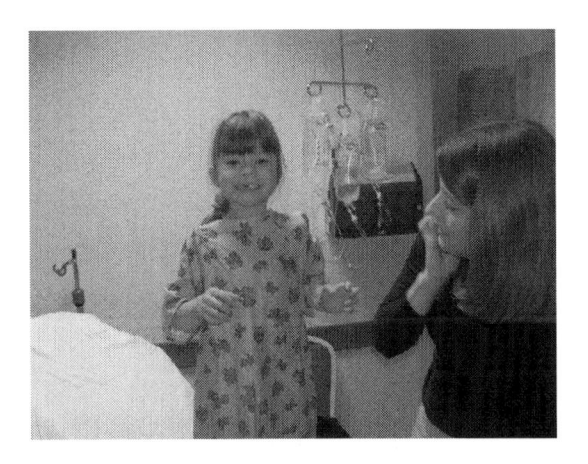

Moments later Juliana, with her hair up on a pony tail, walked down the hall as if she owned the hospital. She wore a light colored shirt and pants with flowers on it. She hopped from square to square that was inlaid into the linoleum floor. She was not worried about anything.

The time came for Juliana to get a biopsy of her arm. Tammy took Juliana by her right hand and they walked to the end of the hall and made a left turn into one of the rooms. Tracy, the nurse said,

"Hi, girlfriend!" I said, "this is a great place to take a nap." I was trying to ease any anxiety that Juliana might be getting now.

Juliana climbed up on the hospital bed like a professional and turned around and laid back on it. Tammy asked her, "Are you comfortable?" Juliana nodded yes. The nurses told Juliana they were going to put some stickers on her to monitor her heart beat. Tammy took off Juliana's black boots she was wearing. Tracy, the nurse, covered Juliana with a warm blanket. Juliana took her pony tail out so she could lay back all the way. Another nurse brought her a stuffed cat to hold. Juliana smiled so big. Juliana's hair was half-way down her back. I said, as they put the probes (stickers) on her chest, "Julie, I am so proud of you. You are so big." Juliana held the stuffed cat in her left arm while her right index finger had a pulse-ox on it.

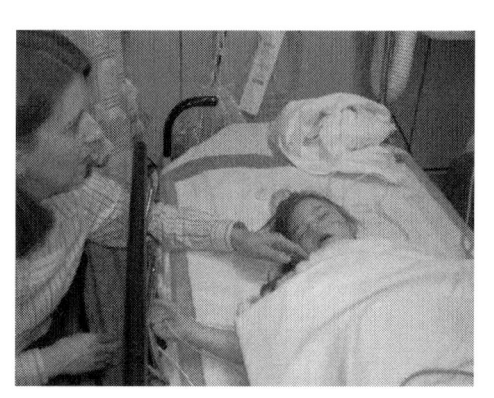

They put a blood pressure cup on her leg. She asked if

it was going to hurt. The nurses assured her it would not hurt. Tammy stood to Tammy's left side. The anestesiologist came into the room and, with Spunge –Bob clothes on put Juliana to sleep. A lot of people, at that hospital, called him Dr. Sponge-Bob. His real name is Dr. Aaron Zuckerberg. His kindness is extraordinary.

A little while later the procedure was done and Juliana was trying to wake up in the recovery room. Juliana smiled as she opened her eyes. Her stuffed cat was to Juliana's left as she stretched her arms, over her head, and gave a big yawn. As she woke up, more, Tammy rocked her in her on her lap.

In the following days more scans and tests happened. A few days later, we took the kids back to our new house to see that the sheetrock was up. Juliana walked, in the door, and with her left hand covered her mouth with amazement. The rest of the kids said, "WOW!" The kitchen cabinets were up and they were screaming as they ran through the house. Tammy and I could hear the echo of the kid's feet as they ran up and down the hallway on the second floor.

The kids ran, back, downstairs and onto the enclosed back porch which was, almost, completed.

Juliana said, "Dad, watch me jump" as she jumped over a long box of siding sitting on the back porch. The inside of the house was still being put together so we couldn't move in yet. We were, still, trying to sell our current home.

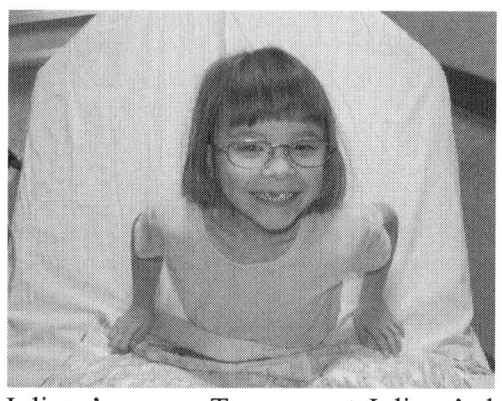

A few days later, we were back in the hospital, for another one of Juliana's scans. Tammy got Juliana's haircut really short since it would be falling out. I put her pony tails in a bag (which I still have today). Juliana colored in a coloring book before being put to sleep again. After the procedure, Tammy rocked her until she woke up. One of my goals was to keep Juliana laughing as much as possible as she was fighting cancer. The hospital put a port in Juliana's chest to make it easier to get chemotherapy.

In early March 2007, Juliana was admitted to the hospital for her first round of chemotherapy. My mother, Edna, called to speak to Juliana.

Juliana, using my cell phone told my mom, "the whole thing is fun, I got my own clock and my own blanket and I can put my feet up if I do this (then she pushed a button on her bed to make her feet go up)" and gave me a big smile. Matthew, Juliana's big brother, got on the phone and she told him, "I'm at the hospital in my own bed…for a sleepover." Within moments, Juliana asked to speak to Tim (her other big brother) on the phone. Tammy and I, both, kept telling Juliana that this is "no big deal" even though we were scared out of our minds.

A little more than an hour later Juliana received her first dose of chemotherapy. She was wearing pink pajamas sitting up in bed and watching television as a nurse, covered in a yellow gown, put the chemo in Juliana's IV. Tammy gave her some bubbles to blow to help pass the time. My sister, Michele, came by for a visit to Juliana's hospital room.

The next day I brought the rest of the kids, to the hospital, and found Juliana in the hospital play room. Juliana was wearing pink pajamas as Tammy pulled her IV pole behind her. We, all, walked back to Juliana's hospital room. Juliana was very proud to show off her hospital room. The room was very small but we, all, squeezed in to hang out with Juliana and Tammy. A nurse walked in to check Juliana vital signs. Everything was normal. Every time the nurses would check and clear Juliana's port they would put heparin in it. Juliana kept calling it "peppermint" so that's what Tammy started calling it.

In March we celebrated Rebecca's birthday as Juliana sat next to her as Rebecca opened her birthday cards. Juliana went back and forth to the hospital a lot. The kids would accompany Juliana as much as possible. Tammy continued to home school all the kids. In one of Juliana's first clinic appointments Dr. Jason Fixler (Juliana's mail oncologist) examined Juliana's right arm and said, "it doesn't feel as dense…as full as before…good"

On March 19, 2007, Juliana received round two of chemotherapy. She was wearing a white shirt and pink pants. She, still, had her hair at this time. Juliana, always, insisted on taking the tape off her the area where her port was located. She was in charge. Juliana started playing a video game while the nurse began to insert a needle into the port in her chest. Tammy had put EMLA cream to numb her chest before we came back to the hospital that day. EMLA became a life-saver for many years. Lindsay looked on as the nurse was getting the needle ready to give Juliana. The nurse placed the needle into Juliana's port and Juliana didn't even flinch. The nurse said, "so brave." Juliana said, "doesn't hurt." Tim said, "I would cry if that happened to me."

When we were done we drove back to our new house to find them putting the hard wood floors down. Juliana hopped down the basement steps. The gentleman who put up the kitchen cabinets, Dale Yingling, put the boxes they came in the breakfast room. Shortly after we arrived Dale cut holes in the boxes to make them into little houses. The kids LOVED them. Lindsay said, "Look Dad, they have doors and windows." I said, "Those houses were built a lot faster than our house." Lindsay climbed out of one of the box-houses and said to me, "Let me give you a tour…here's a door and here is a window." Matthew found some tape and put a "lock" on his house. Dale would become an amazing and faithful friend for many years to come.

Finally, moving day arrived while some "finishing touches" were being done on the new house. A couple hours later I walked upstairs to find Juliana asleep on the floor, covered with a blue blanket, of her new room. The chemotherapy treatments were making her very tired. The following weekend several friends, from church, came over to help us pain the kid's bedrooms. Days later the kid's rooms were finished and their beds were in place. Juliana loved her new room. It was painted purple which one of her favorite colors.

We celebrated Kristina's adoption day...the first one in our new house. We bought the kids some walkie-talkies as our land was so large we wanted to be able to reach the kids wherever they were on the property. All the kids were very patient with Juliana as she endured cancer treatments. Juliana's hair started to fall out and she was losing weight. Juliana wore a scarf on her head as the kids colored Easter eggs. On Easter morning you could really see how thin Juliana's hair was getting from the chemotherapy. Lindsay and Rebecca had poison ivy from playing in the woods. The, other, kids guided Juliana to where her Easter basket was hidden.

Within a week Juliana's hair was, almost, gone. By the end of Juliana's, daily, radiation treatments the burns (from them) were horrible even though Tammy would put cream on where the radiation was hitting Juliana's little body. We took all the kids to several of Juliana's radiation treatments. Juliana was losing weight. I could see her ribs. Tammy would lift Juliana up onto the table where Juliana would get radiation treatments. Dr. Cardella Coleman was Juliana's radiation oncologist. She was amazing with Juliana and us too. Juliana would giggle when a radiation technologist would use a "Sharpie" pen and mark, on Juliana's arm and chest, where the radiation would go. Juliana remained very brave and positive through months of treatment. Juliana carried her little stuffed cat to most of her hospital visits.

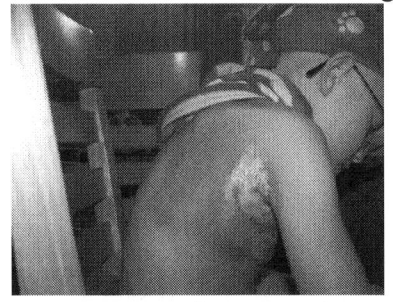

By April 26, 2007 Juliana's her hair was totally gone. In the early Summer, my friend, Bradd Atkinson, invited us to his house to see his ducks and go swimming. A couple weeks, later, David Hall, came by our home and built the kids a tree house. The kids were so excited. Tim, Rebecca and Matthew helped some too. Juliana had lost weight. Juliana looked at me, while David Hall, was building the tree house, with a red scarf on her bald head and said, "Dad, I love you billions and billions." I said, "I love you zillions and zillions." Juliana said, "I love you that much too" and walked over to Tammy as she watched the construction of the tree house with the rest of the kids. Juliana hopped up, from Tammy's lap, and found a stick and began to use it as a microphone and sing a song then she walked over to a swing and sat beside her big brother Timothy.

The kids continued to be kids, laugh and enjoy their new home and the outdoors. In early June, we celebrated Tim's sixth adoption day. Tim insisted that Dale Yingling, the man who built the kids the houses out of cardboard boxes, sit next to him when he blew out the candles on his adoption day cake. The other kids remained in martial arts until it was just getting too much to do with Juliana's cancer treatments.

July fourth came and we had a cookout on the back porch and lit ground-based fireworks on the driveway. In mid July we were invited by Mike

Hunter to his ranch in North Carolina. We stayed in one of his cabins. The kids rode horses and had all kinds of fun that week. Mike was so kind to invite us.

We celebrated Tammy's birthday on August 8 with an ice cream cake. Juliana helped her blow out the candles. Later in the month we took the kids to Ocean City Maryland for a few days. As we arrived to the beach Juliana was wearing a pink shirt, blue shorts and a dark blue bandana on her head. The kids loved the beach.

In October we went pumpkin picking with all the kids. The kids enjoyed the outdoors as the Fall was in full force. Juliana was able to run and play and tried to keep up with the rest of the kids. Tammy got the kids involved in a home school gym club which they really enjoyed. The day came when it was time to cut out the pumpkins they got from the pumpkin patch followed by going trick-or-treating the following night. Juliana walked, the entire way, and was so excited. She wore a little bandana on her head.

By this time, I started a YouTube channel sharing pieces of Juliana's fight against cancer. I was hoping that as more people followed Juliana and they would say prayers for her that God might hear those prayers and keep Juliana healthy for the rest of her life. I thought, for sure, that God would pay attention, to Juliana's war against cancer, if thousands or hundreds of thousands of people would pray for Juliana from around the world.

A few days later (in early November) a home nurse, Judy, came by the house to check on Juliana. Juliana wore a purple long-sleeve shirt and blue pants. She was so tiny sitting in our lounge chair as the nurse took her temperature. The nurse brought some medicine to put into a little "ball" that Juliana would carry around until the medicine was gone. She didn't have to drag around a medicine poll while getting her medicine. The nurse accessed Juliana's port while Juliana sat in our blue lounge chair. Eventually, the nurse left and Juliana and a few of the other kids sat on the sofa and watch television while Juliana's medicine went in her little body.

Thanksgiving Day, as always, was full of our extended family. Tammy does a fantastic job preparing Thanksgiving Dinner each year. We got the other kids involved in a home school soccer group which they enjoyed. Indoor soccer would come to be one of Matthew's passions. The day after Thanksgiving Tammy and I pulled out the Christmas decorations. Most of the kids jumped in to help decorate. Juliana asked me, "are you going to take a picture of me with my presents." I said, "Of course." This was our first Christmas in our new house.

On December first we celebrated Lindsay's eighth adoption day (we celebrated each of our kids adoption days each year). A few days later we celebrated Juliana's sixth birthday. She was so excited to have her, future uncle Thomas, Aunt Michele and her grandparents at her party. She had a, serious, crush on her future Uncle Thomas. Her birthday cake was white with a dachshund dog on it.

Christmas Eve came and the kids were very excited. They opened gifts that they had gotten each other. Later that night, I walked up to Juliana's room (when she was in bed). I asked her why everybody is so excited so she looked up at me, with her beautiful bald head and said, "because it's Christmas tomorrow morning....you and mom have to go to bed soon." A few minutes later she "tooted" which caused her to giggle. I said, "stinky poo." She "tooted" a second time and laughed even harder. She sat up and said, "I love you Daddy." I, then, walked into each of the other's kid's rooms and chatted with them for a few minutes.

Christmas morning came and Tim sneaked into Rebecca's room and climbed under her covers. Juliana was, already, awake when I checked on her. Lindsay said she heard "pitter patter" of something on the roof. It was 6:23 in the morning. The kids got up and got ready to go downstairs to open their gifts. It was lots of screaming and excitement. As was our, long standing custom, all the kids came down the steps at the same time. Sounds of paper ripping and screams filled the air.

The day came, a few days after Christmas 2007, that it was (we thought) Juliana's last chemotherapy treatment. Juliana was wearing a green outfit and all of us were very excited to get cancer behind us forever. Juliana pulled out the binder that had a calendar of all her treatments and scans in it and used a yellow highlighter to highlight her last chemo treatment. After she got back from chemotherapy we got a cake for Juliana and we all sang, "Congratulations to you." She giggled, so hard, as she blew out the candle.

A couple weeks later Juliana had some scans to make sure the cancer was gone. The scans were clear…a HUGE relief for all of us…especially Juliana. Juliana was starting to gain weight again and feel good.

Tammy continues, from a conversation I had with her back in January 2015 describing part of Juliana's first battle against cancer. "We (Juliana) started her treatments in the beginning of March (2007) and by January 2008 she got all of her off treatment scans and we were expecting good news. They said something showed up on her (Juliana's) PET/CT that it lit up on the PET and they looked at it on the CT and it looked like there were lesions on her lung and that she relapsed. The oncologist (Dr. Jason Fixler) was really upset. They managed to do a lung biopsy for the following day and did surgery through. Come to find out it wasn't lesions at all. It was "radiation recall" because part of her lung was hit from the radiation (treatments). The chemotherapy, we were giving her, was causing it to flare up."

Chapter 6

February 2008 rolled around and Juliana was due for her scans to make sure she was, still, cancer free. These scans went on for years. The scans, she got in February, she wore a pink sweat suit with a black bandana with good footprints on it. Tammy brought some spelling words for Juliana to work on. Juliana was, always, a great student who strove for perfection in everything she attempted. Her scans were clear. The same month we celebrated Rebecca and Matthew's tenth adoption anniversary.

The day came when Juliana had her port removed from her chest. The doctor joked with Juliana and asked her if she wanted a tattoo or a belly button ring during the surgery. After the surgery Juliana was trying to wake up in the recovery room. Juliana was six years old. A couple days later Juliana and Lindsay were performing a dance and singing performance for us. A few days later, for Rebecca's birthday, we all went to the mall. Rebecca wanted her ears pierced. Easter, soon, followed so the kids colored Easter eggs. Juliana's hair was starting some come back. This time it was much darker in color. On Easter Morning the kids looked for their Easter baskets.

In late March we had a big party to celebrate Juliana being cancer free. A lot of people came to our house to help us celebrate the great news. Juliana received lots of gifts.

Mary Bohlen was the social worker, at Sinai Hospital in Baltimore Maryland. She put us in touch with organizations that offered trips and other fun activities to families of critically ill children. One of the organizations she contacted, for us, was the Lighthouse Family Retreat (https://www.lighthousefamilyretreat.org/). In early

April 2008 we drove to Florida for a week at an event sponsored by the Lighthouse Family Retreat. It was a magical week for all of us. The kids had so much fun as we were with about a dozen other children who were fighting to live.

Lindsay would, regularly, have singing and dancing performances with Juliana and Kristina in our basement. We continued to celebrate the other kid's adoption anniversaries and birthdays. It was time for more scans. May came around and Juliana's hair was getting so thick.

Make-a-Wish contacted us for Juliana pick something she would like to have as she beat cancer. After lots of thinking Juliana chose an above ground pool for our yard. She LOVED that pool…all the kids loved that pool.

It was, now, August 26, 2008 and we celebrated Juliana's adoption day with a white cake with red letter on it. Her hair continued to grow and get thicker. Mary Bohlen put us in touch with Believe in Tomorrow (https://believeintomorrow.org/) who offered us the opportunity to spend a few days in their cabin in Western Maryland. Believe in Tomorrow would help us, several times, in the years ahead. We had a great time.

When we got home, through the rest of the Autumn, the kids enjoyed the outdoors. In October we had a big Halloween party, at our house, and invited relatives and friends of our kids. It was time for more scans. Juliana's port was out so she was SO scared, as Tammy held her on her lap, when she got to get the needle to put the dye in her for the scans. She was so brave. Her scans, thankfully, were clear. Several weeks later Tammy and the kids decorated for Christmas. December 4, 2008 and Juliana's seventh birthday arrived. Christmas was full of fun and excitement.

2009 rushed into our lives. Juliana's hair was, now, really dark and curly. By now she had lost another front tooth. It was time for more scans in February. Juliana was so nervous about getting the needle for the dye to get the scan because her port had been taking out so she would have to get a needle in her arm. Tammy stooped down to Juliana's right side as Juliana held out her left arm for the needle. Juliana was so tense and squinting her eyes. Tammy said, "You're very brave." She wore a pink short-sleeve shirt and blue pants. The scans were clear again. When it was all over and

Tammy and Juliana were getting ready to leave Juliana held a white stuffed dog in her right arm. The days and weeks were full of school work, day trips and the kids playing.

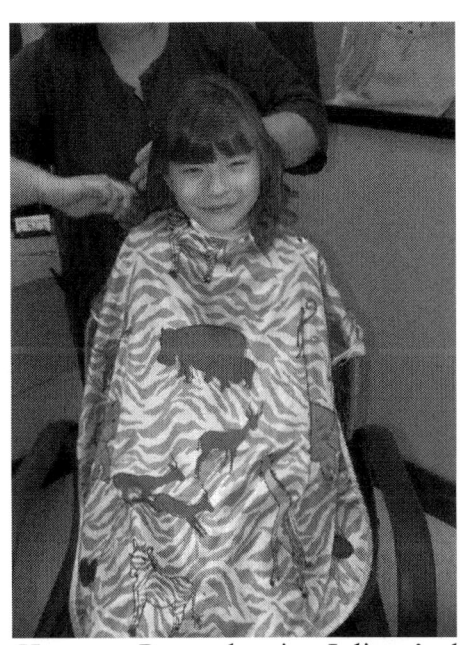

Juliana got her, first, haircut in a long time on April 4, 2009.

By the time April 2009 arrived we were taking the kids to the park on a regular basis. Their favorite park is in Hanover Pennsylvania. Juliana's hair was thinker than it had ever been in her life. The four younger kids (Lindsay, Timothy, Kristina and Juliana) loved to swim and play in our sprinkler. Lindsay got her ears pierced for her birthday. Lindsay and Timothy celebrated their tenth birthday in May. Juliana sat between them as they blew out their candles. Juliana started learning how to ride her bike without training wheels. Juliana got so upset when she fell. Lindsay said to Juliana, "You can't get mad at yourself." Lindsay was trying to help teach her. A few days later Juliana wanted to show me that she could ride without falling. She was wearing a black shirt, blue shorts and had her hair in a pony tail. She rode, her bike, all the way down the driveway looking like a professional. She's always been a perfectionist.

May came along and we were headed to the Carolinas for my sister's wedding. We were so excited for my sister Michele. The kids enjoyed the pool and the beach. We were able to tour a World War Two ship (USS North Carolina) that I toured when I was a little kid.

In early June it was time for more scans for Juliana. She wore a pink shirt and black shorts. Juliana was, always, so brave. By early June she had lost another tooth so three teeth were missing in the front of her mouth. The day, of the scan, she was very focused. Tammy stood to her right side and held her other hand. Juliana closed her eyes and started breathing very heavy. She hated needles. Tammy kept talking to Juliana to keep her mind off of the stress of the moment. Both, Juliana and Tammy, were wearing a pink shirt. Juliana shed no tears that day. Juliana learned, after received so many scans, going back to 2007 when she was five years hold, how important it was to be still during the scans. It went much faster that way. After the scans she was examined by Dr. Jason Fixler when went to the 5-Below Store. Dr. Jason Fixler always teased me about video- taping and taking lots of photos. The scans were clear.

Juliana was turning into a "professional" badminton player in our front yard. She was determined to win at everything she attempted to do. Most of the kids loved to play the game a few times a week. July fourth came and we, as always, had a cookout followed by sparklers and ground-based fireworks. On this day, Juliana was" grading" the quality of the fireworks. One she gave a B+ and another an A+. She was so funny. It has, always, been a special day for our family since we adopted Rebecca and Matthew in 1998. We celebrated each of our kids birthdays and adoption days until they reached the age of eighteen. A couple weeks later we celebrated Matthew's birthday. A week, for so, later we took the kids to a local 4H fair where they saw a lot of farm animals. Juliana's hair was getting so long and thick. It was much thicker and darker than before she had cancer back in 2007.

In August 2009 our church, Faith Outreach Chapel, had a birthday party for Tammy's 41st birthday. We had one, for her, a day or two later at home. Juliana held Tammy's left hand and moved it up and down as most of the kids sang Happy Birthday to Tammy. The same month we celebrated Juliana's sixth adoption anniversary with a white cake and purple icing. A couple weeks later we took the kids to their favorite park in Hanover Pennsylvania.

September 2009 came and it was time for more scans for Juliana. She wore yellow shorts and a white shirt. The scans became a "routine" for our lives. Tammy and I lived in terror that the cancer would return. Again, Tammy stood by Juliana's right side comforting her while she got the needle, in her left arm, for the scans. We never had her stuck with a needle in her right arms because of all the damage the cancer and radiation did to that right arm. Tammy said, "take a deep breath" as Juliana turned her head toward Tammy and closed her eyes. Tammy had engulfed Juliana's head with her left arm and covered Juliana's left ear and cheek with her hand. Tammy has been, beyond, amazing throughout Juliana war against cancer. Thankfully, the scans were clear…again.

A few days later, Lindsay arranged for another one of her concerts, in our basement, when we got home. Juliana and Lindsay worked on a song and dance routine for us to watch. Tammy continued to home school all the kids. Later in the month we took a trip, with other home school families, to the Baltimore Zoo. I gave the kids a disposable camera in case they wanted pictures of the animals for themselves. Fall arrived and Juliana kept getting better a riding her two-wheel bike. We had signed up Lindsay and Kristina in dance classes to see if they would enjoy it. They did dance class for about a year. In October 2009 we went to the Baltimore and Ohio Museum. In October 2016, Juliana, Tammy and Kristina were there for a Cool Kids Campaign (childrenscancerfoundation.org) fundraiser. Juliana, in October 2016, was fighting cancer for the eighth time. I will share that horrible story later in this book.

Thanksgiving came and went as Tammy prepared dinner for a lot of family members. The day after the kids helped put up Christmas decorations. Matthew was active in indoor soccer which he has developed a passion and I attended as many of his games as possible. We celebrated Juliana's eighth birthday with a chocolate cake with strawberry's on top of it. A couple weeks later we, all, attended a dance recital which Lindsay and Kristina performed along with several other girls.

On December nineteenth we received several inches of snow. The kids got their coats and boots on and had so much fun playing in the snow. Christmas Eve arrived and the kids exchanged gifts with each other. Christmas morning arrived and the kids, of course, were so excited. Juliana asked me, as they waited at the top of the steps, if Santa ate the cookies we left for him. They raced down the steps and tore open their gifts.

In mid February 2010 we received a blizzard which dumped several inches of snow in our area. By now, Rebecca joined Matthew in playing soccer. Tammy and I felt, nervously, that cancer was behind us forever. The terror, that the cancer could return racked our minds every-single-day. May arrived and Tammy continued having the kids involved in various home school groups.

We continued to enjoy the outdoors as much as possible. Once again, it was time for Juliana to get scans. She did it like a professional. Tammy said, "You always worry about nothing." She was quoting Juliana's words as Juliana would get upset at herself about stressing, in her words, "about nothing." Thankfully, the scans were clear.

The family celebrations continued for the kids adoption days and birthdays. Summer time brought lots of time in the pool and a trip to pick peaches. In late August we celebrated Juliana's seventh adoption day. Later in the week we took the kids back to the park to play in addition to lots of fun at our house and going to pick pumpkins. Thanksgiving came and went and Christmas came and the kids were so excited.

I continued to share Juliana fight, on my YouTube channel, and asked people to say prayers for her because we didn't want her to get cancer again. We wanted Juliana to stay healthy and grow up to reach all her hopes and dreams.

At this time Lindsay joined a soccer team and really seemed to enjoy it. In February 2010 we celebrated another adoption anniversary for Rebecca and Matthew. We did the same to all the kids throughout each year.

In March 2011, our world imploded for the second time. Tammy shares, from her looking back on this time in 2015:

March 2011 - "Juliana had been off (cancer) treatment for three years. She was nine years old and we really thought she beat cancer. She had her scans less than a month (earlier). She (Juliana) told me that she had a bump in her groin area and she thought since she was playing home gym class at the time and got it by a volley ball and she thought it was a bruise of some kind or a lump from getting hit by a ball. At first, we didn't think anything of it and then she mentioned a week later something about that bruise. I was like Julie that should be getting better and be gone by now. Let me see this bruise. When she showed me the bruise I knew that was not a bruise. Where it was located, I thought maybe it's not a swollen lymph node maybe it's a hernia or something like that so I took her back to the pediatrician and told her "please tell me that's not a swollen lymph node." She looked at it and said, "It is." So, we started looking and we found she had a swollen area

in her right thigh. We went, directly, from the pediatrician's office right back to Sinai Hospital (in Baltimore Maryland) to see her Oncologist and started the whole process again.

She had to have all the scans done again, another biopsy done of her right thigh and we had to come up with a new treatment plan. She ended up having to get another twelve weeks of chemotherapy..a totally different type of chemotherapy she had the first time. She tolerated that chemo really well. We finished it then she did five weeks of radiation into both areas (the right thigh and the groin where the lymph node was). She flew through the chemo, that time, easy and didn't have any neutropenic fevers (like she did the first time Juliana fought cancer). We thought "maybe it was gone, for good, this time."

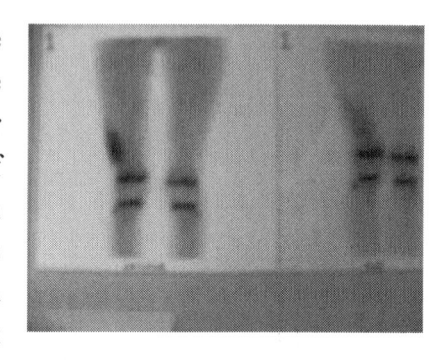

One day, in March 2011, Juliana said to Timothy (her big brother), "Why does this have to happen to me? At least I know what I have to do."

Her courage continued to blow my mind. Juliana is the strongest human being I have ever known.

Juliana had another port put back in her chest. During 2011 and while Juliana was getting cancer treatment for the second time Juliana wanted to get her ears pierced so we took her to the mall to make that happen. Juliana was SO excited. Tammy remained by her side just like she would do, every time, Juliana was in the hospital. Over the next several weeks Juliana's hair began to fall out again but this time it only fell out on the top of her head. Her long, dark hair on the back of her head didn't fall out.

I brought the rest of the kids, to the hospital, to hang out with Juliana. I would keep up the other kid's sports schedules while Juliana and Tammy were in the hospital. On one of Juliana's first, multi day, stays at the hospital for this fight against cancer Rebecca made her a Welcome Home Cake.

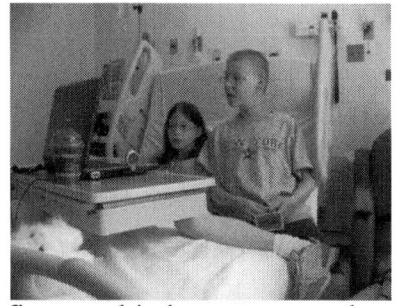

Juliana couldn't wait to get back home, after each chemo treatment, so she could continue being a little girl. She didn't let cancer stop her from having fun. May came around and the kids spent a lot of time in our pool. June 6, 2011 was one of the days I brought the rest of the kids to see Juliana in the hospital. Timothy crawled in bed with her to hang out; Juliana put her left arm around Timothy's neck and gave him a big hug. Juliana was wearing a pink shirt and Tim was wearing a grey New York shirt. Juliana was being treated, like last time, by Dr. Jason Fixler and Dr. Joseph Wiley and now, Dr. Yuram Unguru. Juliana's hair was starting to get thin on the top of her head. Nurse Tracy, who helped Juliana when she first got cancer in 2007, stopped by the playroom to see Juliana and give her a big hug. The weeks passed and Juliana, as much as possible, went swimming with Lindsay, Kristina and Timothy.

Juliana spent so much time in the hospital and never complained. She never whined. Tammy and Juliana were together through it all. Our other children were beyond understanding to Juliana's fight against cancer. In late June, Tammy and I bought new mattresses and box springs for all the kids just as Juliana had lost, almost, all her hair on the top of her head. The kids were so excited about their new bedding. They were screaming with excitement.

As was our custom, we had a cookout on July fourth. Tammy, always, backed a cake that looked like the American Flag using white icing, strawberries and blueberries.

The kids continued to enjoy the rest of the summer between Juliana's cancer treatments. Mary Bohlen, the social worker from Sinai Hospital, asked if we would like to have family photos taken by this amazing organization so we agreed. They were so kind. Casey Cares (Caseycares.org) made it possible for us to go to a Baltimore Orioles Baseball Game. September came along and Matthew was, still, very much into playing soccer. He did so well and scored lot of goals that I tried to get all of them on video. I missed a few of them.

Lindsay and Juliana used to love playing the Wii game where you sang popular songs and danced to choreographed dance moves. Also, in September the chain broke on the front swing, while Tammy was on it, and sent her flying and broke her wrist. Tammy pushed on, after she got her wrist in a cast, because Juliana was still getting chemotherapy. Winter came and the kids continued to love playing in the snow. Thanksgiving came and

Tammy, once again, fixed a fantastic meal for about eighteen people. Juliana was starting to get her hair back on that day. The day after Thanksgiving, per Tammy's custom, the kids helped decorate for Christmas.

It was time, in early December 2011, for Juliana's tenth birthday. Friends and family came by including Juliana's pediatrician Dr. Sara Spinner-Block. We were so thankful Juliana made it to her tenth birthday. She had a chocolate cake that Tammy made for her.

Later, in the month, we went to the annual skating party sponsored by the Children's Cancer

Foundation. They asked me to join their volunteer Board of Directors a couple years later.

Christmas morning was another blur. The energy, in the room, was (as always) so amazing to watch the kids open their gifts. Tammy and I waited so many years to be able to see something like this, for our own children. It was incredible.

## Chapter 7

On January 3, 2012 I was invited to go with my parents to meet Mr. and Mrs. Youkers. They are the parents of Bethany. Bethany is a young lady, who passed away, and donated her heart. My mother, Edna, would receive her heart. My mom's heart was damaged by cancer treatments as she fought cancer a couple of times. The meeting was so emotional. The Youkers are an amazing family.

January 12, 2012 came and Juliana continued to receive radiation treatments. If I couldn't make it to the treatments, as well, Tammy remained close to Juliana as the radiation technicians adjusted the radiation beams to help Juliana. Juliana was, always, to brave as she had to be locked in a big room, alone, while she received the treatments. We could talk to her and hear her through a microphone but it seemed, to me, that we were so far away. On this day, she just crossed her arms over her chest and waited until she was finished. Cancer treatment was, quickly, becoming a part of our lives…especially Juliana's life.

The next day, I took the other kids to their home school gym class. January 21, 2012 was here and the kids went out and played in the snow. Most of the kids enjoyed playing in it and sliding down our back hill. The sounds of their screams, as they were sledding, gave me so much joy.

In February, Juliana was honored at a StrongHope Foundation (stronghopefoundation.org) swim meet. The founder of StrongHope is my friend Bradd Atkinson. One of his closest friends passed away when they were young and it left a huge hole in his heart. StrongHope raised money, through sporting activities, to find ways to helps families fighting pediatric cancer and fund pediatric cancer research. The swim group, of kids, wanted to show all the swimmers how brave Juliana is and did not let cancer stop her from pushing to be the very best. They had a group photo taken, with Juliana in it, and they signed it. The framed photo hangs in Juliana's room as I write these words.

On March 6th Juliana received more scans. Tammy, as always, stayed by her side.

March 13, 2012 came along and it was such a warm day the kids played outside and they roasted marshmallows. On March 18th, another warm day, the four younger kids had a water balloon fight. It was so fun watching them run around the yard. I continued to take Matthew and Lindsay to their soccer games and video a lot of them. On March 23rd Juliana had another surgery. The hair, on the top, of her head was getting so thick. I called her "the champion of champions…the best of the best" as she had her hospital robe on sitting in the pre-operation room. She turned on television and watched Tom and Jerry to get her mind off of what was happening. She was so nervous.

They gave her to "loopy medicine" to make her less stressed before the surgery. She wore a dark blue puffy cap as they rolled her into the operating room. I gave her a kiss. She said, "I feel loopy." One of the doctors told her a knock- knock joke as they rolled her down the hall. After the surgery Tammy and I walked back to see Juliana. The nurse said Juliana is "doing great." She, eventually, woke up and we got her a pop sickle. She said, "Now, I don't have to worry about it." She was referring to the surgery since it was all done now.

April came along and there was more coloring of Easter Eggs, going to the park and enjoying Easter. On April 15$^{th}$ we took a family trip to Washington DC to go to the Smithsonian Museum. We had a really nice time. Juliana was feeling good and it was a bright and sunny day. Our friend, Dale Yingling, came along with us.

In early May we celebrated Tim and Lindsay's birthday. On May 12, 2012 we had a, very rare, earthquake. I was at my office when the entire building started shaking and I heard screams, from the hall way, and people running up and down the hall. Later in the day, when I got home, Matthew said the shelves in the garage were shaking. The next day, Kristina and Juliana went swimming even though the pool water was pretty cold. On May 16$^{th}$ we took the kids back to the zoo and as always they had a great time. The end of May involved more soccer for Matthew and Lindsay.

It was just a couple days into June 2012 and Juliana's life was about to take another turn for the worse.

Tammy shares, from her looking back on this time in 2015 then I will share details of the balance of 2012:

"Juliana was only off treatment four months from her first relapse until we found out she relapsed again. It was really weird. We were, actually, at my uncles funeral at the graveside service and we're standing there listening to the minister speak and she (Juliana) had this awful pain. It was so bad I thought she was going to pass out. I had to pick her up and carry her back into the church. Finally, the pain subsided after ten or fifteen minutes. It went away by itself but we knew something was really wrong because she never had that kind of pain ever and Julie has a really high pain tolerance. She had off-treatment scans that were coming due and already scheduled for two days later. I called her oncologist, brought her in (to the hospital), did an exam and didn't find anything from the exam but decided that if I could talk them into it they would add another scan to where the pain was so I called up the radiology place and talked them into doing three MRIs back to back which they do not ever do but I begged and pleaded and they agreed to do it for me.

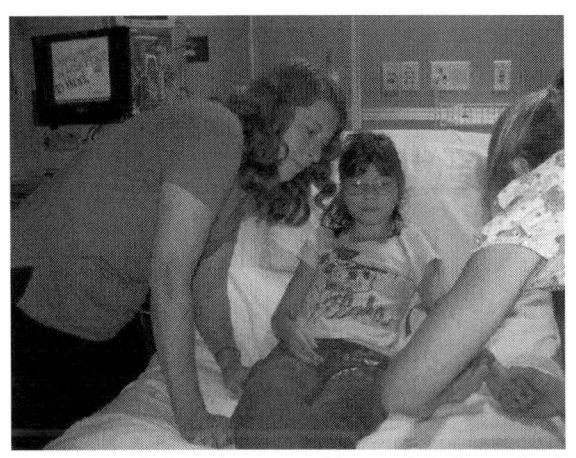

I took her the next day and Juliana had three, very long, MRIs. Afterwards, I waited, and had them burn (the scans) onto a disc because I knew something was really wrong. We went home from there and had dinner and then we got a phone call right after dinner. The doctor said, "I want both of you (me and John) on the phone. We knew it was not good news. He told us she had relapsed again that the MRI showed that her vena cava was either a clot or being constricted and couldn't tell which from the MRI as it wasn't very clear and they need to do another scan as soon as possible to see what, exactly, what was going on. It was serious enough that she needed to be admitted that night.

We told Juliana and packed a suitcase, went to the hospital and were admitted. We thought we were going to be there two or three nights but it ended up...we had CT scans that night and they showed, not only was it defiantly pressing the vena cava but there was another one in her chest that was

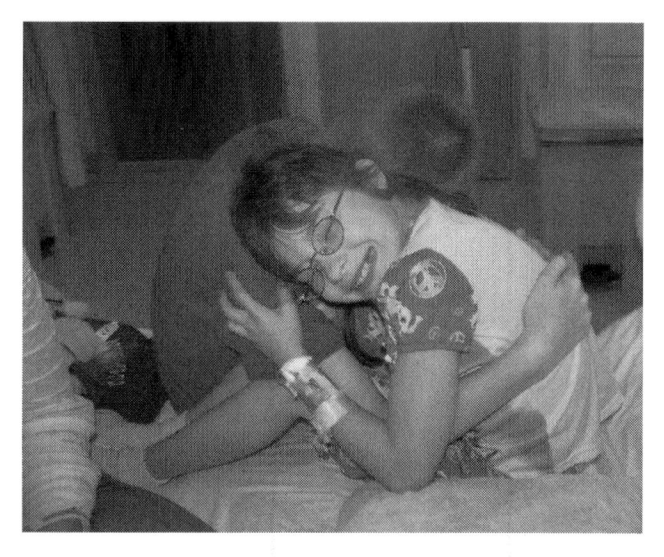

pushing against her aorta causing increased pressure which was dangerous.

She relapsed, not to another muscle, but it was in the mediastinum and retroperintoneal lymph nodes. We ended up staying (at the hospital), they talked to us and came up with another treatment plan. This time it was going to be a harsh treatment that would have to be given all in patient for five days in a row every-single-round and they needed to start it right away because we had to do something about those tumors. We had to fix it with chemo or surgery because you can't have it (the tumors) compressing on the vena cava because it will stop blood flow to the lower part of (Juliana's) body.

They scheduled her for surgery. They put Hickman Lines in (Juliana's chest) because they needed two lines to do the treatment they planned. The next day, they started the first day of the five-days of chemo. It was really, really, really nasty. They started with some serious anti-nausea drugs but once she started throwing up from this chemo they couldn't get it stopped. We ended up staying, not just the five days of chemo and three days before that but a few days after the five days of chemo because they couldn't get her to stop throwing up. Until we could get her to keep down her anti nausea medicine we couldn't go home.

Ten days later we were finally able to get home. They sent her home on fluids. She was, still, really dehydrated. That was the beginning of an entire year of treatment that was just nasty. We were there for a week for treatment (Monday through Friday) then off for two or three weeks depending on Juliana's counts. On the off weeks we would be there two or three days a week getting blood and platelet transfusions....during that time, I think, she got over eighty (80) blood/platelet transfusions. It was just really nasty.

She, also, got two neutropenic fevers. One of them, actually, had bacterial infection in her (Hickman) line which was life threatening in and of itself. We ended up, in the hospital six days for that. She got massive amounts of antibiotics. Finally, we made it through the treatment and then went into seeing about getting radiation therapy. We found out that they wouldn't be able to do (radiation) both areas at the same time like they had done previously because there were such large areas and so much bone marrow was going to be hit they were afraid it was going to drop her counts too low and her immune system had not come back from all the chemo she just had.

We ended up having five weeks of radiation to each area and we did the five weeks bacl-to-back so we went for ten straight weeks every day, back and forth, to the hospital (80 miles round trip) to get the radiation therapy. It took about fifteen/sixteen months for that treatment plan before it was, finally, finished. It was a long hard treatment but she made it through it and was cancer free, at the end of it, again."

The week of June 2012 Juliana and Tammy were in the hospital and Juliana was feeling horrible on some days. We, really, hoped Juliana had beat cancer but, now, it came back again. We started getting emails from places like Rome and South America checking on Juliana. I knew, now, many more people around the world were saying prayers for Juliana. I asked her if there were three wishes what would she like to have. She thought about it and said, "not to have cancer, a billion dollars and a puppy." I told Juliana that we are working on the first wish and I wasn't sure about the second wish. The third wish, I thought, "let me see what we can do." Tammy and I agreed that we should get Juliana a dog. Tammy and Juliana started to search, for a dog, online.

Juliana smiled, so big, when she found out we were going to get her a puppy. Secretly, Tammy and I didn't think she was going to make it as the doctors didn't give us hope back then so we wanted to give Juliana as much happiness as possible.

Our friend, and the kid's former Martial Arts instructor Wil Lerp, came by to see Juliana. This was the beginning of many visitors Juliana would have in the coming months. On June 14, 2012 Juliana and Tammy walked out of the hospital to head home. Juliana was so excited to go home. Juliana began to receive cards and gifts from around the world. On June 16$^{th}$, while Juliana was hooked up to a medicine pump, we drove to the SPCA in York Pennsylvania and Juliana picked out a Shih-Tzu puppy that she named Maddie. Juliana and Maddie became so close. In October 2016, it was Juliana's last wish to "look good for Maddie," as she brushed her hair, when she went home from the hospital. All the kids loved Maddie. Maddie brought so much joy and laughter to our home.

In late June 2012 Juliana had sores, in her mouth, from a blood infection. Believe in Tomorrow (believeintomorro.org) offered us the opportunity to take a trip to Ocean City Maryland for the week. We went on boat rides and invested lots of time on the beach. Juliana's favorite place, on the planet, was on the beach. One of her favorite hobbies was fishing. She loved the challenge. Our friends watched Maddie for us while we were away.

In July 2012 Juliana, and for months after, continued her chemotherapy treatments. On July 2$^{nd}$ I arrived at the hospital to find Juliana smiling and sitting in her hospital bed. Within a few minutes she asked me to go, downstairs, to the hospital cafeteria and get her some "wings and onion wings" then proceeded to flatter her little eyes at me with a big giggle. Of course, I went right to the cafeteria.

The next day, when I arrived in her hospital room she was getting another blood transfusion and eating more chicken wings at the same time. Later in the day she was really depressed and started to cry because she wanted to go home. She missed her dog and the rest of the kids. Later on, we walked to the hospital playroom where she took a nap instead of played. Thankfully, she had a visit from Jen

Klaput and her amazing daughters. They put a smile on Juliana's sad face.

On July 7, 2012 Juliana was back home and so happy. Later on July 16th, thanks to Casey Cares (carecares.org) we were able to go to Hershey Park Pennsylvania and have a day of fun. All the kids had a ton of fun. July 23$^{rd}$ Juliana was back in the hospital and cried so much. She just wanted to go home. She never did, however, complain. Timothy, Juliana's older brother is very close to Juliana. No child should have cancer. It was so painful to watch her in tears because all she wanted to do is be healthy.

In August 2012 Cool Kids Campaign (coolkidscampaign.org) was invited by the local Fox News Channel 45 to be on their morning broadcast and talk about a fundraiser program they were doing. Juliana was invited to be interviewed. Tammy and I drove Juliana to the studio. Juliana did an amazing job. Juliana continued to receive cards and gifts from all over the world.

In the same month, Amy Baldwin, started a page on Facebook called "Angels for Juliana" (https://www.facebook.com/Angels-For-Juliana-250289225091998). I had never met Amy but the page started getting more and more followers. I can't thank Amy enough for coming up with the idea to start the Facebook page. I've been able to keep a lot of people updated on Juliana's journey. As of the year 2020 Juliana has more than 107,000 followers on that page.

The kids continued to enjoy time in the pool. On August 13th Juliana was back in the hospital for more cancer treatment. I continued to bring cards and gifts from her fans that extended to various parts of the world. It was humbling to know so many people love Juliana. I was hoping that God would hear those prayers, answer them and make Juliana healthy for the rest of her life.

On August 16' 2012 Sinai Hospital coordinated with Batman (Lenny Robinson) to visit children in the cancer ward. Mr. Robinson traveled around the mid Atlantic area putting smiles on children's faces. We made sure that most of our other kids could be there as well. On August 17th Juliana was able to leave the hospital and go home. The next day we took the kids ice skating. They had so much fun. On August 21st I was back, with Matthew, at one of his soccer games. He was really getting good as he practiced quite often.

The time came to celebrate another adoption anniversary for Juliana. Tammy baked a sheet cake as Juliana watched Tammy put white icing it. When that was done Tammy helped Juliana put red lettering on it.

George Stein, who knows some people that we know, and a lot of his friends who ride motorcycles, held a fundraiser for us on August 25th. Those friends included 2012 Louie Sauer, Tim Scott, Dwyane Staub, Bill Bryson, Kevin McCarrey, Ben Freels, David Scott, Neal Moose, Tom Myers, Scott Timberman, Jared Mays, Terry Woods, Scott Staples, Steve Yingling, Tim Thompson, Chris Matz, Corey, Matz plus their wife and/or girlfriends. It was amazing. All these "biker dudes and biker gals" rallying around our family along with a lot of other people (we never even knew) came out to support us. George and his friends have helped so many families and continue to do so to this day. They called the fundraiser "Give the Girls a Hand." They were helping another family, that day, as well. They even had a derby race. It was Awesome!

On August 30' 2012 I asked Juliana to make a short video encouraging others who might be going through a difficult time. In the video she said, "Hi. I'm Juliana Carver and I've been through some stuff. I don't really know some people out there (on the internet). If you're having a hard time you can get through it. If I can get through it then you can and I know you can."

On August 31$^{st}$ Rebecca, Tammy and Timothy went to a American Red Cross blood Drive and donated blood. Each blood donation helps up to three people. Between 2007-2016 Juliana received more than 240 transfusions.

By September 10$^{th}$ Juliana was back in the hospital for more cancer treatment. She had some friends and a few of our kids that stopped in for a visit which lifted her spirits. Tammy would take her on walks around the hospital, attached to her IV pole, to get out of her hospital room for a little while. Juliana, Tammy and I always knew so many people were praying for Juliana. We, at the time, believed that it might help Juliana beat cancer and live a long and healthy life.

On September 19, 2012 I recorded a video of Juliana. She was wearing a Believe Big (believebig.org) shirt and gray pants. She said, "Hi everybody. I'm Juliana Irina Carver and I would like to thank all of you for helping me get through cancer for the third time. Your prayers mean a lot to me and my family. It's a bit hard going through it and everything at this age…it's hard for me and my family so thank you so much for praying. I love you all (then she gave a big hug to all those watching the video)."

The kids continued to enjoy the outdoors and have lots of fun. On September 27th Bradd Atkinson (founder of StrongHope – stronghope.org) was going to run an Iron Man Race ad asked Juliana to sign a hat that he could wear to give him courage during the race. Bradd went on to do very well in that race. On October 1st Bradd came back to our house. Bradd sat next to Juliana on the sofa and looked at Juliana and said, "you know I had my race yesterday…that Iron Man thing…I had a great day and I did the best I've ever done in a Triathlon. I wanted to let you know that I thought about you a lot during my race because you have a lot of time to think during those races…you helped me stay strong. You helped me push and, believe me, when I was doing the rough parts about half-way through and I was getting a little tired. I started to think about you…I have to keep going. I have to keep these feet moving. I'm doing this for Julie. I had my StrongHope stuff on…you and I inspired a lot of people yesterday. There were people asking me about StrongHope and about what I was doing. They were asking me about my hat. People have emailed me today. It's really exciting that you helped me the way that you did.

You inspire a lot of people. Remember, a while back, I told you how you touch a lot of people (Julie nodded yes) and inspire a lot of people. I know you've been going through some things and I know you've had some tough times. You're a tough little girl and you, always, stay so happy. You stay so positive and you don't let things get you down. You stay so energetic all the time even when you're not feeling so good and that is so special. You touch so many people. I don't think you realize, in your ten-and-a-half little body how many people you really touch and you really inspire. You're a special little girl and you really helped me a lot yesterday…I brought you a little something (Bradd reached into his right pocket) that I got yesterday and I want you to have it. I want you to have this medal. (Bradd began to get chocked up) What do you think about that? They give you these when you finish those races and when you come across the finish line (Bradd placed the medal over Juliana's head and placed it around her neck) they put them around your neck like that and they give you those medals like that because you've accomplished something that pretty difficult and I want you to have it because you're a special little girl (Juliana looked down at the medal hanging from her neck)." Juliana said, "Thank you." Bradd said, "Give me a hug…ahhh…you're the best…you're the best."

On October 6, 2012 we took the four younger kids to a church fair, in Hanover Pennsylvania, where they had games, face painting, hay rides and other fun activities. They had so much fun. Two days later Juliana was back in the hospital for more cancer treatment. Dr. Joseph Wiley, Dr. Jason Fixler and Dr. Yoram Unguru and quite a few nurses continued to be amazing with Juliana. Each had their own way the helped Juliana and we appreciate all three of them more than they will ever imagine. Dr. Wiley agreed to have Maddie (Juliana's dog) come to the hospital lobby so Juliana couple play with her because she missed Maddie so much. This, kind act, from Dr. Wiley helped Juliana so much!

I kept a few of the other kids active in their home school gym activies. October 28, 2012 arrived and we were invited by the Children's Roads to Recovery Inc fundraiser (http://www.childrensroadstorecovery.org/). Their founder's son passed away from the same type of cancer Juliana was fighting, now, for the third time. Children's Roads to Recovery would send us Exxon gas cards to help us with the gas to get back and forth from the hospital. They were a huge help to Tammy and she made hundreds of trips back and forth to the hospital. The gas cards came for a few years. We appreciate them so much!

A couple days later the kids decorated pumpkins and went trick-or-treating and, of course, had lots of fun. November 5th Juliana was back in the hospital. I would bring her fan mail and video her opening it so her fans could watch it. We were able, thanks to Dr. Wiley, bring Maddie to the hospital lobby which let Juliana have a little fun with her dog. When Juliana was able to come home she and a few of the other kids played in the leaves in our front yard. A few days later we took the kids bowling. Juliana would get so frustrated because, as she is right handed, she couldn't throw the ball without using both hands. Her right arm was so radiated, back in 2007, that it shrunk the muscles in her right forearm. Juliana's right arm remained weak for the rest of her life.

On November 13, 2012 Juliana got another blood transfusion. They became a regular part of Juliana's life. Thankfully, people who donate blood (American Red Cross) are so selfless that Juliana could get those transfusions. Tammy, once again, prepared an amazing Thanksgiving Dinner for a lot of family members. The kids and their cousin, uncles and a couple aunts went outside for some football. Juliana played right along with them.

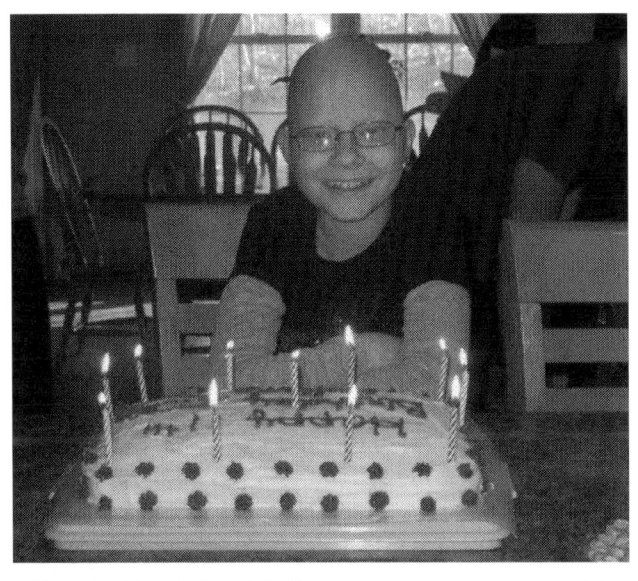

The day after Thanksgiving Tammy was baking cookies with Juliana's help while the other kids helped decorate for Christmas. December 1$^{st}$ we had a 11th birthday party for Juliana because, on December 4th (her birthday) Juliana was stuck in the hospital getting more chemotherapy.

Casey Cares (caseycares.org) just so happened to arrange for several of the Baltimore Ravens Football Players to visit the children on the floor where Juliana was getting treated. Juliana was so groggy, from her medication, she didn't even remember much of them being in the room. It was very kind of Casey Cares and The Baltimore Ravens to do that for the children. A local news crew interviewed Juliana but she had just been crying before the players walked in the room.

Thanks to her fans, on Angels for Juliana (on Facebook) a lot of people sent Juliana birthday cards because I told them she would not be home for her birthday. Maddie was able to come back, to the hospital, on December 5th and give Juliana some joy for a couple hours. Juliana just wanted to be healthy and be a normal little girl.

By December 8, 2012 Juliana was back home so we went to the Children's Cancer Foundation Christmas Party at a local skating rink. A couple of her doctors were there, too, having fun with their children. Juliana was determined to live life to the fullest when she wasn't stuck in a hospital or her blood counts were too low for her to run and play.

The next day, The American Red Cross invited Juliana and I to the Washington Redskins Football Stadium in a private suite. Tammy and I agreed, a year or two earlier, to let the American Red Cross, use Juliana's photo to help people understand how important it is to donate blood. At the stadium Juliana and three other members of the American Red Cross would walk out to the fifty yard line while the announcer told the huge crowd about the importance of donating blood. It was an amazing experience.

December 13th I was back at one of Matthew and Lindsay's soccer games. I went to a few more of their games, that month, too. Christmas time was, finally, upon us. The kids, eagerly, waited on the steps to go downstairs to open their gifts. They were getting older so it was less screaming, in excitement, as they ran down the steps. December 29th brought more snow so the kids ran outside and had so much fun. The last day, of 2012, Juliana was back in the hospital.

## Chapter 8

January 2, 2013 brought on another home school gym class which Juliana participated and even did some sit ups and Tim held her feet. As I will say, many times, in this book Juliana did not want cancer to stop her from having fun and being a kid. A week later, on January 7$^{th}$, Juliana was back in the hospital for more cancer treatment. We were, again, able to bring Maddie to the hospital lobby for Juliana to have a little fun. Juliana continued to receive mail from all over the United States and other countries. On January 15$^{th}$ we celebrated Maddie's first birthday but we don't know her exact birthday. The kids loved it.

Tammy and I didn't want to get a pet because we have six children. We felt that we would be the ones to take care of a dog once the kids got tired of it. That all changed when we thought Juliana wasn't going to make it as she fought cancer for the third time. We wanted to grant as many wishes, to Juliana, as possible because we thought we were going to lose her back in 2012.

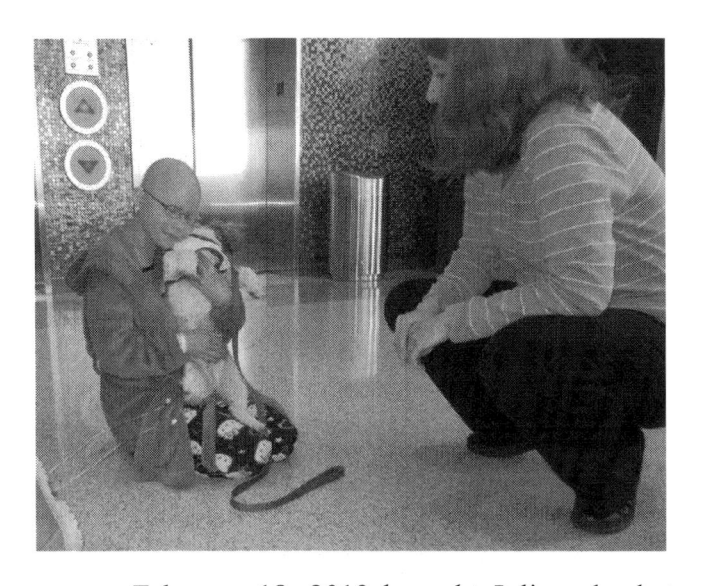

February 18, 2013 brought Juliana back to the hospital for more chemotherapy where she would stay a week at a time like in the past. Since Maddie wasn't allowed upstairs in the Oncology floor we would wait in the hospital lobby. When we arrived I would call or text Tammy. I remember standing by the elevator door hoping to hear Juliana's voice to know when to start the video camera to capture her joy seeing and playing with Maddie.

March rolled in and we could tell Juliana would need another blood and platelet transfusion soon. On March 5$^{th}$ she got more blood and platelets. It's amazing how blood transfusions helped Juliana. In the days before a transfusion she had no energy, couldn't walk up steps and, definitely could not run and play. When she received a blood transfusion she could do all those things and more. On this, particular, day after her transfusion we stopped by the grocery store to pick up a few things. She insisted on carrying a gallon of milk to show how good she was feeling. She was all smiles. It was awesome!

Maddie, Juliana's dog, played a huge part in her life. Maddie gave Juliana times of joy, laughter and comfort. On March $8^{th}$ I gave a speech, in Arlington Virginia, to a room full of American Red Cross employees and volunteers. I was able to call Juliana, from the speech while she was getting another transfusion, and they I put my phone on speaker and up to the microphone. Juliana was able to share what blood transfusions mean to her and she thanks everyone in the audience. It was so powerful for people to meet or hear Juliana's voice. The experience gave people a much better understanding about what cancer does to children.

March 24 brought another Children's Roads to Recovery fundraiser luncheon. They shared, at each table, a thank you card I sent to them for the

Exxon gas cards they sent us which helped Juliana go back and forth from the hospital.

On March 27th Casey Cares (caseycares.org) invited us to the Ringling Brothers and Barnum and Bailey Circus in Baltimore Maryland. It was a wonderful evening of fun and forgetting about cancer for a couple of hours. March 30th brought on more coloring of Easter eggs followed, the next day, by Easter. Easter, in our home, has always been fun. The kids would dress up for Easter Church Service, come downstairs and begin a hunt for their Easter baskets.

April 1, 2013 Juliana was back in the hospital for more chemotherapy. We were able to, once again, bring Maddie to the lobby to play with Maddie. Tim, reached around Juliana's shoulder and placed his head on her head and said, "I missed you." They were so close. There was something about the connection between Tim and Juliana that lasted for her entire life. As I looked back through photos and video of all the kids Tim took his role, as big brother, very seriously and compassionately.

April 5th Juliana was able to go home. That same evening she said, "Mom is really tired so I wanted to do something nice" so she proceeded to help fix spaghetti for dinner after putting on her red and white apron. Remember, she JUST got out of the hospital after receiving five days of chemotherapy. The next day I took the kids to the park and, as always, they had so much fun. Juliana was back in the hospital on April 17$^{th}$. We went to a different park a few days later. It was so important to me to provide as many outdoor activities, for all the kids, as possible especially since Juliana was in the hospital so much.

May 2013 arrived and the kids were outside a lot enjoying the days that were getting warmer. Matthew was still playing indoor soccer quite a bit so I attended several of his games. Juliana's fan mail continued to arrive. By May 6$^{th}$ (two days after Lindsay and Tim's birthday) Juliana was back in the hospital for several days. Once again, Maddie was able to break the boredom so Juliana could see her furry friend. We continued our trips to some local parks and, as the temperatures increased Juliana, Kristina and Timothy went swimming. The kids loved the pool but, especially, to play with Juliana. They knew the pool gave Juliana so much joy and enabled her to forget about cancer even for moments at a time.

June brought much of the same as May except that, on June 10th, Juliana was back in the hospital for another surgery. Five days later we were back at the park in Hanover Pennsylvania and Juliana was playing soccer with Matthew and climbing on the monkey bars. Juliana was determined to be a regular kid and not be defined by cancer. On June 18th I took Matthew on a day trip to Philadelphia. It was nice to both of us to be together and do some sightseeing and go to a baseball game. June 19th brought radiation treatments for Juliana. The radiation technicians used a permanent marker to draw, on Juliana's belly, where the radiation would be focused. It was about half the size of a dinner plate. The radiation would upset Juliana's stomach so much she wasn't able to eat too much but, yet, she continued to play outside and swim. Very little slowed her down which enabled her to enjoy fun at our fire pit that Lindsay's built in our yard. I never heard Juliana complain.

In late June we were invited by Casey Cares (caseycares.org) to take a boat ride in the inner harbor of Baltimore Maryland. It was scheduled for July 1st. It was a picture-perfect day. Juliana wore a white shirt and hat and a blue skirt with polka dots on it. She was feeling really good. Later that day,

Juliana had more radiation treatments (this happened daily, for weeks, so I don't document all of the times in this book). July 4$^{th}$ came and we had our cookout, the kids went swimming and we lit our ground-based fireworks. Tammy, every year, sets all this up. She's awesome in so many ways. At one point she walked over to me and sang (as she held a lit sparkers in her hand) "we love sparklers…we love sparklers…what do we love…we love sparklers."

Juliana was starting to get her hair back, again, for which she was excited. She, really, missed having hair to brush and fix up. On July 20, 2013 we took the kids to the local carnival and bowling a couple of days later. The afternoon of bowling was made possible by Casey Cares (caseycares.org) who, also, invited one of the Baltimore Raven Football Team Players. Tammy and I tried, our best, to keep Juliana's mind off of cancer and on fun activities as much as possible. At the end of July I took Juliana and Kristina to a local pond so they could feed the ducks. It might sound so simple but those things meant so much to the kids. Juliana spent so much time, stuck, in the hospital I really wanted her to experience and enjoy life.

Juliana loved to laugh. Timothy, one of Juliana's big brothers, was fantastic in getting Juliana to laugh...a lot. He did that for years. On August 16th we invited a couple of Juliana's friends over, who had been getting treatment at the same hospital, for a cookout, dancing and swimming. They had so much fun. Ten days later we celebrated Juliana's adoption day with a delicious chocolate cake. The day after brought more radiation treatments followed by a WMAR-TV's Jamie Costello who did an interview, on Juliana, Tammy, Dr. Joseph Wiley and me, for a news story about Juliana and pediatric cancer. The news story aired on September 20, 2013. Juliana was outstanding.

Casey Cares (caseycares.org) invited us to an outing at Segamore Farm on September 7th.

Shortly after we arrived Batman appeared. It was the same Lenny Robinson who visited Juliana and other children in the hospital. He has a heart of gold. Toward the end of our time, at the farm, Juliana was getting tired. The radiation was starting to wear her down. She bounced back, pretty quickly, so Tammy and I took the kids for a walk on a local path close to our house where we saw a bald eagle. Watching Tim hold Juliana's hand, on part of the walk, filled my heart. Tim looked at me and said, "I think you're going to fill that memory card before we get home" as he watched me video them walking. I can't express to you how close Tim, Kristina and Juliana were…it was precious. The kids had fun.

Several weeks Mary Bohlen, from Sinai Hospital, told Tammy about the organization Give Kids the World (http://www.gktw.org/). Tammy contacted them and within a short amount of time arranged for us to fly to Orlando Florida. We flew, out of Baltimore, on September 29th, for a week of fun at their Give Kids the World Village, Disney World, Universal Studios and Sea World. It was an incredible week with so much laughter, fun and exciting rides. It's, way, too much to list all that we did in this book. You can find so much what I've shared, so far, in this book on YouTube. My channel is https://www.youtube.com/user/johnwcarver/

On the evening of October 4, 2013 something happened that would make waves around the world. We got back to the Give Kids the World Village and went back to our bungalow. Tim, Kristina and Juliana wanted to do some fishing so I took them to the pier that was on their property. Tim was helping Juliana catch a fish. Juliana wasn't catching anything and Tim was focused on helping Juliana catch a fish before he attempted to catch one for himself.

The sun had set and no fish were caught. Tim and Juliana kept working at it. Tammy asked Juliana if she wanted to head in, for the night, and try again tomorrow. I was standing to Juliana's left and she baited another hook. She looked up, at her mom, and said these words that have made waves around the world. She said, **"I'm not a giver upper."** Shortly after those words Juliana caught a fish and then another. Kristina and Tim did the same thing. "I'm not a giver upper" has given thousands of people courage in their most difficult times. Juliana said it, first, On October 4, 2013 in Florida.

By October 19th we had been back home in Maryland. That evening Juliana, Tammy and I went to the Children's Cancer Foundation (http://www.childrenscancerfoundation.org/) annual fundraiser banquet. That organization has raised tens of millions of dollars to help fund researchers who are looking for cures for the many types of pediatric cancers. I'm proud to serve, as a volunteer, on their Board of Directors. The end of October brought more pumpkins and Halloween fun.

Juliana's hair, by November was getting so thick. On November 20th Juliana was back in the hospital for more chemotherapy. The kids enjoyed the last few days to nice weather before it started getting cold. The day, after Tammy's amazing Thanksgiving dinner, most of the kids helped Tammy decorate for Christmas.

In early December we celebrated Juliana's birthday. She invited Emily and Sadie, her hospital buddies, and their families as Emily, Sadie and Juliana spent so many days and nights stuck in the hospital. They became very close friends. After the cake and ice cream and Juliana opening her gifts Tim and Juliana did a little magic show for everyone who was there that day. Later that day we took Juliana to Wal-Mart and she picked out a new bike with some of her birthday money. The next day brought several inches of snow. The kids couldn't wait to get outside and play in it.

December 11th brought more scans for Juliana. She, always, did so well for being a little kid. The hospital staff was so kind and patient with Juliana. She scans were clear once again. December 14th we took the kids to the Maryland Science Center which let them experiment and have lots of fun with other kids. We invited Aubrix who is a friend of the our kids. A few days later we attended the Children's Cancer Foundation's Christmas party at a local skating rink. The kids loved to skate and this gave them time to let loose and have a blast. Four days later Juliana was back in the hospital getting more chemotherapy. The hospital arranged for Santa Clause to make a visit. He put a lot of smiles on some sick kid's faces that day.

On December 21' 2013 my, long time friend, Arthur Hawkins, came by our house and took some beautiful photos of our family as a gift to us. Arthur has his own photography business. His work is incredible. Christmas morning arrived. Juliana woke everyone up that morning. As Juliana waited, on the steps for the rest of the kids she said, "I got everyone up this year. Everyone was asleep. I looked at my clock and…ran down the hall…I'm pushing Timmy…it's 7:01 (A.M.). He got up…went into Kristie's room…it's 7:01." In the past, Timothy would get everyone up as he would be jumping up and down the hallway waiting to come downstairs. I miss the days of that kind of excitement more than I can ever describe to you.

Per our custom on Thanksgiving Day and the day after Christmas the kids, their Uncle Thomas and Aunt Michele would have their Nerf War where they would run around the house (on two different teams) shooting Nerf guns at each other. It was so much fun to hear the roaring laughter echoing around our home.

Chapter 9


On February 3, 2014 we got another several inches of snow which meant Kristina, Tim and Juliana were outside enjoying every inch of it. Less than an hour south, of us, they got no snow at all. They were sledding and throwing snowballs. February 12$^{th}$ brought another hospital visit and chemotherapy for Juliana. On February 13$^{th}$, overnight, we received another fourteen inches of snow on top of the several inches that was, already, on the ground. Of course, the kids loved it and went back outside in the 13$^{th}$ and had so much fun.

On February 17' 2014 Casey Cares (caseycares.org) gave us tickets to the Ripley's Believe it or Not museum in Baltimore Maryland. The kids really enjoyed themselves with all the hands-on items they had on display. Ten days later our oldest daughter, Rebecca, came over and played charades with the rest of the kids. Timothy, Kristina and Juliana love when Rebecca would hang out with them. Juliana hair was really growing fast…so much so she was twirling her hair.

March 2014 - By late February or early March I had been noticing, in several of the photos I had taken of her that her right eye lid was lower than the left. I told Tammy about it and was insistent that we get it looked at by her oncologists.

Tammy shares from a video I taped in January 2015 "While we were, already, in the midst of Juliana's radiation therapy done in the Summer of 2013, her doctor decided to put her on maintenance chemotherapy. We went ahead and started with the oral chemo while she was, still, getting the radiation therapy and then when that finished, which was the end of August (2013), then we started with some IV chemotherapy too that was supposed to be maintenance to stop her from relapsing again. We continued giving her that every other week for the IV and giving her the daily oral chemo at home. Everything seemed to be going well and then the middle of March (2014) we started noticing her right eye lid was drooping. We took her back into the hospital and they looked at it and agreed, definitely, it was drooping but not being eye doctors they didn't have a clue to start with it.

I suggested, since we were already in Baltimore, if I can get her as an emergency visit with her regular ophthalmologist (Juliana wore glasses since she was very small) who had seen her for (crossed eyes) when she was a little baby. I took her a few miles down the road and took her back and her ophthalmologist looked at it and started feeling her eye and he said to me it's a tumor. He called her oncologist and told him it's, definitely a tumor there and he told me don't worry I know somebody who can help you. He called a friend of his who happens to work at Sinai Hospital (where Juliana had been getting cancer treatment) who is an ophthalmologist and a plastic surgeon.

He got me in with them about a half hour later…he said he wanted an MRI done of it ASAP. They called and tried to get us in and they couldn't have anything open, for outpatient, for several days…so they admitted us. The doctor said he was going to come back, to Sinai Hospital, and do surgery on Juliana the next day and try to get as much of the tumor out as possible so there would be a lot less there to do radiation therapy. We didn't want to get it (radiation) too close to her brain. We went ahead and had the MRI and surgery the next day and, fortunately, he was able to get all of the visible cancer out but he wasn't able to get margins. Everything else he got out. That was really good news.

We were really concerned, though, because we were afraid it (cancer) could be in other places in her body. It's odd for it to relapse, like that, in just a tiny little place. We came home, the next day, after surgery. You can't have a PET scan, while your inpatient at the hospital, because our insurance wouldn't pay for it. We went back to the hospital the next day and had a full body PET/CT scan done and waited anxiously to hear the results of that and finally they called us. They said it (the cancer) was no-where else. It was just in her eye. We had to come up with another treatment plan.

We decided to do, just, one more round of major chemo. Her counts had never, fully, recovered from what (treatment) we had done previously and we were afraid we would make her really sick. She went back to radiation oncology and they set her up to do radiation on her right eye orbit. The cancer wasn't anywhere near her brain, it didn't penetrate the dura, it was just right in that little muscle that controls your eyelid blinking. They (the radiation technicians) put a mask-thing on Juliana and hooked her to the table with the mask on so she couldn't move so they could zap her eye with radiation while she was awake. She had it done, everyday, for five weeks again.

When we finished that we decided that we would go back on maintenance chemo…some low dose chemo. We've done several different things since then. We've done a couple different types of oral chemo and we added some more IV chemo along the way but she tolerates it very well…"

Let me, now, fill in some of the other details from 2014 for you. Juliana was diagnosed, with cancer, for the fourth time on March 17, 2014. On the day of Juliana's surgery (March 18$^{th}$) to remove as much of the cancer as possible in her right eye orbit she was so calm. It was like "here we go again." I walked, on the left side of her bed, as they wheeled her down the hallway. Tammy walked behind Juliana. Juliana waved "bye" to the nurses, at the nurses, station as we made our way to the elevator. I said to Juliana, "You are so brave." Juliana reached out her right hand and took Tammy's right hand and gave her mommy a big smile.

The elevator was just enough to fit Juliana's bed and a few more people. Juliana sat there with her fingers interlocked. We got off the elevator and turned right and into another corridor. We approached the prep area and Juliana said, "I'm scared." I reached down and kissed her and said, "I love you so much!" Tammy, now, stood at Juliana's right side and Juliana looked up at her from her hospital bed waiting to be taken into another surgery. Tammy reminded Juliana that Juliana always said that she "worried about nothing" as Tammy rubbed the top of Juliana's head then kissed her on her forehead.

A nurse was commenting on Juliana's small finger nails at they put a pulse-ox on her right middle finger. Juliana waved to me swayed her hand back and forth. The doctor came in and used a permanent marker to mark Juliana's eye where the operation was to happen. Tammy put on a blue operating suit to walk with Juliana into the operating room. Juliana waved to me again. A nurse were teasing me about videoing everything. The same nurse put a silver hat on Juliana. The nurse told Juliana what to expect in the operating room and gave Juliana a choice of where to put certain things like the blood pressure cup.

Juliana did not like, ever, having the mask put on to make her go to sleep. The nurse understood and told her that she would give Juliana some extra "loopy medicine." Juliana smiled and clapped her hands in relief. They began giving her the "loopy juice" to help Juliana relax a little more before being wheeled into the operating room. Juliana sat there, calmly, with her fingers interlaced.

The nurses began to wheel Juliana, from the small room, down the hallway toward the operating room. Tammy walked to the left side of Juliana's bed as it rolled out of the room. I said to Juliana, "let me give you some kisses" as I reached down and gave her a kiss and said, "I love you." I said "you're feeling it (the "loopy juice") already aren't you" as I could see it on her face. She nodded and said, "ah ha." Her fingers remained interlaced. Juliana waved to me, with her right hand and said, "bye," and had the look of being on the "loopy medicine." She said, bye" one last time and let out a big yawn and her bed rolled passed me. Watching them go past the point where I could not follow was, and always has been, so emotional because I never knew how everything would turn out and to play our baby's life in other people's hands is never easy.

After the operation Tammy and I were escorted into the recovery area. Juliana's right eye had a plastic covering and was bandaged as she was just waking up. Juliana waved to us with her right hand and coughed because of the breathing tube that was down her throat during surgery. Tammy rubbed

Juliana's head with her left hand and asked Juliana if her throat was sore. Juliana nodded yes. Tammy asked Juliana if her eye hurt. Juliana said, "a little." The nurse asked Juliana if she wanted a little ice. Tammy said, "it might help." Juliana nodded yes. Juliana, then reached up with her right hand and tapped the bandage that was covering her right eye. The anesthesiologists had dug her right cheek (close to her mouth) with the tubing during surgery. They apologized before we went back to see Juliana.

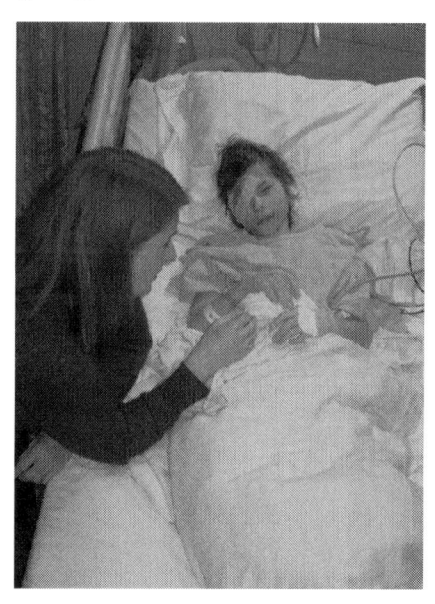

Tammy told Juliana that the doctor said, "you did a such a good job" as Juliana reached her left hand up to grab Tammy's right hand. Juliana dozed off to sleep as Tammy sat to her right side keeping an eye on our little girl who has fought so hard since she was five years old. Moments later Tammy was holding Juliana's right hand and was caressing it gently with her thumb. A minute or two later Juliana was holding Tammy's hand. Tammy and Juliana were inseparable.

About an hour or so later Juliana was wheeled back to the Pediatric Oncology floor. Later, Juliana arrived home. She got out of the car, with Tammy's help, and gave me a big smile. Juliana was wearing her, "Hello Kitty" pajamas. Juliana walked in the door, smiled so big, and said, "Hi, Maddie…I haven't seen you in so long." Maddie was jumping up onto Juliana's legs wanting her to pick her up. I said, "look…she (Maddie) missed you so much" as Juliana reached down to pet her while shielding her covered eye from Maddie. Juliana couldn't resist so she picked up Maddie as she licked Juliana's face. Tammy reminded Juliana, "Don't let her near your eye. Be careful."

Juliana walked, on her own power, into the family room (while carrying Maddie) and sat on the sofa. She began hugging and petting Maddie as she licked Juliana's fingers. Big brother, Tim, sat to Juliana's left and reached his right hand behind Juliana and gave her a hug and leaned his head on Juliana's head while rubbing her back. He asked Juliana, "do you want to take off your coat?" Juliana said, "sure" as Tim helped her take it off.

When she got off her coat Maddie jumped back up on Juliana's lap. Juliana gave Maddie a kiss on her right cheek. Juliana's eye was not covered with a bandage. You could see where it was cut for the operation. Juliana was all smiles as she hugged Maddie and said, "My little fuzzy…you're so soft." Maddie gave Juliana a kiss on her chin. Maddie knew Juliana was hurt (from the operation). Later, Tammy washed Juliana's hair in the kitchen sink.

The next day I found Juliana, in Tim's room, playing a game. I can't describe how much Tim took an active role in trying to help Juliana have fun and enjoy life. He is beyond awesome! Two days later Juliana was outside playing hopscotch with Lindsay and Kristina. Maddie and Juliana were so close. Maddie brought more joy, to our family, than I can tell you. Maddie is Juliana's baby.

On March 27, 2014 I was invited to York Pennsylvania to give a speech. York is about an hour from our home. Part of my speech was to share part of Juliana's story (up to that point in time) so I invited Juliana and Timothy. She was very excited to go. She received a standing ovation and helped me sign autographs, in one of my books, for those in the audience. It was awesome.

March 31st rolled around and we, several days before, were invited by Casey Cares (caseycares.org) to a kid's indoor park where they were able to play with other families who had children struggling with health challenges.

On April 1st Juliana was back in the hospital for more treatment but was able to go home after she was done the same day. That evening a nurse came by the house to give Juliana more fluids and hooked up a pole for her to drag around while the fluids were going into her little body. On April 3rd Casey Cares (caseycares.org) made it possible for us to go to the circus again.

The weather was starting to get warmer, in our area, so Kristina, Tim and Juliana would play outside as much as possible. On April 8th, while Juliana was back in the hospital, Lynn from the

American Red Cross came by and gave Juliana a big bag of crafts to work on when she got bored. April 19th brought more coloring of Easter eggs and, the next day, the kids getting their Easter baskets.

On April 29th I was able to go to radiation treatments with Tammy and Juliana. Watching the radiation techs set Juliana up for the treatments and placing the mask on her face then bolting the mask to the table was difficult to watch. To this day, I am humbled and amazing by Juliana's courage through all she endured. In addition, Tammy's tender love and attention to the smallest detail of Juliana's care has been amazing. After radiation, that day, my long-time friend Mark Jenkins invited Juliana and I to have dinner with him as he was in the Washington DC area for a few days. We had a wonderful evening with Mark.

On May 4, 2014 (Timothy and Lindsay's birthday), Juliana decided to make omelets for dinner for all of us. She put her apron on and proceeded to gather the ingredients. Juliana wanted to be a chef when she grew up. Her dinner, as always, was delicious.

Radiation treatments continued, daily, for several weeks. May 6, 2014 we lit a bon fire that Lindsay built a year or two earlier and another trip to the park two days later. Later in the month, on April 22$^{nd}$, we were invited to a television news station, in York Pennsylvania, to talk about how blood donations help kids like Juliana.

Finally, by June 3$^{rd}$ it was getting warm enough for the kids to go swimming in the pool, even thought the water was chilly, that Make-A-Wish gave Juliana a few years earlier. Juliana was a little fish in the water. The next day we made another trip to Hershey Park Pennsylvania thanks to Casey Cares (caseycares.org). The kids had so much fun. Juliana loved the roller coasters and would scream so loud when the roller coaster was going around the sharp turns. On June 12$^{th}$ we were invited to the Children's Cancer Foundation Crab Feast and Fundraiser. Juliana loved steamed crabs and shrimp. More and more the kids would play outside around our house.

On July 1, 2014 Juliana recorded a message to her fans that might be going through a difficult time. She said, "I know some of you are going through some struggles and I've been going through some struggles for a few years now. I just wanted to tell you that you can do it no matter what."

Juliana's, incredible, patience astounds me to this day. Every time Juliana came back, from the hospital, Juliana would squeal with happiness to see her dog Maddie. She'd look at Maddie, pick her up and say, "I missed you." Maddie was a huge part of Juliana's life from the time we adopted Maddie when Juliana got cancer for the third time. The fourth of Juliana brought friends and family for a cookout, sparkler and ground-based fireworks. July 11$^{th}$ I had the kids back another park to run and play and so they could just be kids.

We were so excited, when July 27$^{th}$ came around because Believe in Tomorrow (https://believeintomorrow.org/) made it possible for us to stay at their House on the Bay in Ocean City Maryland. Juliana, and all the kids, love the beach and fishing. John and Wanda Thompson were kind enough to watch Maddie for us. We were, also, able to meet the Kolenda family in Ocean City as well. Emily Kolenda was getting treatment at Sinai Hospital. Juliana and Emily would spend a week at a time, in the hospital, and would have movie nights in each other's rooms. Juliana loved the challenge of catching fish. It was a goal and she was very goal oriented in everything. On July 30th Juliana said, as she walked on the beach, "I love sand and I wish we could stay here forever and ever and ever….but we have to get Maddie" Later in the week our friends, the Bromley's came by to hang out with us. The week was filled with laughter, relaxation and forgetting about cancer…at least for a little while.

In August Casey Cares (caseycares.org) provided more fun places to go for our entire family to have fun. They are an amazing organization. August 22nd was a pretty big day for Juliana. She got a haircut. Most people would not consider getting a hair cut a "big day" but when someone, like Juliana, fought cancer for so many years and was bald for a few of those years getting a hair cut is a really big deal. She smiled, in the mirror, as the lady cut her hair. Juliana was radiant. On August 25th we took Juliana to an American Red Cross blood drive, lead by Bonnie Rill, where big sister Rebecca and her friend Ben donated blood along with several other kind blood donors. The next day we celebrated Juliana's adoption day with a chocolate cake that Tammy made. We celebrated all our kid's adoption days in the same way. We cannot imagine if Juliana would have been in the orphanage when she, first, got cancer in 2007.

In August Tammy got a call from Believe in Tomorrow (https://believeintomorrow.org/) and asked if she and Juliana would be interested in taking a ride in the MetLife Blimp in Frederick Maryland. They, both, agreed that it would be a lot of fun. The blimp ride took them high above Frederick. Tammy and Juliana really had fun.

In mid September 2014 Juliana had an eye lift after the incision healed to get much of the cancer out of her right eye orbit. On September 22$^{nd}$ Juliana had an operation to get another port. We, also, found out that the port, in Juliana's chest was leaking. There was a tear, in the tubing, that went into her heart. It was very scary, to me, to see the leak happening right on the X-Ray machine.

On September 25, 2014, starting around 5:30pm, Juliana recorded a message for her fans. She said, "Hi, this is Juliana Carver and I just wanted to let you know what has been going on this week. We went to the doctors a few days ago…and they found out that there was a cut in my port so we needed to get surgery for that, of course. Then we thought while they were doing surgery for my port they should do it for my eye too. So, we did that…we did both of them…this is three days after surgery (she showed her fans, on video, her eye). It's looking pretty good. It's strengthening the muscles so I can't close it all that well. It hurts a little bit to close it so that's pretty much what's been going on this week…."

October brought more playing outside and attending the Children's Cancer Foundation Annual Gala (http://childrenscancerfoundation.org/). Juliana was very involved in raising awareness for the need to find cures for Pediatric Cancer. By the end of

October the kids were having fun going trick-or-treating.

In November there were, continued, blood transfusions and chemotherapy. It became a way of life for Juliana. She never complained. She never whined. She loved helping Tammy in the kitchen. Thanksgiving dinner was delicious and the next day the kids helped Tammy decorate for Christmas and Juliana helped Tammy start baking Christmas cookies.

In December 2014 Juliana turned the big thirteen. She was a teenager! Juliana invited the Kolenda family to her birthday party. The afternoon was full of fun and laughter as Juliana celebrated her special day.

On December 8th Matthew earned the right to be honored by a prestigious fraternity (Alpha Beta Gamma) in his college. Matthew has done very well in college.

Christmas morning was a lot of fun. Even though the kids were getting older, the four younger ones really got excited about the big day. The next day, we had a big fiftieth wedding celebration for my parents. Our home was full of family and friends wishing my parents well on their big day.

Chapter 10

It was January 15, 2015 and we celebrated Maddie's third birthday. We don't know the exact birthday so we guessed it based on her age when we adopted her from the SPCA in York Pennsylvania. Four days later, we were all invited by Casey Cares (caseycarees.org) to an a place where the kids could play games including laser tag. They had a lot of fun.

On January 21$^{st}$ we received more snow so the kids put on all the winter gear and went outside to play and go sledding. They loved playing in the snow. A couple months, earlier, Juliana was asked by Giant Food (giantfood.com) to be one of their Ambassadors. Giant Food, their employees and customers have raised millions of dollars to help find cures for Pediatric Cancer through the Children's Cancer Foundation (http://childrenscancerfoundation.org/). Juliana's picture and biography would be posted in all the Giant Food Stores in the region. Giant Food arranged for Juliana's photos to be taken at our home.

February 8, 2015 arrived and the owner of Sunnyday Studio arrived, at our home, and took photos of Juliana and our family. It was so amazing to know that more people would see Juliana and put a "face" with pediatric cancer so more people can help find cures for the disease. In late February we took the kids ice-skating which they really enjoyed.

March 11' 2015 Juliana was back in the hospital for more chemotherapy. Tammy remained by Juliana's side, as always, every moment. The next day was the big Giant Food meeting with about six hundred managers in a huge banquet room. We walked in and there were big posters of Juliana, and a few of the other Ambassadors, in the lobby and the banquet room.

Juliana had been rehearsing her speech for several days. Tammy was going to make a speech as well. I could feel the energy in the room as so many people, from Giant Food, were about to hear from a few kids who were fighting cancer. As Juliana and Tammy were announced, from the stage, I was so proud of both of them. Tammy spoke first.

Tammy said, on March 12, 2015, to a group of more than 500 people: "My name is Tammy Carver

and I'm Juliana's mom. When she was diagnosed with rhabdomyosarcoma back in February 2007 it changed life as we knew it for our entire family. It is a surreal experience, one minute you think you have healthy child and the next you find out she is critically ill with a disease you never knew existed (rhabdomyosarcoma is a pediatric muscle cancer). I have six children and at that time Rebecca was 13, Matthew was 11, Kristina was 8, Lindsay and Timothy were both 7 and Juliana was 5. I was home schooling all of them and we were in the final stages of building a house and packing to move. Fortunately we have family nearby who were able to help with babysitting as we ran back and forth to Sinai Hospital—40 miles one way from our house—for many scans and surgery then daily radiation therapy and weekly outpatient chemotherapy. After a few months, the whole family got used to a "new normal" where kids had to help out around the house more, Mom was home less often and all of our plans could change at a moment's notice when Juliana got a fever.

A year later, after fourteen rounds of chemotherapy and six weeks of radiation therapy, Juliana was cancer free. For the next three years she remained cancer free and except for the scans and blood work she had every three-four months, life slowly returned to normal. Then in March 2011 she found a swollen lymph node and a new tumor in her thigh. Her relapse protocol called for an overnight stay for the first day of each of the 12 rounds of chemo plus weekly outpatient chemo followed by five more weeks of daily radiation therapy. Nearly a year later she was once again cancer free, but we barely had time to celebrate before she relapsed for a second time in June 2012.

Her new relapse plan included 12 more rounds of chemotherapy, only this time she'd be inpatient for a week for each round. This treatment was the worse yet—Julie had several neutropenic fevers, dozens and dozens of blood and platelet transfusions, severe nausea, neuropathy and severe electrolyte wasting. Julie and I spent as much time at the hospital as we did at home most months. After chemo she had ten weeks of daily radiation therapy—five weeks to her abdomen followed by five weeks to her chest—she had radiation every weekday for her entire summer vacation in 2013. Juliana then started maintenance chemotherapy which consisted of a combination of daily oral chemo and every other week IV chemo. She was still getting maintenance chemo when she relapsed for the third time in March 2014.

By this time Juliana had been taking chemotherapy continuously for three years and her bone marrow was shot so our chemotherapy options were limited. Fortunately, the new tumor was in her right eye orbit and she was able have it surgically removed although they couldn't get margins without destroying the muscle. Juliana had two more rounds of outpatient chemo and five weeks of radiation therapy and was cancer free again. We then changed her maintenance chemotherapy protocol and started giving her mistletoe injections. Next Tuesday will mark a year since her last relapse and Juliana remains cancer free although she is still taking daily oral chemotherapy and getting mistletoe injections three times a week at home plus she gets another round of IV chemo at the hospital every three months.

During our family's eight year journey with pediatric cancer there have also been many "positives." Countless friends and family members have made us dinner, babysat and given Juliana and her brothers and sisters gifts. Many wonderful organizations have helped with everything from tickets to shows and sporting events to vacations in Ocean City and Disney World. Our children have grown up spending lots of time at the hospital playing with kids who are sick and injured and it has made them into caring, compassionate teenagers and young adults. It has also brought our family closer together and made us stronger.

Two of Juliana's four cancer protocols were clinical trials; even so none of the many chemotherapy drugs Juliana has taken over the last eight years was developed for rhabdomyosarcoma or even for pediatric use. Pediatric cancer research receives very little public funding which makes private fund raising like this so important. Your contributions will make a huge difference to brave children like my daughter.

When Juliana spoke she said, "Hi, my name is Juliana Carver and I am thirteen years old. I am home schooled and am in 8th grade this year. I like playing video games, swimming, making crafts, baking and cooking. I also really love playing with my dog, Maddie.

While I was in the hospital after relapsing the second time my Dad asked if I had three wishes what they would be. I said not to have cancer anymore, a billion dollars and a dog. The day after I got out of the hospital we went to the SPCA and adopted Maddie—so I got one of my wishes right away!

When I grow up I want to be a chef and open my own restaurant. My favorite foods are seafood and anything with barbeque sauce on it, like barbeque ribs, chicken and pulled pork. I also really like baking cakes and cookies.

I was only five years old when I found out I had cancer. I showed my parents a bump under my right arm that was bugging me. The next morning Mom took me to the doctor and that afternoon I had my first MRI. The next day my parents told me the bumps under my arm and in my forearm were cancer. I really didn't understand exactly what it was back then; I just knew I had "sick" cells in the bumps and needed lots and lots of medicine for a really long time to get rid of them.

Over the last eight years I have relapsed three times and gone through chemotherapy and radiation four different times. I remember when I found out I had relapsed the first time, after crying for a couple minutes I dried my eyes and said, "Well at least I know what I have to do to get rid of it again."

None of it was easy, but the worst was the chemo after my second relapse when I had to be inpatient for a whole week for each of the 12 rounds. My Mom stayed with me, but I would really miss my sisters and brothers, my Dad and my dog. Everyone would come to the hospital to visit—even my dog, Maddie, was allowed to visit me, but it wasn't the same as being home.

I have always been home schooled so I just did my school work in the hospital, but I did miss a lot of home school events and didn't get to see my friends as much. Lots of people, many I really didn't even know, sent me cards and gifts to help cheer me up during treatment. It made me feel better knowing lots of people were thinking about me and praying for me.

I would tell other kids with cancer that if I can do it, you can do it, you just can't be a giver upper!"

A couple days later I was back, with Matthew, at one of his soccer games. He is really good and it mirrors how he handles most things in life. He doesn't wait around for things to come to him. He goes out and gets it done. As, in years past, we continued to celebrate all the kid's birthdays and adoption anniversaries.

Believe in Tomorrow (believeintomorrow.org) asked me to give a speech at their annual fundraiser on March 19th. Juilana's photo was on the cover of their programs that were available for everyone who attended. Juliana didn't want to speak at that event so she stood by my left side as I spoke. My goal was to share how important it is when people give to families who have children who are fighting cancer. Among other things I said, "Believe in Tomorrow gave us the opportunity to rest, have fun and try not to worry for a few days. Your love is very very powerful to us." As I told them the best part of staying in their House on the Bay was fishing off the peer being the house. Juliana looked up at me, when I said those words, and gave me the biggest smile.

On March 22$^{nd}$ we were back at the annual Children's Roads to Recovery (http://www.childrensroadstorecovery.org/) Fundraiser. They are the ones who send out gas gift cards to help with the transportation in taking Juliana back and forth to the hospital.

April 2015 came along which included coloring Easter eggs and Easter morning. Back in July 2014 we heard about Believe Big (believebig.org). Their organization, with the help of scientists and doctors, found a form of mistletoe that can cure some cancers. We applied to add Juliana to it and were accepted. Juliana would receive, sub-q (just under the skin) shots three days per week. It seemed to help keep the cancer away. On April 11$^{th}$ Tammy was asked to speak at their annual fund raiser dinner.

The next evening we were at the fire pit, in our yard, roasting marshmallows. Later in the month we went to our local carnival where the kids got on rides and had lots of fun. May brought lots more time at the fire pit as well. It was a place, for all of us, to relax and enjoy the outdoors. May8th was a beautiful day. Juliana and Tammy worked on planting flowers and herbs in the flower bed at our house. Juliana's hair was long and pulled back in a pony tail. She looked into my video camera and said, "We are going to put some mulch in the flower garden and we're making an herb garden also and we got some more herbs..." She has always a perfectionist in everything so she made sure she did it right. She said, "if you don't like getting dirty you should not be doing this."

May 14$^{th}$ came and we were invited to the Giant Food (giantfood.com) Annual Softball Game, at Ripken Stadium in Aberdeen Maryland, where a lot of their employees would have an afternoon of fun. Our four youngest kids attended and have fun playing softball. Juliana was feeling really good. A few days later the American Red Cross, with the local leadership of Bonnie Rill, held another blood drive. Tammy and Lindsay rolled up their sleeves and donated blood that day. Juliana walked over to each of them and held their hand as they gave blood. The kids continued to enjoy the nice weather, swimming and playing badminton in our front yard.

On June 3$^{rd}$ Casey Cares (caseycares.org) made it possible, once again, for us to go to Hershey Park Pennsylvania. Juliana was so full of energy. All the kids had so much fun. By mid June, the Cool Kids Campaign (coolkidscampaign.org) who is the same organization who invited Juliana to be on the local news a couple years earlier, invited us to stay at their condo in Myrtle Beach South Carolina for a week. It was AWESOME! We arrived on June 13$^{th}$ and went right to the beach in the early evening. Juliana looked up at me and said as she jumped up and down, "Daddy we're at the beach..at the beach...at the beach." Tim, Lindsay, Kristina and Juliana walked right up to the water and let the water get their feet wet. Juliana's hair was blowing in the breeze. She jumped up and down, again, and sang, "I love the beach...I love the ocean!" To see our kids having fun was such an amazing feeling. She said, "I need morning to come now. I need to swim in this water."

The next morning Juliana was wearing a Believe Big bathing suit as she, and the rest of the kids, went swimming in the ocean. Juliana was sitting on the beach, for a minute, and said to me, "I love the beach" then she got up and walked deeper into the water. Tammy walked out to meet her while the other kids were out in deeper water. It was a beautiful day.

Tim walked back to the beach and started building a sand castle. He loved playing in the sand since he was really small. Juliana put on some swimming goggles and walked deeper into the water as he approached Matthew and his girlfriend Ashley who drove down separately. All our kids were growing so fast. Tammy and I hoped, so much, that cancer was behind us forever.

The smiles and laughter was so refreshing to see and hear from all the kids. Juliana grabbed a "boogie board" and went deeper in the water. She was having so much fun. At that moment, cancer seemed so far away. As she walked back to us, on the beach blanket, Juliana stopped to pick up some sea shells. My sister, Michele, her husband Thomas and son Thomas Ellis, joined us on the beach as they lived not far away. A little while later Juliana was digging a hole, in the sand, just like Tim had done then ran back into the ocean. The other kids were throwing a football, in the ocean, with their Uncle Thomas.

Cool Kids Campaign offered us this opportunity and we appreciate it so much! The next day, while sitting on the beach, Juliana recorded a message which said, "Thank you Cool Kids for an awesome week at the beach…" It was, now, June 15th and the day was beautiful as the kids played on the beach and in the ocean. We stayed on the beach most of the day and, after dinner, went back to the beach.

The next evening, the wind was kicking up and it didn't matter, on bit, to the kids. Tammy and Juliana went for a walk on the beach and collected sea shells and put them in a bucket that Juliana was carrying. Right around 8pm, while Juliana was sitting on the beach as the waves got her wet she said again, "I love the beach!" She began to put sand over her legs and said, "I'm a sand maid." I asked her, "how to you like Myrtle Beach?" She said, "I love it...wooo!" The entire week was much fun. We arrived back home on June 20$^{th}$ and went to pick up Maddie from John and Wanda Thompson's house (we used to live next door to them) who, graciously, watched Maddie for us while we were away.

June 23$^{rd}$ brought another trip, for Juliana, to the hospital. During her exam, Juliana told Dr. Jason Fixler, that she was having pain inside and on Juliana's right hip. The first, three, times Juliana had cancer it was on the right side of her body. He continued to exam her as he asked her lots of questions. Juliana had an MRI and the scans were clear. There was some point, in June, that Juliana said, "you gotta find another way around your problem" That was her approach to cancer. She was determined to beat it and grow up to be a chef.

In June 2015 Giant Food (giantfood.com) contacted us through the Children's Cancer Foundation and asked us if we would like to come to Washington DC where Chef Robert Irvine (chefirvine.com) was going to sign some autographs. Chef Irvine starred in a cable tv show called "Restaurant Impossible" which we loved as a family. In addition, Juliana wanted to be a chef when she grew up so this was a huge deal for us. On July 1$^{st}$ we drive to a Giant Food Store, in Washington DC, to meet Chef Robert Irvine. Gordon Reid is the President of the Giant Food Region and developed a love for Juliana.

As we approached Chef Irvine, in line, a Giant Food employee attempted to introduce Juliana to Chef Irvine. Chef Irvine took over the conversation.

He was wearing his Robert Irvine Foundation (robertirvinefoundation.org). He looked at Juliana and said, "Hi cutie pie." Robert looked at Juliana and asked her "how old are you?" She said, "thirteen." He said, "no way no way." He stooped down on one knee and looked at Juliana. He asked her if she cleaned her room then gave her a high five. The next question was "do you have a boyfriend?" Juliana said, "no" and she got another high five. He asked her about school and gave her another high five. He asked her if she runs around and go crazy. Juliana said, "sometimes." He asked her to shout as loud as possible, then screamed really loud to show her how load to scream. Juliana's pretty shy but she did yell pretty loud. He gave her a "pinky swear" and he promised to be her BFF. HE stood up and signed a couple cook books for Juliana and our family.

Less than an hour later we were lead to an elevator where we were going to have lunch with Chef Irvine and his wife Gail. Gail, at the time, was a professional wrestler on television. The lunch was a lot of fun. At one point, Robert Irvine, looked to his right where Juliana was sitting and promised he was going to stay in touch with her. As her Dad, I thought it was such a kind gesture but this guy is busy, has several businesses and there's no way he could take that kind of time to communicate with Juliana. I was so wrong. In fact, over the next year he did exactly what he said with many Facetime chats and phone calls. Make no mistake, Robert Irvine is a man of his word.

July 4th came and we had another cookout, playing in the yard and watching ground-based fireworks. Juliana was feeling okay. Juliana's life (and ours too) was about to implode again. One day I asked her why she never complains about all that she has endured. She said, "Don't complain about something you can fix. If you can fix it then fix it."

Juliana started to have pain in her chest so we had another scan done. Remember, just a few weeks earlier there was a scan and everything was clear. Juliana said, "You gotta do what you gotta do to make it work."

July 12' 2015 came and we got the horrible news. The cancer was back for the fifth time. This time, Relapse to mediastinum and retroperitoneum lymph nodes, right cardiophrenic angle and left anterior upper chest. All of us were devastated. Juliana was so upset. It was horrible to see the disappointment on her face. Juliana was admitted to the hospital.

July 13th Juliana gave her fans an update. She said, "Last night we got the MRI and it showed I had another tumor, not fun, and hopefully we can go home today because we're going to talk some stuff out about radiation and what the game plan is so, hopefully, we can go home today." Juliana was really motivated to get out of the hospital that day.

Casey Cares (caseycares.org) contacting Tammy and asked if Juliana would like to go see Taylor Swift in concert. Juliana jumped at the chance to see one of her favorite singers. We received a few tickets and Juliana invited her friend Emily Kolenda who had been her "hospital buddy" at Sinai Hospital in Baltimore Maryland. On July 14th Tammy, Juliana, Emily and myself drove to

Washington DC for the concert. It was one day from when we found out Juliana had cancer for the fifth time. The entire concert all I wanted to do was sob and sob and sob. Not again, why won't this cancer leave our baby girl alone?!?! Juliana and Emily had a great time. They sang along with the songs and were just little girls.

On July 16th Juliana recorded another video message for her fans. She was so sad. She said, "Hi everyone, it's Juliana Carver here and I just wanted to tell you, as you probably already know, the cancer is back in my side and on a (pain) scale from one to ten some days it's a three and, also, sometimes it's like a six. It's really bugging me so we're taking some pain medication and sometimes that helps sometimes it doesn't. Please pray for me because, starting Monday, we should be starting chemo to make it shrink and get smaller so please pray for me and hope I get better. Thank you."

The next day brought more scans. She started getting Chemotherapy – Vincristine, Irinotecan and Temozolomide. She received five rounds before getting severe stomach pain that required hospitalization for pain management, fluids and TPN.

On July 19$^{th}$ we were invited to a banquet, in Pennsylvania, hosted by Giant Food (giantfood.com) and to celebrate a lot of money being raised to fight Pediatric Cancer. Gordon Reid, the regional president, knew Juliana had cancer again. When he got up to speak to talk about Juliana he got so emotional and asked Juliana to stand as the audience gave her a standing ovation for being so brave.

Once the chemotherapy started, again, Juliana was getting so sick. The prior several months she was feeling really good, having so much fun on the beach at Myrtle Beach and, now, the cancer is back for the fifth time. Why? Why won't God answer our prayers to make Juliana well and keep her healthy?!?!

On July 27, 2015, Chef Robert Irvine (http://chefirvine.com/) Facetimed her to encourage her to keep fighting. His wife, Gail, was wrestling behind him while he was chatting with Juliana. He let her watch a few minutes of the wrestling match. He reminded Juliana that the wrestling is all "story…it's not real…so you don't get scared." He said, jokingly, "Don't mess with my wife…kind of tough." The crowd started chanting "Let's go Gail…Let's Go Gail." He introduced Juliana, while on Facetime, to a couple of Gail's friends. Chef Irvine's compassion is amazing.

The next day Juliana was back in the hospital getting chemotherapy. My parents and most of our other kids come to the hospital to visit with Juliana that day.

We began hearing chatter that there might be a way for Juliana to get a bone marrow transplant to cure her of cancer. August 3' 2015 I told Juliana's fans that Juliana had been in the hospital for the last seven days. Her intestines were not functioning because of the chemotherapy taken away the ability for her to absorb food. I told her fans, that we heard a couple weeks earlier, that Juliana might be able to get a bone marrow transplant but we had to find Juliana's birth mother to see if she would be willing to come to America to be a bone marrow donor. I contacted the embassy in Belarus, Washington DC and New York a few weeks before this day. The country of Belarus found Juliana's birth mother.

We were so hopeful this transplant would be a cure for Juliana. She began to lose weight because of not being able to keep food inside her for more than an hour or two. Her eyes were looking so weak. The next day, August 4th, Juliana found out she was able to go home after another week in the hospital. Juliana's hair was starting to show the signs of coming out. It would come out in clumps as Tammy brushed it. Her hair had gotten so long and she was so sad that she was losing her long and beautiful hair.

The next day, August 5th, Chef Robert Irvine called to Facetime with Juliana again. He was on the set of one of his Restaurant Impossible shows. He asked Juliana to tell the crew, who were on the call with them, what she always says..Juliana said, "I'm not a giver upper." He called and Facetimed Juliana several times.

On August 7th Juliana and I went for a walk in our woods. She recorded a short message for her fans. She was losing weight, weak but determined to get better. She said, "Hi, It's Juliana Carver here and I wanted to update you again. I've been battling cancer for eight years now…really hard…the fifth time. Since we started it's been really hard 'cause everything is just so stressful…all the pain and the hospital and stuff. It's just really hard but with your friends and family by your side and people who care about you it really helped. Right now I'm just taking it easy…thank you for your prayers."

Juliana was now bald...again. Juliana was losing more weight. She was back in the hospital, again, on July 11$^{th}$ and seen by Dr. Joseph Wiley. Dr. Wiley was in charge of building the new Oncology wing at Sinai Hospital. It was so much better than when Juliana was getting cancer treatment in 2007. Juliana started to cry from the stress of fighting cancer again. She just wanted to be a healthy teenager.

On August 13$^{th}$ Cool Kids Campaign invited us to the Maryland State House where Governor Larry Hogan was fighting cancer. Justin Berk and several of his friends had, almost, completed a trek across the State of Maryland to raise money for Cool Kids Campaign. The visit with Mr. And Mrs. Hogan was amazing and Mrs. Hogan would continue to stay in touch with Juliana including coming to visit her in the hospital.

Juliana continued to get several blood transfusions in the coming weeks. Juliana found it difficult to run and play so she would watch her siblings play from a chair. On August 26$^{th}$ we celebrated Juliana's twelfth adoption anniversary. Our friends, Mike, Tori and Aubrix, were there for the celebration. Tammy made a chocolate cake. Juliana was able to eat a little cake.

Tammy continued to teach most of the kid's home school. On September 2$^{nd}$ Casey Cares (caseycares.org) invited us back to Hershey Park Pennsylvania. This time Juliana was pushed in a wheelchair. There was no way she was strong enough to walk too far. The kids had fun like in the past. September 3$^{rd}$ Juliana had more scans to see how the chemotherapy was impacting the tumors.

While at the library, on September 4$^{th}$, I told Juliana that the three tumors that Juliana had two of the three were gone and the third one was half the size. We were told they were going to try to move forward on the bone marrow transplant. Chemotherapy would continue. Five days later Mrs. Yumi Hogan (First Lady of Maryland) visited with Juliana, in the hospital, and showed Juliana how to draw some pictures as Mrs. Hogan is an artist. It was so kind of Mrs. Hogan to visit with Juliana.

September 12$^{th}$ came and it was time for the Cool Kids Campaign (coolkidscampaign.org) annual fundraiser dinner. Juliana and I were asked to give a speech. She wore a grey shirt and black pants with a pink bow on her head. Juliana did an outstanding job. She said, "I had a lot of fun at Myrtle Beach this summer. I love the beach because the water was so warm and calm you could go swimming in it. I, also, like to play in the sand and make castles and help to bury my brother up to his neck (Juliana giggled along with the audience). My next favorite thing was the pool. We could walk across the grass, from the condo and the water was so warm it felt like a hot tub. I, also, had fun going on the sky wheel and eating yummy food. At the condo there were fun things to do like video games, board games, puzzles and movies. I had a great vacation." The crowd erupted in applause.

Four days later Juliana was back in the hospital. September 23$^{rd}$ came around and we took the kids to pick peaches at a local orchard. Five days later Juliana was back in the hospital.

On October 6$^{th}$ I asked Juliana to describe, for her fans, what it feels like to need a blood transfusion. She said, "It feels like you run out of breath really easy like, for me, just walking a few feet or just standing here for a few minutes makes me really tired…doesn't really make sense but…it feels like you're running across the room."

Later that day saw, on Facebook, that Chef Robert Irvine was going to be in Red Lion Pennsylvania on the set of out another episode of Restaurant Impossible. As soon as I found out, I texted him and asked if we could bring Juliana up to see him. Red Lion is less than an hour from our home. He was so happy to know we were so close and welcomed us to hang out with him.

Once Juliana was getting a blood transfusion, on October $7^{th}$, and got home, we ate dinner and drove up to see Chef Irvine. It was "reveal day" when the owners of a local restaurant would see what the Restaurant Impossible crew and volunteers did to transform their restaurant. There was a line of people waiting for the restaurant to open. We parked the car and walked to where Robert Irvine's motor home was parked and waited for him. A few minutes passed and he walked out of a large tent, walked over to Juliana and gave her a hug. Behind him were volunteers and staff.

He stood up, put his left hand on Juliana's left shoulder and said, "A few of my friends want to say Hi. This is Juliana…say HI Juliana." The crowd yelled "Hello Juliana!" Robert said, "I can't hear you." The crowd yelled "HI JULIANA!" He introduced us to several people and took us on a tour, of the restaurant, before the owners (of the restaurant saw it).

After the tour he invited us into his trailer (motor home) where the televisions and wires were set up for the Restaurant Impossible show. We were able to watch, as the owners of the restaurant, walked into their newly renovated restaurant. Once that part of the episode was finished Robert came back to the trailer to hang out with us for about an hour. He's such a tender man beneath the tough guy image.

October 15$^{th}$ came and Flashes of Hope (flashesofhope.org) invited us, again, to have family photos taken. We drove back to Sinai Hospital with most of our kids for some pictures to be taken. They did a great job. The next day I was back at one of Matthew's soccer games. He is really good but, also, knows how to work as a team to win a game. The following day we took Juliana, Tim and Kristina bowling. When Juliana was fighting cancer, at age five, the radiation shrunk the muscles in her right forearm which made it really weak and shorter than her left arm. It didn't stop Juliana from trying to keep up with the rest of the kids. Juliana was very competitive in everything. That evening Juliana fixed breakfast for dinner for several of us. She loved to cook.

The next day we were invited by the Children's Cancer Foundation (childrenscancerfoundation.org) back to Sinai Hospital for Juliana to appear in a video clip with Dr. Joseph Wiley about the importance of funding research to find cures for pediatric cancer. Juliana did a great job. Later that day, Juliana was examined by Dr. Jason Fixler. He has been awesome with Juliana.

October 24, 2015 brought decorating pumpkins and getting really for Halloween night. The next night took us back to the Children's Roads to Recovery Annual Banquet. My father and Juliana got up and danced for a couple seconds. Tim walked around and did magic for a lot of people. Everyone had a lot of fun. A few days later, Chef Robert Irvine called to FaceTime with Juliana again. His mom was with him, from England for a couple of months, so he asked Juliana to wave hi to her. He is such a kind man. He was, always, trying to encourage Juliana and get her to laugh.

The first week, of November, brought another week-long stay in the hospital for chemotherapy. Juliana was eating a little more food even though she was on TPN (food in a tube). A few of our kids, and their friend Aubrix, came up to visit and play with Juliana. Emily Kolenda was, also, in the hospital that week so they invested more time together. November 8$^{th}$ Tammy and Juliana were able to come back home, from a week in the hospital, to the joys of seeing Maddie again. It was, always, so beautiful to see the joy on Juliana's face when she was able to play with Maddie again.

Tammy, as always, prepared a wonderful Thanksgiving Dinner for a house full of family and friends. The next day, per Tammy's custom, they decorated for Christmas. Juliana said, "I'm always in a good mood when Maddie is around" then gave her dog a big kiss. It would be the last time Juliana would celebrate Thanksgiving and Christmas.

The next day, Juliana and Tammy started baking Christmas cookies. Juliana had been helping Tammy, bake Christmas cookies, since she was about four years old. Juliana wanted to be a Chef when she became an adult.

During the prior few months I had been communicating with a representative of the Government of Belarus in attempting to coordinate getting Juliana and Kristina's birth mother to the United States to help with the bone marrow transplant in early 2016. The Belarussian government was so helpful and kind through the entire process.

On December 3, 2015 Chef Robert Irvine Facetimed Juliana from a LIVE seminar he was doing for several hundred people. He asked her, while the audience could see on her on a big screen, "What do you say to people who are having a bad day?" Juliana said, "You should never give up because you can fight it no matter what…I'm not a giver-upper." He asked her how they met. She said they met in July 2015. He asked her, "if you could say one thing to all the folks in this room what would it be?" Juliana said, It's a crazy journey…expect the unexpected."

Juliana had a "Birthday Weekend" for her fourteenth birthday which is December 4, 2015. She had family and friends over the house, went to a craft store and painted pottery with the Kolenda family and her friend Aubrix and went to a Mexican Restaurant where the employees sang Happy Birthday (in Spanish) to Juliana. Maryland Governor and Mrs. Hogan sent her a fruit basket for her birthday.

I went to one of Lindsay's basketball games and Matthew's soccer games. We had breakfast with my brother, Chris, and his family who live in Florida on December 8th. Juliana was feeling pretty good and we had her laughing a lot that month as we had done in prior months and years. Laughter, we felt, helped her feel better.

December 21st Chef Robert Irvine and his wife Gail called to Facetime. He talked to her about Christmas and her school work. He was saying this he knew that she was a good girl. He said he wanted to make sure he called her as soon as he got back from Afghanistan to encourage the troops. Christmas Eve was upon us so we drove to my parent's house to open some gifts. Once again, Chef Robert Irvine (as he promised) called to Facetime with Juliana again. He is such a genuine man. We love him and his wife, Gail, so much!

Christmas morning came and everyone was so excited to open their gifts. Tammy and I, always, spent the same amount (within $5-$10) for each of the kids although it may have looked like we spent more on others because of the gifts they chose to receive.

December 29, 2015 I posted, on Facebook, "Tomorrow (Wednesday) Juliana is getting her first set of scans in four months to see the status of the last tumor that was wrapped around toward her spine. It, normally, takes a day or two to get the results. Our expectation is that cancer is gone...we shall see.

We, also, found out that a doctor at Johns Hopkins was contacted by a Dr. Anna Zborovskaya, Director of Belarusian Research Center for Pediatric Oncology and Hematology (I didn't even know they had such a center in Belarus). She reports that she received permission from the Ministry of Health in Belarus to ship the sample (mouth swab of Juliana's birth mother to confirm she's a match for the transplant). She also offered, an alternative, to run the test in Belarus and send Hopkins the results. Now, the government of Belarus is getting involved (again) to help us...that's a HUGE step. Next week we have another appointment with the bone marrow transplant team at Johns Hopkins Hospital."

As I write these words, in my original rough draft of this book, it is December 31, 2017 at 1:56pm. The agony of what I am to write in this paragraph and the next chapter is beyond description. On December 31, 2015 Kristina, Tim and Juliana stayed up, with us, and watched 2016 arrive. Juliana said to the right of me on our sofa. Behind Juliana and I was a Happy Holidays blanket draped on the back of the sofa. She was wearing her pink pajamas.

She was so excited for 2016 to arrive and to receive her bone marrow transplant, at Johns Hopkins Hospital in Baltimore Maryland under the direction of Dr. David Loeb, and be healed of cancer forever. She began to chant, "2016…2016…a New Year..Good Year. It's going to be a New Year New Year Good Year." I, then, did a LIVE video on Facebook with Juliana and I watching as 2016 arrived. She was counting down. She said, "Fifty Seven seconds…" as she watched the clock on the television. She said, I like watching the ball (in New York) drop (on TV) even though it doesn't really drop." Juliana counted down some more, "Twelve, eleven, ten, nine eight, seven, six, five, four, three, two….2016…IT'S A NEW YEAR IT'S A NEW YEAR IT'S A NEW YEAR…IT'S GOING TO BE GREAT. Thank you everyone for an awesome 2015 and, hopefully, to be an amazing 2016 and thank you for all your prayers…YEA!!!"

We had no idea that 2016 would be the worst year of our lives.

## Chapter 11

January 4, 2016 took us to Johns Hopkins Hospital as the day was getting closer for Iryna (Juliana and Kristina's birth mother) to fly to America and donate bone marrow for Juliana. We took a tour of where Juliana and Tammy would be staying, in the hospital, for several weeks after the transplant. Our hopes were through the roof that this bone marrow transplant was going to cure Juliana of cancer. She was, also, getting a biopsy done on that day. Juliana was wearing a pink hat, pink sweat shirt with a rainbow on it under her coat and black pants.

As she hopped up on the hospital bed in the pre-op area Tammy helped take off her boots. Juliana was wearing pink socks. She was, exactly, fourteen years and one month old on this day. A nurse brought Juliana a green hospital gown to change into for her surgical biopsy while Juliana passed the time playing on her IPAD. I stepped out of the room, for Juliana to change into her hospital gown, and when I returned she was playing on her IPAD again. She said, "I feel...stressed" about the upcoming biopsy. She was very afraid it was going to hurt.

The nurse brought in some warm blankets for Juliana as they got her ready to take her into surgery. As they began to wheel Juliana away I gave her hugs and kisses. Tammy would walk with the hospital personnel as they wheeled Juliana down the hall. She said, "See you when we're done." I said, "I love you" and responded, "Love you too." She waved, with her left hand to me, as she wheeled away. After the procedure Juliana was awake, when Tammy and I were able to go see her in recovery. I asked her, "how did it go?" She said, "Better than I thought." She said that it didn't hurt.

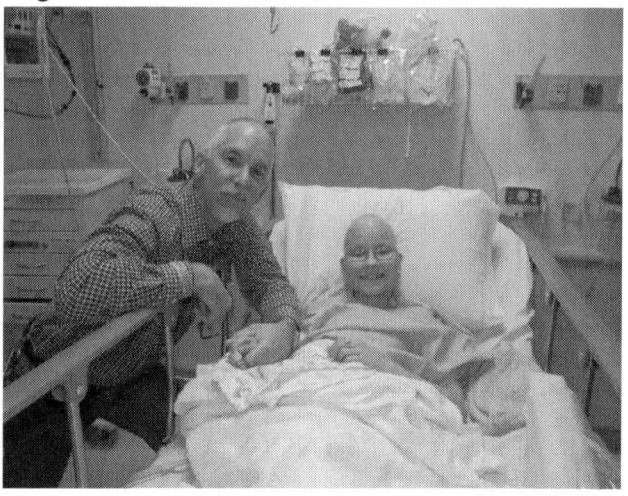

She began to explain, a little more, what happened. She said, "When they put the needle in it...I was like WO WO WAIT...I hold mom's hand like I usually do...I was like OH MY GOSH OKAY...It went well...just a little needle and pressure but it was fine. I only felt the needle and a little stinging."

Moments later I asked her if she could explain more, to me, what happened. She said, "Well, I went on the table for the CT (Scan), I was on my stomach, and I had my (left) arm like this (over her head)...it was really uncomfortable. They took some pictures (scans), then they cleaned the area (where the biopsy would be done) and they let it dry. They put the needle in to put the numbing medication in...that wasn't as bad as a I thought...so all this time this little needle (is what I've been worried about...I always freak out about it and, then, when it's finally done that's not as bad as I thought...it never is...it never is...I always worry about nothin'. After that it was all numb and then they started pokin' it...it felt all weird. I could, kind of, feel it when they put the needle in...not a prick but the pressure of the needle. It felt so weird. It, just feels like someone is pushing down..like pressure. It was a bit creepy."

January 12, 2016 took us back to Johns Hopkins Hospital for more tests. A few days later, we were in our kitchen celebrating Maddie's birthday. The connection, that Juliana and Maddie had, is hard to explain. They were so close. Juliana's hair was starting to grow again.

On January 20th Juliana was scheduled for more scans to get radiation from the most recent discovery of cancer in December 2015. We got to the hospital waiting room and Juliana began to play on her IPAD to pass the time. This time, Juliana had to lay on her stomach because the cancer was on a rib on her back. The technician covered Juliana with a warm blanket and Juliana was facing to her right side. Tammy and I stood close to Juliana. Dr. Carmella Coleman had treated Juliana, for radiation, several times and she was to put stickers and permanent marker on her back to help identify where the radiation would be focused.

Tammy stood to Dr. Coleman's right side as she explained, to Tammy, how the radiation treatments would be done (Tammy studied science, chemistry and biology in college). Juliana, just, wanted to be a healthy girl and do what normal little girls do. Juliana's patience was extraordinary. She never complained. She never whined.

As they prepared Juliana for the scans her arms were over her head, while on her stomach, as she faced the right side of the table. Juliana's eyes closed and she was relaxed. It was time to get the scans so Tammy and I, along with the technician, had to stand behind a wall while the scans were happening. We could see Juliana the entire time. She scan lasted 6.2 seconds each

Dr. Coleman and her team has, always, been amazing with Juliana. On this day, they readjusted Juliana's position, on the table, a little bit and took more scans and still photos to make sure that Juliana's position would be the same during the radiation treatments.

Finally, the scans were done so we went to eat lunch at Don Pablos Mexican Restaurant in Owings Mills Maryland. Juliana was starting to be able to eat much more regular food instead of only being on TPN (food in a tube). When we got home she opened more fan mail. The next day,

Chef Robert Irvine Facetimed her, from another Restaurant Impossible TV Show location. He asked if Juliana was doing okay and wondered what she was eating for dinner. He introduced all the people were working with him. He told his crew to follow Juliana on Angels for Juliana on Facebook. He, also, told his crew that I video tape everything including a time with Robert Irvine Face Timed Juliana while he was in bed (true story). Juliana looked over her right shoulder, at me, at laughed and said, "yes he did!" He said I was a "good guy!"

Two days later we got a blizzard of over a foot of snow. As soon as it stopped snowing and I cleared the driveway and sidewalk the kids got their coats on and went outside to play. It was really deep for our area. Juliana was feeling awesome and had lots of energy. Tim built a snow cave by the pool.

On February 5th Tammy and Juliana baked some brownies with chocolate chips in them. She said, I've been wanting to bake for a while but with radiation and hospital....but today was the last day of radiation so I got to celebrate with brownies!" They were delicious!

Juliana was starting to have pain in her back. February 8th we took her back to Johns Hopkins Hospital (Sinai Hospital, where Juliana had been getting cancer treatment since 2007, does not do bone marrow transplants). We were so scared that the cancer was back for the seventh time. Tammy sat inches, from Juliana, as we waited to be seen by a doctor. Juliana and Tammy encouraged Juliana not to worry although, Tammy and I, were scared out of our minds the entire time.

This time, I was going to go back, with Juliana, before they knocked her out for another biopsy to see what the pain was from in her back. I suited up with a hospital gown and cap. I followed Juliana down the hall, while she stayed on the hospital bed, into a small operating room.

By this time, Iryna (Juliana and Kristina's birth mother) had her passport, visa and plane ticket to fly to America, several days later, to donate bone marrow for Juliana. Juliana spoke up and was talking with a nurse, named Julie, who was standing to her right side. Another nurse, standing to Juliana's left side asked if she would like a warm blanket. Juliana nodded yes and smiled.

They injected medicine to put Juliana to sleep and I went back to the waiting room after I gave Juliana a kiss. After the biopsy, we met Juliana in the recovery room. She asked how I liked going back with her into the operating room. I said, "it was cool…it was different." Juliana grabbed Tammy's hand and Tammy gave her a kiss on the forehead. I caressed her left check and said, "You're so beautiful." Juliana lifted her head and kissed my hand.

Once she woke up she asked for some pain medication. They gave her oxycodin around 2:18pm. We had been, at the hospital, since 7am that day. Shortly, thereafter, we were led into a small room for Juliana to get some more scans and an EKG. Juliana put on another hospital gown and waited for the scans to begin. The technician turned out the lights, in the room, in order to see the screen better as she pushed the probe on Juliana's body to get clear images.

On February 10$^{th}$ we found out Juliana had cancer for the seventh time. She had a 3cm tumor near T-9, T-10 and T-11. As Tammy told her, in our home, Juliana said, "We were so close" and started to cry. The next day, Juliana was back at Johns Hopkins Hospital for a breathing test which is normal for pre-bone marrow transplant patients. Two days later, when I texted Chef Robert Irvine, that Juliana had cancer for the seventh time, he called to Face-Time her again. He said, as Juliana held my cell phone, "What's UP!?!? He said, "how are you?" Juliana said, "Good." During the conversation he encouraged her to be strong and that cancer is "just another bump in the road and we're going to do it all over again like we did six times before." Juliana said, "sadly...yes." Robert said, "I know it's sad." He told her he was in another Children's Hospital and he showed Juliana's picture to other kids who were sick. He made Juliana laugh and smile.

He said, "I wish I could have had you with me to tell them, listen, don't be whining...fight...because that's what you do." She said, "It would have been more fun than being at the hospital all day." He said, "we got to do what we got to do, right?" Juliana said, "Yup."

Robert Irvine said, "I know it's upsetting. Here's the coolest thing...you have the best family on the planet." Juliana said, "Yes!" and looked up at me and smiled. Robert continued, "You have a lot of people, in this big world that are like, you know, reading your Dad's posts (on Angels for Juliana) and I follow you on Twitter too." Juliana said, "I saw." Robert said, "Now I can tweet you. All the people that I work with think about you every day and, although, it's a little setback we'll just get back on that horse and we'll keep (riding) that horse, right?" Juliana said, "Yup."

Later that day our friend Joe DiMaggio and his children came by the house and brought Juliana some gifts. It was very kind of them.

We found out that Johns Hopkins Hospital, in Baltimore Maryland, agreed to freeze Iryna's bone marrow because Juliana could not receive it if she had active cancer. February 15$^{th}$ arrived, which was the day, Iryna was to arrive in America. Days before I posted, on Facebook, how we needed help with Russian translating. Thankfully, several people offered to help us. The day Iryna arrived Gregory Krupkin, who knows my sister Michele, offered to go with us to the airport and to help translate for a couple days.

We drove to Dulles Airport and waited for Iryna to arrive. Juliana, Kristina, Tim and Tammy sat in the waiting area. I was too hyper to sit down. Moments seemed much longer. Finally, I saw Iryna being escorted by a representative from the Embassy of Belarus named Oleg. Iryna walked toward me and I ran up to her and gave her a huge hug and thanked her (in Russian). I am sure I freaked her out.

Gregory walked up to Iryna, shook her hand and introduced himself. Iryna saw Kristina and

Kristina saw Iryna and walked toward each other. Iryna had not seen Kristina since she was four years old and Kristina did not remember Iryna. She stood and looked at each other. I am sure Iryna wanted to embrace Kristina but was not sure if the hug would be accepted.

Tammy walked up, with Juliana, and she waved to Iryna. Iryna had only known Juliana for less than a few hours after she was born. Timothy was kind enough to take still photos for me while I was videotaping this amazing day. All our hopes and dreams were that the bone marrow transplant would cure Juliana of cancer. Iryna kept looking at Juliana. I wonder what was going through her mind.

We gathered her bags and walked to the van to leave the airport. New friends, of ours, Mr. and Mrs. Daniels (parents of Melissa Daniels) agreed to have Iryna stay with them for several days because Juliana was going to start new chemotherapy treatment the very next day.

My sister knows a woman, who speaks Russian and lives in the mid west. She agreed to fly to our state to help translate for us and stay for several days. Her kindness blew my mind. Her name is Yelena. The same day, February 16$^{th}$, I found Iryna being briefed, with Yelena at her side, on the bone marrow transplant. Juliana started receiving Vincristine, Irinotecan and Temozolomide. She received two rounds of this type of chemotherapy this time.

By February 18$^{th}$ Juliana was feeling really bad from the chemotherapy.

On that day, we sat on our sofa, with her translating for Iryna, and looking through photo albums of Juliana and Kristina growing up in our family. Iryna brought photos of her son and her parents and brother. We had lunch but Juliana was feeling so bad, from the chemo, she couldn't enjoy Iryna being in our home.

A couple days later Iryna was, with Juliana, as she got more chemotherapy. This time, we went back to Sinai Hospital to get the chemotherapy. Juliana had been treated there since 2007. My parents arrived to give Iryna a big hug and thanked her for helping Juliana. Gregory Krupkin came to the hospital to help us translate.

Juliana started receiving TPN (food in a tube) because the chemotherapy was doing so much damage to her digestive system.

On February 23$^{rd}$ Iryna was at Johns Hopkins Hospital for some pre-transplant tests then we went back to Sinai Hospital to invest some time with Juliana. Iryna and Juliana sat on the sofa, in Juliana's hospital room, quietly as they didn't speak the same language. Iryna is a smoker and I kept encouraging her to quit smoking because we want her in our lives for a long time.

Later, that evening, Iryna was back at our house. She was going to sleep in one of our bedrooms for the remainder of her visit to America. Kristina, Tim and Iryna (Juliana was still in the hospital getting chemotherapy) and tried to communicate with each other using Google Translate. They laughed and Iryna tried to teach them Russian. The kids tried to teach Iryna a little more English.

February 24, 2016 came and it was the day Iryna was going in for surgery to donate some bone marrow and, we hoped, would save Juliana's life. I was with Iryna, in the pre-op area. She was calm and eager to help Juliana. The hospital provided a translator for Iryna. We agreed that Iryna should be put to sleep during the procedure so she would not remember anything.

A nurse put a "pulse-ox" (oxygen saturation) on Iryna's finger. By the look on Iryna's face she had never seen such a thing. She asked the translator to ask the nurse what it was for so the nurse explained it to Iryna. After the bone marrow procedure I stayed, with Iryna, until she was coherent. Her blood pressure was all over the place so, after many hours of waiting for it to regulate, the hospital agreed to have her spend the night for observation.

On the 26th Juliana and Tammy came home, from the hospital, as Iryna and the rest of us waited for their arrival. Spending a week, in the hospital, and getting chemotherapy is so hard on Juliana. Maddie ran up the van to see Juliana. She picked up Maddie and then Maddie gave Juliana some kisses. Tim hugged Juliana and said, "I missed you so much!" Maddie continued to kiss Juliana's chin. Juliana kissed the left side of Juliana's head.

As Juliana walked into our house, Iryna held the door open for her. Juliana walked over, to me, and gave me a hug. As I hugged her I said, "You're so Awesome!" Tim gave Juliana another hug.

Iryna's face was swollen from the bone marrow procedure. We had gotten a poster made with photos of Juliana and Kristina on it. She liked it very much as she gave me a thumbs up. We didn't have a translator, at the house, at that moment. Later, we sat around our table as Juliana received a lot of fan mail and opened cards and packages. Iryna held Maddie on her lap. Iryna had no idea what we were saying.

A couple days later, Dariya Baker, who saw Juliana's story on Facebook came over to help translate for us. Dariya was such a huge help to us. It was getting close for Iryna to fly home to Belarus. Tammy helped pack her bags so everything fit in the luggage. We could feel the sadness as we may never be able to see Iryna again.

The next morning we took lots of pictures and video. Iryna had developed a real fondness for Maddie. Iryna looked on as Juliana took a lot of pills and Tammy disconnected Juliana's TPN pump. Iryna looked up at me, as Tammy was disconnecting the lines from Juliana's port, with confusion in her eyes. Iryna stooped over and looked, to her right, to watch what was happening. I could see the concern, for Juliana, on Iryna's face.

We picked up Greg Krupkin on the way to Dulles Airport for Iryna to get her flight back to

Belarus. Juliana was too sick to join us. Iryna and Kristina sat beside each other waiting for the time for Iryna to board the Aeroflot plane. There was a familiarity that Kristina felt, toward Iryna, but had no memories of her time when she lived with Iryna before living in an orphanage. Greg and Iryna were chatting about something (not sure what). Tim sat to Kristina's left playing with his magic cards.

Iryna looked over, at me, and said (in Russian) that Kristina is shy. I said, "very." Kristina smiled. Iryna joked that all I know is a few words in Russian. The time came when Iryna had to go to another area of the airport to board her plane. She stood up and put a bottled water in her purse. I asked her if I could hug her (Greg translated for me). Iryna outstretched her arms for me to give her a hug. Now, Iryna had tears in her eyes as it was time to give Kristina a hug. I hadn't seem such emotion, in Iryna, the entire two weeks she was in America. Now, it was time to say goodbye.

I said, "it's okay to cry." Kristina and Iryna embraced. Iryna hugged her so tight. She rubbed the back of Kristina's head and was speaking to her in Russian (I couldn't hear it). The hug lasted several seconds. Iryna waved goodbye as I said, "Thank you" again. She wiped away more tears as she said "bye" (in English). I said, to Iryna, "I miss you already and you're not even gone yet." I gave Iryna another hug and said, "Thank you so much!" Greg told me that Iryna said she will come again and write us. Greg was kind enough to escort Iryna to the place where we could not follow any more at the airport.

Iryna hesitated and Kristina walked up to her and they embraced again. They didn't want to let go of each other. Iryna said, "bye" and gave Kristina a kiss on her right cheek. They hugged again and, now, the tears in Iryna's eyes were flowing. Kristina was, now, wiping away a few tears from her eyes too. They embraced again. Iryna waved goodbye, again, to all of us and turned to go down an escalator until we could not see her again. I was sobbing by that moment as Iryna waved when she was going down the escalator.

Juliana continued to remain on TPN (food in a tube), when March arrived, but she was trying so hard to not let her inability to eat food stop her from having fun. March $8^{th}$ was a beautiful day so Juliana, Kristina and Timothy (and Maddie) were outside enjoying the nice weather. Juliana ran and played in our front yard as if she had never had any worries in her entire life. Juliana was planning for a bonfire, in our fire pit, for later in the day.

March 17, 2016 was day four of Juliana's chemotherapy, that week, and she came home. She was resting on the sofa with Maddie. I said, "What would we do without Maddie?" Juliana said, "It would be very bored. What would Maddie do without us?"

A few days later I took Lindsay out to take some nature photos with a camera that the Bromley family bought her for Christmas. The Bromley's have been very kind to our family.

Juliana had to carry around a pump, for a few hours a day, would feed her the TPN since she had great difficulty eating solid food. Tammy has been such an outstanding mom to Juliana and all our kids. Literally, Tammy was Juliana's full time nurse for nine years.

March 23$^{rd}$ arrived and I was at one of Lindsay's soccer practices. A few days later it was, once again, time to color Easter eggs. Juliana was feeling good and helped Tammy bake resurrection roles. She loved to cook and bake. Juliana and Tammy were a team in the kitchen as much as possible especially when it came time for baking. Juliana was determined not to allow cancer to keep her from enjoying life. They, along with Timothy and Kristina, also colored Easter eggs.

Easter morning came and Juliana was wearing a beautiful dress with a white bow wrapped around her head. Tammy started a custom, years ago, to give the kids some fun on Eastern morning for the kids to hunt for the Easter baskets in our house. March 26$^{th}$ we went to see the movie Zootopia. We, all, loved it and laughed at different parts of the movie.

Two days later, on March 28$^{th}$, Juliana was back in the hospital. She was having problems with her Hickman line working properly. The TPN (food in a tube) is known to clot blood which may have caused the Hickman lines not to work correctly. Juliana said, "Lovely morning." She was so frustrated and she just wanted to be a healthy teenager.

She had to get a needle instead of using the port that wasn't working. Juliana hated needles. Tammy held Juliana's right hand as the nurse gave Juliana a needle to find out what was wrong. Ever since Juliana started fighting cancer, Sinai Hospital, had an understanding with Juliana. When she had to get a needle Juliana would tell her nurse when she was ready to get poked with the needle. She would say, "wait, wait, wait….go." Johns Hopkins Hospital did not abide by Juliana's request in that regard. Juliana did not cry when the nurse put the needle in her left arm to get blood to get some cultures. Sinai Hospital and its many nurses were, always, to kind and patient with Juliana.

Ever since Juliana heard that a bone marrow transplant could cure her of cancer her focus was like a laser. She knew that if she got through the transplant her life would be so much better because that's what Johns Hopkins hospital led us to believe.

Once Juliana received an IV she started to receive fluids. Less than ninety minutes later the nurse had to clean the area where Juliana's port. This was done very regularly. Juliana was always scared that Tammy or the nurse would pull on her Hickman lines and hurt her. On this day, Tammy held Juliana's right hand to calm some of her fears.

Juliana held her head back as the nurse cleaned the area on her chest. Tammy says, "It's going to be okay…it really is…" They began to try to access Juliana's port again so Juliana said "wait…wait…and….go!" The nurse pushed the needle into Juliana's chest. YES! The port started working correctly. Tammy said, "Oh my gosh…it didn't clot…thank you…it's been almost three hours with nothing going through it."

No child should have to fight cancer. Tammy continued to hold Juliana's hand. A bit later Juliana started receiving platelets. Platelets look like orange juice. While Juliana was getting platelets we walked to another part of the hospital to a room on the Pediatric Oncology floor. I was joking with the nurse that I "married way up" as Tammy knew as much as many of the nurses that treated Juliana over the years.

When the platelets were done going into Juliana she laying on the hospital bed. The nurse disconnected her and Juliana looked over to me and smiled. Tammy leaned over to Juliana, as she was about to have an endoscopy done, to see what was going on with Juliana's stomach. Tammy was trying to explain, to Juliana, what was going to happen. Juliana looked calm but so frustrated.

After the endoscopy we found Juliana in the recovery room. Tammy held Juliana's right hand as the nurse was telling Tammy what do look for when we got Juliana home. Juliana slept while the nurse was talking to Tammy. Eventually, Juliana began to wake up. She said, "My mouth is dry." The nurse offered a Sprite for Juliana which she accepted. Juliana started eating some "Teddy Grahams." Juliana was eager to get out of there and go home. The nurse, in the recovery area, was awesome!

The next day, March 29, 2016, I was at one of Lindsay's soccer games. Juliana had a PET/CT of her head to knees. Juliana was diagnosed with H. Pylori (bacterial infection) as a result of the findings of the endoscopy.

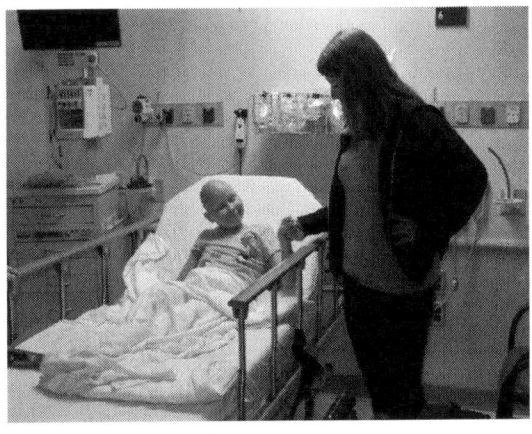

The following day we celebrated Kristina's twelfth adoption anniversary with a chocolate cake. Juliana sat to Kristina's left as she blew out the candles on the cake. We celebrated all our kid's adoption anniversaries, each year, until they reached the age of eighteen.

April 1$^{st}$ took us back to Johns Hopkins Hospital. She was there to get blood work done in preparation for her bone marrow transplant that, was, rescheduled. It seemed they were taking so many tubes of blood she wouldn't have any blood left in her body (exaggerating, of course). Juliana was so patient. Again, Juliana believed (Tammy and I did too) that the bone marrow transplant would cure Juliana of cancer.

The nurse, who had a poodle, got Juliana to talk about Maddie. The nurse asked Juliana if Maddie was like her dog, a princess, and didn't like to get wet. Juliana said, "Maddie didn't go outside (to use the bathroom) for a whole day because it was raining." Juliana had another biopsy done that day as well.

April 5$^{th}$ took me back to one of Lindsay's soccer games. The next day we went to the Baltimore National Aquarium thanks to some tickets provided by Casey Cares (caseycares.org). We had not been there is quite a few years so it was a lot of fun for all of us. Juliana took pictures and, really, enjoyed the dolphins.

The following day, April 7th, we were invited by Believe in Tomorrow (believeintomorrow.org) to their house in Canton Maryland. This is where Juliana and Tammy would be staying for a few weeks, immediately, after Juliana was able to leave the hospital from getting a bone marrow transplant.

During our visit a few volunteers brought in their therapy dogs. Juliana loved petting and playing with the dogs. Also, someone was giving free massages so Juliana and I encouraged Tammy to get one. The lady giving Tammy a back massage talked about giving Tammy a foot massage. Juliana laughed as she looked at me and said, "That's his job." I said, "Hmmmm." You could hear Juliana's TPN pump giving her the food through the port in her chest.

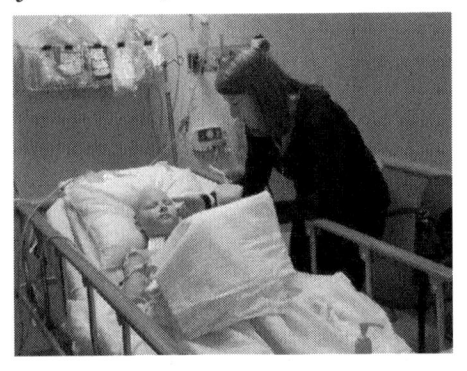

The very next day, Juliana was back in

228

the hospital to have a procedure done where they had to go through a vein in her neck. After she put on her hospital robe she whispered, to me, "sleepy...got up at 5am...it's cold." She, then, reached up her right hand to me and we clasped hands. I said, "I love you very much." She looked at me, right in my eyes, and said, "love you too." I whispered, "You're Awesome."

A little while later a nurse came into the pre-op area where we were waiting and looked at Juliana and said, "I am so proud of you. You know what's going on and you ask such good questions. I'm impressed." I said, "She's a pro..unfortunately." The nurse began to clean the line where the "loopy juice" was going to be injected. Juliana smiled, because she knew what was coming and said, "It feels weird." Juliana watched the "loopy juice" get injected and she said, "It goes in pretty quickly through the IV." Within seconds Juliana felt the effects of the "loopy juice."

Tammy went to put on her "bunny suit" (a paper suit to escort Juliana into the operating room). She walked, with Juliana, down the hall toward the operating room. Juliana looked up at me and said (in a very loopy voice), "I remember, one time, they asked my name and I just couldn't say it."

After the procedure, when we could see Juliana in the recovery area, Juliana's face was swollen and there was a bandage covering the right side of her neck. She was very uncomfortable and in pain. A nurse gave her some IV pain medicine. Tammy stayed at Juliana's left side comforting her and trying to help as much as possible. Juliana looked over to me, as I stood to her right side and said, "Hi." I said, "You're awesome." Tammy caressed Juliana's left cheek and the top of her head. I said, to Juliana, "You Rock...I love you." She said, "love you."

Eventually, around dinner time, we got home. Juliana, slowly, walked in the door. She said, "It feels weird to be home...I'm sleepy."

April 11, 2016 came and Juliana was sitting on the front porch wearing a purple sweat shirt and black pants. She had a huge smile on her face. She was excited to have three days off from having to go to the hospital. We waved her arms up in the air to show her excitement. She was very excited about getting the bone marrow transplant. We, all, were led to believe that it could really cure Juliana of cancer. Juliana continued to get mail and packages from people around the world. Several days later I was back at one of Lindsay's soccer games watching her play.

April 16$^{th}$ (our wedding anniversary) was another beautiful day so Juliana was outside enjoying it with Maddie. Tammy was getting the herb garden ready for the Spring. Tammy, Juliana, Maddie and I went for a walk in our woods. Juliana was feeling so good and couldn't wait to get the bone marrow transplant behind her so cancer could become a distant bad memory.

On the walk, Juliana and Tammy talked about the upcoming stay at Johns Hopkins Hospital. On April 21$^{st}$, the day before Juliana and Tammy were going to have to go to the hospital, for many weeks as the bone marrow transplant arrived, our daughter Rebecca came over to play some games with the kids. One of the hardest parts, for Juliana, is that she would not be able to see Maddie for a long time. Johns Hopkins Hospital doesn't allow dogs to visit like Sinai Hospital allows it. The kids sat on the sofa and floor and laughed while they played video games on our television. I love to hear our kids laugh. Juliana was so passionate about everything she did in life.

## Chapter 12

It was April 22, 2016, the day Juliana and Tammy would leave our home and stay at Johns Hopkins Hospital for several weeks in order for Juliana to get a bone marrow transplant. Juliana was, still, on TPN (food in a tube). As Juliana was drinking tea, in our kitchen, she said, "It's finally getting done…finally. First, it's going to be five days of chemo, then full body radiation, transplant then the rest of the time will be, like, recovery."

Juliana finished her tea, got up, and carried her pump that was feeding her TPN and walked into the living room and called for Maddie. Juliana picked up Maddie and snuggles and petted Maddie. She missed Maddie, so much, already. She hugged Maddie and said, "I 'm going to miss you so much!" Juliana gave Maddie several kisses. Their friendship was so special. Maddie gave lots of kisses, to Juliana, too.

Before lunch we arrived in Juliana's hospital room, at Johns Hopkins Hospital in Baltimore Maryland. The room looked over the east side of Baltimore City. There was a bed, a chair and a sofa what would be converted to a bed for Tammy to sleep. If only we could turn back time, we could have not done the bone marrow transplant. You will see why in the coming pages. Donna was the, first, nurse that came into her room and introduced herself. Donna was very kind. Juliana would have many nurses, doctors and other hospital personnel during her stay. It was, almost, impossible to remember all of them. We could hear sirens outside the hospital window. We, truly, felt that this transplant was the beginning of a life free of cancer for Juliana.

Tammy got the idea of starting a journal, for Juliana, so she could look back on this time and remember what happened. On April 22$^{nd}$ Tammy wrote, in the journal:

"T-Minus 7 – Today, I was finally admitted at Johns Hopkins Hospital to start my transplant. I got two kinds of chemo – cyclophosphamide and fludarabine. My room is small, but the nurses are really nice. I played card games with Mom and played video games on the X-Box and my IPAD to pass the time."

The next day, April 23$^{rd}$, I brought Kristina and Timothy up to see Juliana and Tammy. We videotaped a message to my brother, Chris, whose birthday is April 23$^{rd}$. It was so boring for Juliana and Tammy. At one point, all three kids and Tammy began to play a card game. Juliana was so happy Timothy and Kristina were there to play and pass the time. Our friend, and Maddie's groomer Shelley Ordway, let Maddie stay at her house for the weekend so we could be with Juliana. Lindsay, at the time, was staying with the Bromley family who we appreciate more than they may ever understand.

On April 23$^{rd}$ Tammy wrote, "T Minus 6 - Today was my second day at the hospital. It was hard getting to sleep last night and I'm tired today. Dad, Kristie and Tim came to visit Mom and I. We taught Kristie and Tim how to play Skip-Boo and I won the game! We went down to the cafeteria for lunch and I got chicken strips-I only ate one because my stomach still hurts from H.Pylori. So far the chemo is not making me sick."

On April 24$^{th}$ Tammy wrote "T Minus 5 – Today was my third day of chemo and I started feeling sick to my stomach. I had to get IV ativan that makes me feel loopy. I watched Alice in Wonderland and played Skip-Bo with Mom, Dad,

Kristie and Tim who also came to visit again for a little while.

April 25$^{th}$ arrived and I was back at the hospital. Juliana's blood counts dropped to 8.8 due to the chemotherapy. I brought some more fan mail for Juliana to open. Tammy and I decided to get Juliana some sunlight so we took her to a court yard in the older part of the hospital. It was a beautiful and sunny day. It was nice, for Juliana and Tammy, to get out of the hospital room and get some fresh air. Juliana was attached to a pole with medicine as Tammy pushed her wheel chair. She said it was easier for her to push both the wheelchair and the pole instead of me pushing either. Tammy is an awesome mother. Juliana was in a good mood. She said, "I can't wait until the transplant is done." She's very goal driven and all of us knew that this transplant would cure Juliana forever.

The Cohen Family (Larry, Bonnie and Danielle) were, so, helpful as they let Kristina, Timothy and Maddie stay at their house for several weeks (a couple times) while I was with Tammy and Juliana. Their kindness is beyond extraordinary. We thank them so much!

Once Juliana was ready to head back inside we walked around the old part of the hospital for a little while. We got back up to the floor, where her room was located, and she wanted to walk around for a few minutes. As she walked Juliana held some of the tubes that were hanging from the pole that Tammy was pushing for Juliana. We got back to Juliana's hospital room so she and Tammy played a card game called Phase-10. Juliana was very competitive and loved to win. Juliana was laughing and smiling.

Out of the blue she said, "I love it when we go to the beach walking on the sand barefoot. I love the feeling but I don't like it when you get it all (sand) in your bathing suit...I don't like that."

The days, in the hospital, were so long for Juliana and Tammy. Juliana, still, wasn't eating. While I was there Tammy and Juliana discussed what to write in her journal. Tammy wrote: "T-Minus 4 – Today I took a bath for the first time since I was admitted then I walked two laps around the floor. After that Dad came to visit and we went downstairs and sat outside to get in the sun because it was a nice warm day. I had just one kind of chemo again this afternoon. Then Dad brought me a taco for dinner but I could only eat a little because my stomach still hurts. Finally, after dinner I did two more laps then played Phase-10 with mom before my TV shows came on."

April 26th arrived and, as I arrived on the floor where Juliana's room was located, I found Juliana and Tammy walking a lap around the hospital floor. Each week the hospital would have "Hospital Bingo" where the kids could pick a prize if they won the game. My parents, John and Edna, came up for a visit. She told my parents that she was excited to go back to Ocean City Maryland, in August 2016. The trip would be thanks to Believe in Tomorrow (believeintomorrow.org). After my parents left we took Juliana, back outside, for some sunshine and fresh air.

Later in the day, Tammy wrote in Juliana's journal, "T Minus 3 – Today was my last day of fludarabine chemo. I only have one more day of chemo before the transplant. Dad, Grandmom and Pop Pop came to visit me. After Grandmom and Pop Pop left Mom, Dad and I went down to the cafeteria. I only ate one bite of chicken because my stomach was still hurting. Mom and I watched "Back to the Future" which I had never seen. Tonight, I'm going to watch "Marvel Agent's of Shield" then try to get to bed earlier because I'm tired from being woken up two or three times every night."

On April 27$^{th}$ I brought Kristina back to the hospital to visit with Juliana. They played Phase-10 together. My parents came back up the hospital for several hours. Juliana showed my mother some funny videos on her IPAD. Later in the day some volunteers dressed up in Super Girl costumes to bring some joy to Juliana. Moments later Juliana had an appointment with the occupational therapy people in another part of the hospital. They were trying to help strengthen her right arm that was, severely, damaged by radiation treatments when Juliana fought cancer back in 2007 when she was five years old. Juliana did a great job. When they got back to the hospital room Juliana won the "Hospital Bingo" game so she won a prize. Juliana was so excited. She chose a toy helicopter.

Later on Tammy wrote the following in Juliana's journal, "T Minus 2 – Today was my last day of chemo before the transplant. I had a busy day. Dad and Kristina were her most of the day and Grandmom and Pop Pop stopped in for a visit. Three Super Girls from "Love Your Mellon" brought me a hat and a cape then I went downstairs for occupational therapy. I had to squeeze theraputty (which is like silly putty), do some arm excercises and play a ring toss game. It made my right hand and arm pretty tired. Next I played "Hospital Bingo" and I won a remote controlled helicopter. Then I had to eat an orange Popsicle and ice chips while I got my new chemo (Melphalan) to hopefully stop mouth sores from forming. After that a lady came into my room with an art cart and I drew a picture. I went to the cafeteria with Mom, Dad and Kristie but I didn't feel like eating anything. Finally, I walked two more laps around the floor (I do two every morning and two every evening). Now, I am tired. Tomorrow I get Radiation."

Several weeks earlier, when we met with Dr. David Loeb, so sign the authorization forms to proceed with Juliana's bone marrow transplant we were in a small room in the Oncology Clinic. A few weeks earlier we met a teenage girl, in the clinic, who had the same type of cancer that Juliana had been fighting since 2007. We found out, just before we met with Dr. Loeb to sign the paperwork, that this other teenager had a bone marrow transplant and it failed. The teenager died.

I looked at Dr. Loeb, before we signed the paperwork, and said, "I know you can't discuss the specifics about (I named the teenager) but, as it relates to Juliana, is her situation "apples to apples or apples to oranges?" Dr. Loeb, in a soft voice, said, "Apples to Oranges." Tammy and I were, now, under the impression that Juliana had a chance to beat cancer forever.

It was, now, April 28, 2016 and Juliana was due to receive full body radiation in preparation for the bone marrow transplant the following day. Juliana was starting to feel so sick from the chemotherapy. I asked Juliana how she was feeling as she and I sat on the sofa in her hospital room. She said, "lousy…tired." I wrapped my arm around her and kissed her on her head. She was, still, so excited about getting the transplant because we were led to believe that the transplant could really cure her of cancer and she could live a long and healthy life.

Tammy came over to the sofa and sat down, with Juliana and I, as we talked about the bone marrow transplant. Juliana leaned her head on Tammy's chest and Tammy kissed her on the head as she wrapped her left arm around Juliana.

A few minutes later Juliana was being wheeled down to receive full body radiation. We were taken into a very small waiting room. Juliana was feeling worse. The wheelchair, she was sitting in, wasn't helping. A nurse came in and offered Juliana a choice of more "courage beads." When Juliana was admitted, to Hopkins, she would "earn" courage beads for everything she had do endure (transfusions, chemo, scans etc).

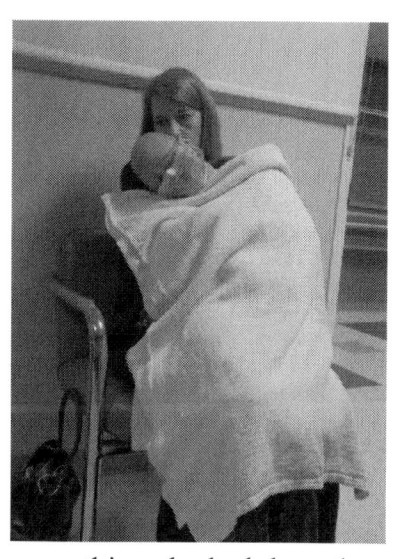

Tammy invited Juliana to sit on her lap. Tammy rocked Juliana and laid her head on Juliana's head. She held Juliana for quite some time rocking her back and forth. She tried to comfort Juliana and reassure her everything will be okay and covered her with a white blanket to keep her warm. I could see the terror in Tammy's eyes. We just wanted Juliana to get better and stay healthy. Tammy held

Juliana for about twenty minutes then it was time for full body radiation.

We wheeled Juliana into a room where the radiation is done and she got up onto a bed. She was wearing a bright pink shirt. The radiation technicians were very gentle with Juliana. When Juliana was her full body radiation we went back to her hospital room to get a blood transfusion. I brought a package, from Force 3, for her to open. It was a blanket, pajamas, candy and some slippers. Force 3 has helped raise millions of dollars, while partnering with the Children's Cancer Foundation, to fund research that tries to find cures for Pediatric Cancer.

As Juliana was receiving a blood transfusion she laid down for a nap on a white pillow pet and covered with a blanket. When she woke up she put her head on Tammy's lap as Tammy caressed Juliana's head. There were seven bags of fluid going into Juliana with, what I counted, nine tubes attached to her little body.

Later that day, Tammy wrote in Juliana's journal "T Minus 1 – Today I woke up feeling awful. My hemoglobin was down to 7.7 and my ANC was only 140. I didn't feel like doing much, but I did take a bath before going downstairs for total body radiation (TBI). TBI wasn't as hard as my last five radiation treatments and afterward I got to ring the bell and got beads and a gift with balloons. When I got back to my room I got a blood transfusion. I spent the rest of the day resting and watching TV. Tomorrow is the big day – TRANSPLANT DAY!"

The following day, while in the "care" of Johns Hopkins Hospital, was going to be the beginning of the worst months of Juliana's life.

Chapter 13

It was April 29, 2016 and we were viewing it like Juliana's new birthday. The bone marrow transplant would give her a new, healthy, happy life and allow her to grow up and live all her hopes and dreams.

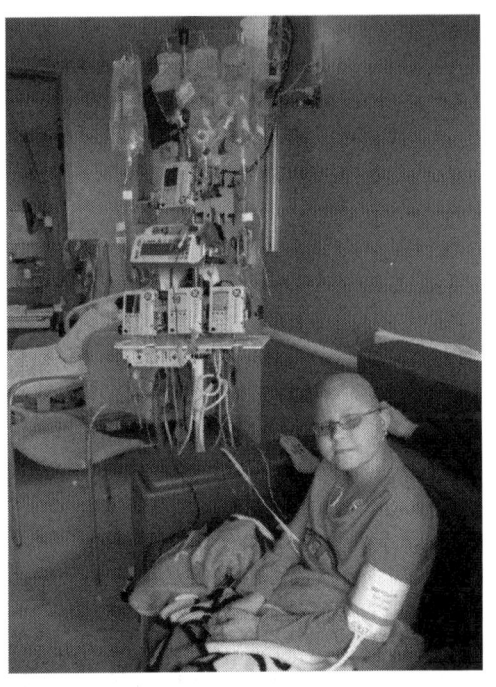

Juliana was sitting on the sofa in her hospital room. She was getting a little chilly, from all the fluids going inside her, so Tammy wrapped her up in a blanket. The moment came for the bone marrow transplant. Juliana said, "Ready Dada?" A woman, wearing a white lab coat, backed into Juliana's room pulling a cart. She was followed by a few more hospital personnel. One of the nurses said, "Happy New Birthday!" All three of us said, "Thank you!"

The cart was wheeled in front of the sink in Juliana's hospital room. The woman, with the white lab coat said, another nurse went to get some saline to thaw that bags that had some of Iryna's bone marrow in them. She said, "we will thaw one bag at a time. Each bag contains about 50 ml. Each bag should go in about five minutes or so." Tammy said, "Oh Wow. That's pretty quick."

They said Juliana will have a funny taste in her mouth because of what the cells, in the bags of marrow, are frozen in. The woman, in the white lab coat, told Juliana how she will have an odor for a day or so, from the transplant and her urine might be pink or reddish.

Juliana waved and smiled, at me, she was about to get her bone marrow transplant. Up until that day I thought that Juliana would have to have another surgery to get the bone marrow transplant. I was wrong. It looked like she was getting another blood transfusion. Juliana said, "I want to see the magic happen."

I walked over to the cart that had Iryna's frozen bone marrow in it as they checked the tubing that would be used for the transplant. Juliana looked very calm but, I know, she was nervous. The woman, with the white lab coat, reached into (what looked like) a steel bucket that had dry ice in it and pulled out the first bag of Iryna's bone marrow. They placed the bag into some solution, after confirming it was for Juliana, and thawed it.

Tammy snuggled closer to Juliana and put her right arm around Juliana. We, truly, believed that this was going to be the, happy, end of Juliana's war against cancer. The first bag of marrow was now thawed. It was a reddish pink color. The room was quiet now. I was doing a Facetime LIVE video as Juliana was getting her first bag of marrow.

They hooked up the first bag of bone marrow and watched it go into Juliana. I thanked Iryna for donating some of her bone marrow for Juliana. The dripping, of Iryna's bone marrow, was fast as it was going into Juliana. Juliana looked at my, with hope in her eyes, and waved at me with her right hand. One of Juliana's nurses, Donna, looked on as Juliana was getting the transplant.

Juliana looked down at the tube and watched the marrow go into her body. She began to smell and taste solution that marrow like the she was told would happen. She made a "yucky" face. She received a piece of chewing gum to help counter the bad taste in her mouth.

The first bag, of marrow, was now empty and the second bag was getting hung on Juliana's pole. Tammy asked Juliana if she was getting sick to her stomach. Juliana said, "If I am I will tell you." Tammy asked the woman in the white lab coat what happens after they harvest marrow from a donor which she explained it very well to Tammy. One of the other people, in the room asked Juliana, "You still doing good…you're a champ." Juliana nodded yes.

The third bag and, then, the fifth bag, of bone marrow, was now dripping into Juliana. As with the others it dripped very fast. Finally, the final bag of bone marrow was hooked up to Juliana. A few minutes later, it was all done. The bone marrow transplant was complete. Juliana just wanted to be healthy and live a normal like just like most kids.

Later in the day, on April 29, 2016, Tammy wrote, in Juliana's journal, "TRANSPLANT DAY!

Today, I woke up feeling really tired. My ANC is zero! I just sat around all day and played on my IPAD, listened to music and rocked on the sofa. At 1pm, my cells arrived. They were frozen in a big metal cylinder inside of flat metal cases. When the technician opened the lid, "steam" came out. After checking and double checking everything, they defrosted the first of the little bags of marrow in some hot water and then hung it. The marrow just dripped into me like when I get platelet transfusions. When each bag was almost empty, they defrosted the next bag until the last was finished. It only took about a half hour then they flushed the line with saline and I took a nap for about an hour until it was time to unhook me from the heart monitor. It was an easy process but I am totally exhausted from not sleeping through the night for an entire week and having really low blood counts. I picked a big purple and red homemade bead and Mom helped me put it on my Beads of Courage. I get to rest over the weekend before having my LAST two days of chemo on Monday and Tuesday. HAPPY NEW BIRTHDAY TO ME!"

The next day I brought Tim and Kristina up to the hospital. Juliana was very tired and up every two hours, the prior night, because of all the fluids she was receiving. Tammy wrote, in Juliana's journal, "T+1 – Today I woke up feeling "blah." I didn't sleep good last night because I was up every 1 ½-2 hours peeing. They are giving me lots of fluids to protect my kidneys from DMSO (used to preserve the bone marrow). I took a couple naps today in between Dad, Kristina and Tim visiting. It's Saturday so I had my Hickman lines changed today. I also had another EKG. I sure hope I get more sleep tonight."

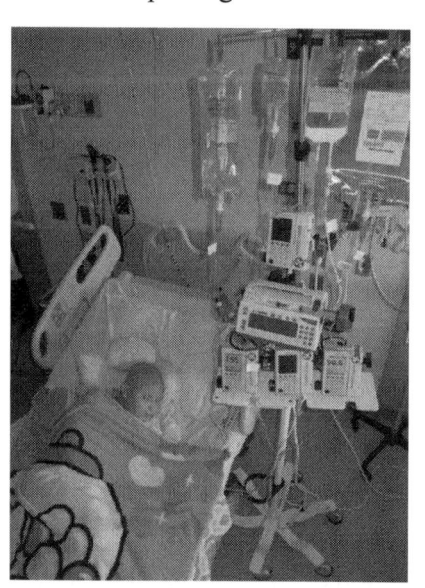

May 1st came and walked into Juliana's hospital room with Tim, Kristina and Lindsay. Juliana was not looking good and in bed. She was swollen from fluid retention and was very red. She was feeling awful. Our happy Juliana was looking really bad. Lindsay and Timothy's birthday is on May 4th so Tammy and I planned to have their birthday party in a conference room down the hall from Juliana's hospital room.

Juliana was telling me that she didn't even have the energy to walk to the bathroom the prior night. Lindsay brought her a Minions coloring book and some bandanas. Juliana said, "Thank you." Lindsay and Juliana started to pay a card game called Phase-10. Even in Juliana's condition she still had the courage to be competitive in that card game. Nothing was going to stop Juliana. Juliana smiled a few times during the game. Next, Kristina came over to Juliana's bed to play the same card game.

Juliana was getting tired but agreed to play the War card game with big brother Tim. Tammy was working with Lindsay on her English school work. Juliana decided to take a nap. Later that evening Tammy wrote, in Juliana's journal, "T Plus 2 – I got a fever just after midnight on May 1$^{st}$. The nurse had to access my port and draw cultures from the Hickman Lines and port. Then they had to stick my arm to draw blood. I didn't get to sleep until 2am. I felt awful all day. Dad, Tim, Kristie and Lindsay came to visit and I played Phase 10 with them. I was so tired I fell asleep before they left. Tomorrow I have to get more chemo."

The next day, when I arrived, Juliana was looking worse than the day before. She was asleep and so red in the face. She continued to swell up with fluid. She, slowly, walked to a wheel chair to be taken for more scans while, still, being attached so a lot of tubes going inside her little body.

When we arrived, at the room, to get the scans the technicians had to get Juliana on the table while being careful of all the tubes and IVs that Juliana had attached to her. Juliana was covered in a big white blanket and feeling horrible. Tammy helped her to her feet to get on the table. They had to be really careful when they slid her into the scanner that it didn't pull out the IVs that were attached to her body.

After the scans we got back to Juliana's hospital room. Tammy sat on Juliana's bed and wrapped her arms around Juliana and laid her head on Juliana's head. Juliana's breathing was so rapid. Tammy and I continued to be terrified. Later in the day Tammy wrote in Juliana's journal "T Plus 3 – Today I felt awful again. All of the cultures have been negative, but I still have a fever and diarrhea plus my cough is getting worse. They did more cultures today – blood, urine, stool, nasal swab but everything is negative. Usually, that is good but right now it would be good to find out what's making me sick. I also had CT scans of my abdomen and pelvis because my belly is hurting but those also came back negative. By bedtime my oxygen level started dropping so they made me have a nasal canula with oxygen which I hate but it does help me. I wish it was next week and I feel better."

I arrived, back at the hospital, on the morning of May 3. Juliana continued to look really bad, breathing was shallow and labored and was gaining more fluid. A technician came in to take some ultrasound scans of Juliana while she was in her bed.

If only we would have known that the teenager, I mentioned earlier, that I asked Dr. Loeb about had the exact same kind of cancer Juliana was fighting and died, after a bone marrow transplant, we would have found another option for Juliana instead of having a transplant.

Later that night I took Timothy to dinner for his birthday. The same evening Tammy wrote in Juliana's journal "T Plus 4 – Last night was rough. I got a platelet transfusion and fluids and had terrible, awful diarrhea. I didn't sleep well. This morning I had to get an EKG, Chest XRay, echocardiogram and another CT of my chest. My diarrhea is slowing down and y fever went away by itself a couple times but it keeps coming back. I still have a bad cough. I slept a lot today and am still tired. I also got my LAST EVER chemo today."

It was, now, May 4$^{th}$. When I got back to the hospital Juliana had just been moved to the sofa wrapped up in a blanket. Tammy sat right beside Juliana. Juliana rested her head on Tammy's shoulder. Juliana made herself get on the sofa. She knew that the more she got moving the faster she could get better. A few minutes later Tammy and I swapped seats so I could sit beside Juliana and snuggle as I kissed her head. A little while later Juliana got back in bed to get another platelet transfusion.

The doctors decided to do a broncosopy so they had to wheel her bed to another part of the hospital. Tammy was able to go back, with Juliana, until she was asleep for the procedure. They wheeled Juliana into the operating room. Roughly fifty minutes later I found Juliana and Tammy in a small room in the recovery area. I thought Juliana was going to die right there and then. She looked, beyond, horrible as Tammy stood to her left side comforting her and rubbing her head. Tammy was holding Juliana's right hand as Juliana was coughing.

Juliana was able to whisper, to Tammy, "when are we going back up (to her hospital room)?" Tammy said, "Not just yet okay?" Juliana started to cry. Tammy stayed right beside Juliana rubbing and kissing her head and holding her hand.

Approximately two hours later we arrived back in Juliana's hospital room. When she got settled in she began to text Lindsay on her IPAD. Three hours later Juliana was trying to sleep again. Her heart rate was 147. Later that night Tammy wrote, in Juliana's journal "T Plus 5 – This morning me fever finally went away. Then the doctors decided to do a broncosoly so they could find out why I have a cough. After the procedure I was coughing worse because they put saline water in my lungs. Also, my throat is sore and swollen from coughing and the procedure. I have to get puffs of breathing medicine now every four hours. The good news is I am starting to feel a little better."

May 5th arrived and she was asleep when I got to her hospital room. Juliana wanted Tammy to write her accomplishments for the day. I told you

Juliana was goal oriented. On the white board Tammy had written "Drinks – 8 ounces 9am."

By the afternoon Juliana was back on the sofa. She, still, had so many tubes attached to her and it was frustrating Juliana so much. Juliana started to cry because the pulse-ox, on her finger, was hurting her. Tammy adjusted it. Tammy sat beside Juliana and put her arm around her. Juliana started to cry, again, because she just wanted to get better.

About a half hour later big brother Matthew and his girl friend, Ashley, stopped in for a visit. Matthew sat beside Juliana. He said, to Juliana, that it's really quiet at the house. Matthew tired to get Juliana to laugh.

Juliana was so weak as the nurse brought in a scale to get her weight. Juliana was starting to fall asleep while sitting on the sofa. She didn't want to get back in bed and take a nap. I said to Juliana, "You're in charge." Matthew got Juliana talking about our upcoming trip to the beach scheduled for August 2016. Juliana was very motivated to get better to be able to make that trip. Ashley slid alongside Juliana and they talked about what was on Juliana's IPAD.

That night Tammy wrote in Juliana's journal, "T Plus 6 – This morning I woke up feeling better. After breakfast I moved to the sofa and sat there watching TV for about four hours. I even drank a big cup of milk. Matt and Ashley came to visit me and Dad too. In the evening I watched "Bones" and "Big Bang Theory." I hope I can soon get disconnected from the heart and oxygen monitors. I hope I feel even better tomorrow so I can go home sooner."

It was, now, May 6, 2016. Juliana was showing her nurse, Laurie, pictures of Maddie that was on her IPAD. Juliana was talking about how much she loved Maddie. Juliana was looking a little better. She put down her cup she was drinking from, looked at me and said, "Watch this." She got up, with Tammy holding her right arm, while attached to her pole with so many wires and tubes hanging from it, and shrugged off Tammy helping her. Juliana grabbed her pole and began to pull it and walked to the sofa and sat down. I said, "Good Job Jul…That's a big deal." Tammy said, "You're amazing girlfriend." I said to Juliana, "You are amazing! You Rock!" Juliana was determined to get better so she could go home.

That night Tammy wrote, in Juliana's journal, "T – Plus 7 – Late Thursday night I started having a lot of wheezing and at midnight Mom and my nurse Ms. Katie took me down to X-Ray to get an x-ray of my throat. As soon as I got back to my room I fell asleep. X-Ray came to my room to do a chest X-Ray. I didn't get much sleep felt pretty bad. This morning the doctors decided to try to give me steroids and more lasix. It only took a couple of hours for me to feel much better. I even got out of bed and sat on the sofa for a little while and listened to music and drank milk. I hope tonight I can sleep and feel even better tomorrow morning because we are having a little birthday party for Lindsay and Tim."

May 7th arrived and when I walked into Juliana's room I could see she was on more oxygen using a cpap. Tammy wrote, that night, in Juliana's journal, "T Plus 8 – Lastnight at 4am they brought me down to PICU because I was breathing hard in my sleep. I was very upset to have to leave my room in the middle of the night. I, also, was unhappy about the larger, very uncomfortable nasal cannula they made me wear. Nurses wake you up even more in PICU and it's very noisy and they don't turn the lights out all night. All day today, between taking naps, I kept asking if I could go back upstairs. I think my breathing was just fine. My x-rays look much better than yesterday and I've lost a lot of extra fluid so I'm feeling better just tired of constantly being woken up. I am supposed to go back upstairs tomorrow."

On May 8th Tammy wrote, in Juliana's journal, "T Plus 9 – I spent all day in PICU again today. I am feeling better and breathing better. In the afternoon they took the pressurized oxygen off of me and put the regular oxygen on (that cannula is much more comfortable). I have lost a lot of fluid and my heart rate has come down some. Also my chest x-rays show my lungs are clearing up and they now sound good. Rebecca, Marina came to visit me which cheered me up. I also had to have my Hickman Line dressing changed and my port reaccessed. IT WAS TERRIBLE. The nurses couldn't get the needle in the right place and they had to stick me four times. I really want to go upstairs...hopefully tomorrow."

I was able to video Juliana, for a minute in PICU on May 9th.. She said that she was breathing better. She said, "That means we can go home sooner...one step closer." She then said, to her fans, "Thank you for all your prayers." Tammy wrote in

Juliana's journal, "T Plus 10 – I woke up in PICU for the third morning and felt much better. I'm using normal oxygen now and they have reduced it to a 2. When Dr. Chen came I asked Mom to tell him I wanted to go upstairs (to her regular hospital room). He said I was ready to go back to the floor but it took about four hours for the nurses finally took me up. I'm in a new room now and Mom had to rearrange the furniture so I could sit on the sofa while I was hooked up to the monitor and oxygen but now I'm happy again. I hope I NEVER have to go to PICU again."

It was, now, May 10, 2016. Juliana was receiving more platelets. She showed me a blown vein from her time in PICU then gave me a thumbs-up. I said, "You Rock." Tammy put some cream on Juliana's legs and back because her skin was so dry and itchy. Juliana's hospital room was right outside the landing pad of the choppers that would bring sick people to the hospital.

That evening Chef Robert Irvine called Juliana again. He said, among much more, "You're like Supergirl."

Later in the evening Tammy wrote, in Juliana's journal "T- Plus 11 "This morning the nurse unhooked me from the heart monitor, but I'm still hooked to oxygen and the oxygen monitor. I have now lost over 15 pounds of fluid and I still have about 5 more to go. I'm getting really tired of peeing every two hours day and night plus I'm still having terrible, awful diarrhea. It's exhausting. It is also getting harder to swallow my medicine. My throat was already sore from coughing and now I have really bad mouth and throat sores from the chemo. The doctor says the sores and diarrhea will start getting better as soon as I have an ANC but that probably won't happen until this weekend or early next week."

On May 11th Tammy wrote, in Juliana's journal "T Plus 12 – Today, Dad came to visit first thing in the morning. I felt really tired all day and slept a lot. My throat is very sore from mucositis and I'm having bad diarrhea still. I also started having bad cramps today and asked to increase my morphine drip. One good thing did happen I got to stop using oxygen. So far I am breathing fine without it. If it's still good tomorrow I will be able to take off the oxygen monitor. The doctor also said they still start cycling my TPN tomorrow so I can be unhooked for a few hours each day. I'm looking forward to being able to take a bath for the first time in two weeks tomorrow."

We can't thank, enough, times the Cohen family for keeping an eye on Kristina, Timothy and Maddie while Tammy and I with Juliana in what, we thought, was a cure for cancer.

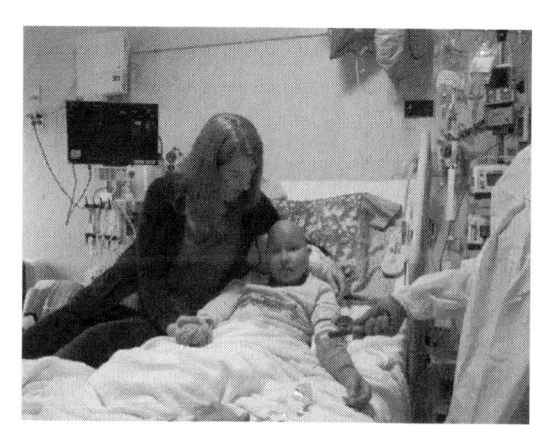

May 12' 2016 arrived and I got back, to the hospital in the early afternoon. Juliana was, still, on a morphine button because of her stomach pain. She was feeling pretty bad. The doctors ordered more blood cultures. They were going to have to get the blood from Juliana's arm instead of her port or Hickman Lines. Tammy sat on the bed, with Juliana, to try to ease her nerves. Juliana gripped Tammy's hand as the nurse got ready to draw blood. Juliana was so scared. The nurse got Juliana to talk about Maddie to distract her from what was happening. As the nurse began to put the needle in Juliana said, "Wait……go" then the nurse put in the needle. A little while later Juliana was able to get disconnected, for a couple hours, from all of the IVs and tubes so Tammy took her down the hall for Juliana to get a bath.

Later in the evening Tammy wrote, in Juliana's journal."T Plus 13 – I am still feeling really tired. My throat hurts a lot and I'm still having bad cramps and diarrhea. The good news is today my TPN is being cycled so I got a two hour break for the first time in two full weeks. It actually felt weird to sit in a tub of water. My heart rate is up today and I've been shaky and my temperature has been up (just below fever level). So my doctors ordered blood cultures. I don't mind the ones from my central lines but I had to get stuck again for a peripheral culture which I HATE. I can't wait to get an ANC so I can start feeling better."

The next day Tammy wrote, in Juliana's journal, "T Plus 14 – Early this morning my peripheral started growing gram positive bacteria and around the same time I got a fever. They have started me on vancomycin again even though it makes me get an itchy rash. Now I'm even more bored because the nurse didn't let me get much sleep last night. I woke up feeling pretty good except, of course, for the sore throat and crampy stomach from diarrhea. I was pretty sad today because I've been in the hospital for three whole weeks and I'm still feeling bad. I also had to get a shot to help my lungs today. Now, I have five more to go."

A year or two earlier I asked Juliana why don't you whine or complain about all you have gone through in your life. She looked at me and said, "whining is for babies."

I can't describe the level of intensity Juliana had to get through this process so she could, finally, be free of cancer. Her target was to be healthy. Nothing was going to stand in her way. Every sign, every hint, every indication, from Johns Hopkins Hospital, pointed to that was a reality for Juliana to be cancer free forever.

May 14$^{th}$ arrived and, ten days late, we were able to celebrate Tim and Lindsay's birthday. Back in early April Juliana knew she was going to be in the hospital so she bought them their birthday gifts at that time. Once again Juliana did not sleep well the prior night. The kids and I were able to give Tammy a, belated, Mother's Day gift to Tammy since Juliana and Tammy were in PICU at the time.

Kristina, Tim, Tammy and Juliana sat on the sofa when Tammy opened her gift. Lindsay sat on the floor next to Tammy. We bought Tammy battery powered candles. She loved them.

My mother, Edna, made a birthday cake for Lindsay and Timothy's 17$^{th}$ birthday. I picked up some decorating icing for Tammy to personalize the cake. We wheeled Juliana, down the hall, to one of the conference rooms to sing Happy Birthday to Lindsay and Tim. My parents were able to join us. Juliana was, still, hooked up to a pole with lots of tubes and IVs. Juliana had to wear a mask because she didn't have an ANC yet. Juliana was singing Happy Birthday under her mask.

Eventually, we headed back to Juliana's hospital room. Juliana was really tired. I cuddled with Juliana, on the sofa, and said, "I love you." She said, "I love you too…I love you too."

Tammy posted, in Juliana's journal, "T-Plus 15 – Today we celebrated Lindsay and Tim's birthday a little late. We were supposed to have the party for them last Saturday but couldn't because I was in PICU. We all went to the conference room for the party. I am feeling pretty good today…my Hickman lines cultures were negative but my port is still positive for bacteria. They are putting and HCl in all of my lines to kill the bacteria and are also giving me vancomycin which makes me crazy itchy—yuck!"

The next day, May 15th, Juliana was crying because they had to give her another needle in her arm. I hate to see her so sad. She just wanted to be healthy. Lindsay, Tim and Kristina were back and all sat on Juliana's bed, with her, and played some games. Juliana was so frustrated that it was taking forever for her to get better. You could still see Juliana's competitiveness while they were playing Phase 10.

That evening Tammy wrote in Juliana's journal, "T-Plus 16 – Today I am feeling better. The diarrhea has stopped, my mouth sores are healing, my breathing is better, even my throat is less sore and I'm coughing less. I even ate a little mac and cheese and some dried cranberries today. Unfortunately, I also found out they are going to take out my Hickman Lines and Port tomorrow and place a double luman PICC line in my arm unless some miracle the cultures from last night are negative. I am EXTREMELY upset about this...I don't want more surgery and I don't want an IV line. I also don't want to have another surgery in a few weeks to put in a new port."

I got back to the hospital around lunch time the next day, May 16th, and Juliana and Tammy were back on the sofa in Juliana's hospital room. I brought Kristina with me that day. Later, in the evening Tammy wrote in Juliana's journal, "T Plus 17 – My cultures were still negative this morning so I didn't have to have surgery today. They are still watching the cultures and if they grow anything I will need surgery but, usually, if it's positive it grows quickly. They put more HCl in all three of my lines today to clean them out and will be running vancomycin through each line every day. I was pretty tired all day because I needed blood. I got two united but they didn't start until 4pm. I am feeling a little better each day. I just wish I'd get a white blood count soon!"

May 17th arrived and Juliana was walking out of her room (not riding in a wheel chair). We stood by a large window down the hall from her hospital room. A physical therapist stood close by in case Juliana fell. The nurse was naming some of the sights across the east side of Baltimore City. All we wanted is for Juliana to be healthy and run and play like most teenagers that are her age. Jliana was still hooked to a lot of hoses and IVs.

The President of the Children's Cancer Foundation, Tasha Museles, came by to visit Juliana. I serve, as a volunteer, on their Board of Directors. Later in the evening Tammy wrote, in Juliana's journal, "T Plus 18 – Still no ANC (White blood cells) but the good news is I now have two negative cultures so no more will be done and I don't have to have any lines removed! Today, I also went for my first walk. I walked out of my room and across the hall to the blue chairs by the windows. The physical therapist is very happy with how I am doing. My throat is still sore, but mostly when I cough and my breathing is getting better and better. Dad and Kristie came to visit me today and Mr. Derrick is coming tonight. I really really want an ANC because I'm tired of being in the hospital now."

The next day, Juliana went on her second walk. She wore her pink knitted hat. She decided to take a much longer walk than the first time. Tammy asked her if she wanted to stop and rest. Juliana shook her head no. She said, "I want to get out of here."

Later in the day, Tammy wrote in Juliana's journal, "T-Plus 19 – Still no ANC. I feel better with each passing day. Today, my throat hurts when I cough. I walked all the way around the floor today and doing arm exercises with the physical therapist. I'm still drinking and today I had some cookies and cream milkshake. It's Wednesday so I played hospital bingo, but I didn't win anything this week. Hopefully, I will win next week. Now that I'm feeling better I'm getting bored and I can't wait to get out of here."

The next day, May 19th, I got back to the hospital later in the day. Juliana was using her IPAD more because she was starting to feel better. She got a bath, earlier in the day, so she said she feels "nice and clean." Later in the evening Tammy wrote, in Juliana's journal "T Plus 20 – Still No ANC! I am feeling even better today-no more diarrhea today and they are going to start switching as many of my IV medicine to oral as possible today. Also, they are going to start weaning me off of pain and itching medicine today. I got a bath today. It's been a week since my last one. I hope to be able to get baths more often when I need less IV medicine. I am getting really bored with being in the hospital!"

The next day, May 20th, Juliana continued to take walks. That evening Tammy wrote in Juliana's journal, "T-Plus 21 – ENGRAFTMENT STARTED!! I FINALLY have a white blood count – it's only .09 so they couldn't do a differential but I do have an ANC…a very small one YAY!!! Today, they had a turtle race downstairs in the courtyard that I got to go watch. Turtles are not very exciting to watch but I enjoyed going outside and sitting in the sunshine. It was a pretty, warm day. I walked two laps around the unit today. I am going to try to walk a little farther each day. I also did my exercises this morning and some occupational therapy this morning. I hope my ANC goes up quickly because I REALLY want to get out of the hospital!!"

I arrived, on May 21, in the early afternoon to find Juliana on another walk around the unit. Her steps were getting more steady and she was picking up speed. About an hour after Juliana did some physical therapy, in her hospital room, big sister Lindsay came up for a visit. Tammy was explaining, to Lindsay, how the Courage Beads worked and how Juliana earned them.

Later in the day, Tammy wrote in Juliana's journal, "T Plus 22 – I, finally, have an ANC today!

It's 130! The doctors said my white counts might drop but they didn't...they went up a lot! Now, I can't wait for my ANC to get above 500 for three days so I can go home. I did two more laps around the unit today plus physical therapy. I'm drinking good and am trying to start eating something each day. They lowered my pain medications again today and tomorrow they're going to turn it all off. I've only got one more medicine that needs changed from IV to oral and they got rid of two pumps off my pole (and two more will go tomorrow)!"

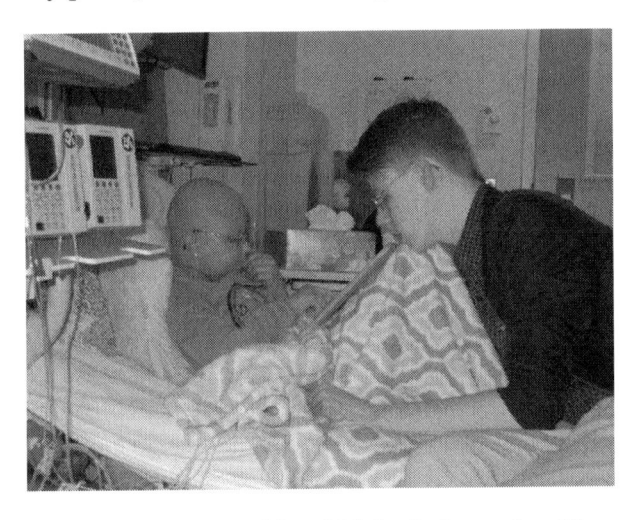

It was, now, May 22, 2016. I brought Tim and Kristina up to visit Juliana. I brought some mail and packages for Juliana to open. Tim was doing magic tricks for Juliana's nurse. Later, Tim sat on

Juliana's bed, with her, and played a game on her IPAD. Later, Kristina joined them to play a game of Skip Bo. Tim could, always, get Juliana to laugh. Most of our kids have developed an extraordinary level of compassion as Juliana fought cancer for so many years.

Later on Tammy wrote, in Juliana's journal, "T Plus 23 – I've been in the hospital for a whole month. My ANC is still going up – it's 220 today---grow neutrophils grow! I'm really bored and so tired of being in the hospital now. I keep doing my exercises and walking laps around the unit to get stronger. Dad, Tim and Kristie came to visit today. I played Skip-bo with Tim and Kristie and Tim won. The nurse disconnected my Ketamine pump this morning and my morphine pump will be disconnected this evening. They are also going to switch to oral cellcept tomorrow so that will be another pump down. The only things I'll be getting by IV tomorrow will be TPN, antibiotics, antifungal and prednisone. I really hope to be discharged by the end of the week!!"

The next day, May 23rd, I got back to the hospital in time to see Juliana doing more physical therapy. Juliana is one of the strongest human beings I have ever met. Her determination was beyond any level I could ever achieve in several lifetimes. Juliana walked another couple of laps around the unit while I was with her and Tammy. She was walking faster and faster. We decided to take Juliana, in her wheelchair, to one of the courtyards at the hospital to get from sun and fresh air.

Later in the evening Tammy wrote, in Juliana's journal, "T Plus 24 – Today my ANC is 350! They are starting to make plans for my discharge but Memorial Day Weekend is causing some problems. The discharge coordinator is working on my home oral and IV medicines and will make sure everything is in place by Friday but I probably won't get to leave until Sunday (the doctors were talking about next Tuesday, at first, but Mom is arguing with them). Dad scheduled a tour of the apartment (Juliana was required to stay near the hospital for a certain time. Believe in Tomorrow has a few apartments near the hospital). I can't wait to get out of here!!"

The next day my parents, John and Edna, came back to the hospital to visit with Juliana and Tammy. She walked around the unit without her pole attached to her…it was AWESOME! A little while later we took Juliana, in her wheelchair, for another stroll outside. At one point she got up, from her wheelchair, to walk to a coy pond that was outside the hospital cafeteria.

That evening Tammy shared, in Juliana's journal, "T Plus 25 – Today my ANC is 610!! Mom is still working on convincing the doctors to discharge me on Sunday morning. She thinks they probably will. Grandmom and Pop Pop came to visit and stay with me while Mom and Dad went for a tour of the apartment. When they got back I took a bath then went downstairs to the courtyard to enjoy the beautiful, warm day. I even visited a coy pond. When we came back upstairs to my room I did some beading with the occupational therapist. We are going to try to get to bed early tonight because we didn't get much sleep last night because of the injector pump kept beeping!"

On May 25, 2016 I arrived back at the hospital. A volunteer stopped by Juliana's room and painted Juliana's finger and toe nails and painted Tammy's toe nails too. Juliana received another blood transfusion while I was in her room. She was swollen due to the steroids she was receiving. Juliana said that the lady was tickling her when she was doing her nails. It was "Hospital Bingo" time.

She was so competitive. A little while later we went back outside for some fresh air.

That evening Tammy shared, in Juliana's journal, "T Plus 26 – Today my ANC was 510 – Day two above 500. I was feeling really tired until they gave me a blood transfusion. It was also spa day and Mom and I got manicures and pedicures. Also, it was Bingo Day but I didn't win again. I hope it was my last Hospital Bingo because I really can't wait to be discharged. Mom and I, also, had to go to a meeting about bone marrow transplants – one more step to getting out of here. Friday morning I am getting a PET scan bright and early at 7:30am. I'm still hoping to go home (Believe in Tomorrow apartment) on Sunday."

May 26th arrived and Juliana and Tammy were so excited because the day was approaching that they would leave the hospital. By now, they had been in the hospital for over one month. I brought Juliana some more fan mail for her to open. The occupational therapist came by and after some exercises in Juliana's room she walked up and down a staircase. She did an outstanding job. They made her wear gloves because of the germs that were on the railings. Juliana was starting to get signs of getting her hair back…just some "fuzzies." Later, in the evening, Juliana was looking at photos of Maddie (her dog) on her IPAD. She missed her so much. Juliana said, "She's so loveable. We're best buddies."

That evening Tammy shared, in Juliana's journal, "T Plus 27 – Today my ANC was 1320 – day three above 500 and day one above 1000! I am feeling a little stronger each day. It was not a fun day because they did surveillance cultures, including a peripheral culture that took two sticks to get, a nasal swab, a bandage change on my Hickman lines and another etanercept shot. I took a bath then did occupational therapy which is always fun and physical therapy. The physical therapist had me walk up and down the stairs (two flights) and then around the unit before finishing up with a new exercise. I'm going to try to get to bed early tonight because I have to be up early tomorrow morning for a PET scan."

A couple nights a week I had been staying at a different Believe in Tomorrow (believeintomorrow.org) house one block from the hospital. That evening, I went for a walk. While I walked I was hoping and praying the bone marrow transplant would cure Juliana of cancer forever and allow her to live all her hopes and dreams.

May 27, 2016 arrived. We took Juliana for a ride, in her wheelchair, to the original part of Johns Hopkins Hospital, for her to walk around a little more. She wasn't attached to her pole and was walking great.

That evening Tammy shared, in Juliana's journal, "T Plus 28 – Today, my ANC was 1810 which is in the "normal" range and I'm still getting GCSF today and tomorrow. I also have just two more doses of vancomycin to get. My PET scan went fine this morning and the preliminary results are negative (NO CANCER). The CT also showed no infection of problems in my lungs. Unfortunately, my bilirubin was a little high today so now I'm not going to get to leave on Sunday which made me cry. I REALLY want to get out of here! Dr. Huo thinks it could be from engraftment, HVG disease or fluor adenovirus so he ordered more blood work. So far, the blood cultures and the nasal cultures from yesterday are all negative and I'm definitely not feeling the least bit sick (except sick of the hospital). Dr. Cooke thinks the bilirubin could be elevated from the blood transfusion I got the other day (it went up right afterwards) andI hope he's right and my bilrubin is back to normal tomorrow."

It was, now, May 28th. Tammy and Juliana had been in the hospital for thirty-six days. Around 3pm we took Juliana for another ride (in her wheelchair) around the hospital to get her out of her room for a while.

Later, in the evening, Tammy wrote in Juliana's journal, "T Plus 29 – Today, my ANC is 2850! Even more important my bilirubin was down to 1.1 today. Dr. Zambidis said he wants to see what it does tomorrow—if it goes down again then I should be able to go home (really to the apartment). He just wants to make sure I don't have VOD or GVH disease. I'm praying hard that it keeps going down. I got my last dose of vancomycin today and the only IV medications. I'll be on tonight are TPN and micefungin-the two I'll be getting at the apartment when I'm discharged. I, still, have to get my last etanercept shot tomorrow and will need another platelet transfusion tonight but if all goes well, I can do everything outpatient at the clinic or at the apartment with Mom."

Finally, May 29th arrived. I walked in her room, with Tim and Kristie and said, "Juliana is getting out of prison (hospital) today!" Juliana got up and gave us all a big hug! I took a photo of Kristina, Juliana and Tim, on the sofa, and Juliana had a HUGE SMILE on her face. She was so excited about getting out of the hospital. I asked her (jokingly), "What's so special about today? She held up her arms in celebration and said, "We're finally leaving!!"

Juliana said, "It feels so good to be disconnected." I can't describe the joy that was in her hospital room. It was the thirty-seventh day after Juliana and Tammy walked into Johns Hopkins for Juliana to start getting prepped for the transplant. She had to get one more IV medication before they could leave the hospital.

I asked her to tell her fans what was happening. She said, "Well, we are all packed up and ready to leave but we have to get one more thing (IV antibiotic). At least we are leaving today." Kristina and Juliana were sitting, on the sofa, and Juliana started going through photos of Maddie on her IPAD again. She said, "I haven't seen her a while…it's going really crazy." Once again, we REALLY thank the Cohen family for letting Maddie, Tim and Kristina stay with them while I was with Juliana and Tammy.

While Juliana was getting her IV Antibiotic I sat beside her on the sofa and snuggled. I would give anything to snuggle with Juliana again. She was SO happy to be able to leave the hospital that day. She said, "Hopefully this is the very last day and last time we will be admitted (into the hospital)…like up here…like no fevers not nothin'. That's the plan!"

She was, also, talking about when her lines weren't working and they had to give her IVs in her arm. She said "it was so cold I couldn't feel my arm." It was, now, getting closer and closer for Tammy and Juliana to leave the hospital. The nurse knelt down to flush Juliana's line. Juliana could, always, taste it when her lines get flushed. She said, while her lines were getting flushed, "I hold my breath (she showed how she was pushing air out of her nose), I breathe it out of my nose because I had my mouth open (then she made a yucky face)."

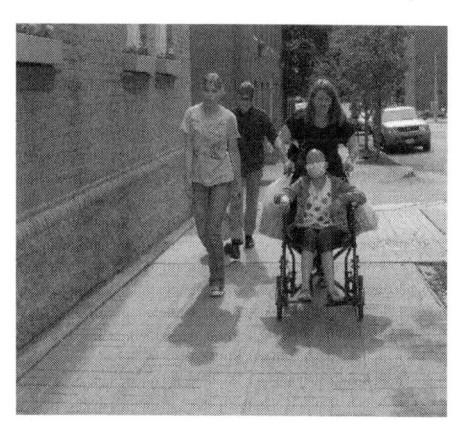

She gave me a "thumbs up" as the seconds ticked closer for her to leave the hospital. She was holding her Hickman lines so the nurse could change the caps, on them, then she could go. It was time!! Tammy was pushing Juliana's wheelchair in, almost, a sprint (slightly exaggerating) as she was walking pretty fast. She was eager to get out of that hospital too. As they turned the corner, heading to the elevator, I heard some nurses yelling "WOOOOO!!!!!We're so happy for you." They were excited for Juliana also.

Tammy was now walking faster as we approached the exit from the hospital. I ran outside to video them leaving. The doors opened and Juliana raised her arms in celebration. She yelled "We're leaving! We're leaving! We're leaving!"

We, really, believed this was going to be the beginning of Juliana's new life to grow up and live all her dreams! We drove a few miles to the apartment, in Canton Maryland, that is owned by Believe in Tomorrow (believeintomorrow.org). It had one bedroom, kitchen and living room as well as a shared deck in the back. Juliana said, as she sat on the sofa, "It's so much better than the hospital....I'm FREEEEEE!" A few minutes later Tim, Kristina and Juliana were sitting at the kitchen table playing Skip-bo. Without a doubt, Tim and Kristina have been the closet, to Juliana, of all our kids. They have been awesome! Juliana was so happy and in a great mood. She was all smiles!

Later that evening Tammy wrote in Juliana's journal, "T Plus 30 – DISCHARGE DAY!! Today, I was finally discharged from the hospital! My bilirubin dropped back down to where it usually us. I didn't get out until 4:30 because the resident forgot I need pentamidine we we had to wait for the pharmacy to get it ready then wait for another two hours for it to infuse. We finally got to the apartment around 5pm. The apartment is nice but I'd rather be home. Hopefully I can go home for the weekend."

The next day was sunny and beautiful. The apartment, where Juliana and Tammy were staying, was on the south east side of Baltimore Maryland and about two blocks from the Baltimore Harbor.

In the middle of the day we took Juliana, in her wheelchair, for a walk/ride by the water. Juliana was wearing black capris, a pink baseball cap and a white shirt. Tammy was in shorts with a pink shirt. Being stuck in a hospital, for over a month, really does something to a person. We could see, in the distance the Domino Sugar factory, in the distance where my mother worked when she was very young.

Tammy was making the apartment into their temporary home. The next afternoon Juliana went out on the back porch to enjoy the fresh air for her to open some of her fan mail. You could hear the police helicopter flying overhead as I started the video camera. Juliana's muscles, in her right forearm, were damaged when she received radiation treatment back in 2007. In order to save time and so Juliana's arm wouldn't get so tired I would slice open the cards and packages for her to open up the contents of them. Moments later she said, "feeling good...out of the hospital finally...nice day out today...eighty-some degrees." Tammy fixed spaghetti for dinner that evening.

On May 30th Tammy shared, in Juliana's journal, "T-Plus 31 – Happy Memorial Day! Today was the first full day out of the hospital and I'm feeling better each day. We didn't get to have a cookout like usual but it was still a good day. I slept in and spent a lot of time resting. Mom, Dad and I went for a walk by the water this afternoon. There are a lot of yachts around here. It was a pretty day so we ate on the deck outside the back door. I ate two small shrimp and a piece of broccoli and so far it's not making my stomach hurt. I really want to be able to eat again so I'm trying to eat a little each day. Tomorrow I have to go to the clinic and I'm sure I'll need a platelet transfusion."

The next day, May 31st Tammy wrote, in Juliana's journal, "T Plus 32 – Today was my first clinic visit after my transplant. As expected, I needed a platelet transfusion. My ANC was 3660- very good because I haven't had neupogen for four days! My hemoglobin is slowly falling but was 10 today. Miss Nancy, from the clinic, was very happy with how I'm doing. When I got back to the apartment, Mom made spaghetti for dinner and I ate a little bit of it and I ate a little bit of vanilla ice cream. So far, my belly isn't hurting. I really hope I can eat more and more each day so I can, soon, get off TPN. I don't have to go back to the clinic until Thursday morning."

## Chapter 14

It was June 1st and Juliana had to be taken back to the hospital because of a fever. Juliana was crying as they tried to put a needle in her arm. I hate to see her cry. Tammy and Juliana were holding each other's hand while they were trying to get blood from Juliana's left arm. A bit later, Juliana was on fluids and so frustrated. She, and all of us, just wanted to be healthy…please God…just let her be healthy for the rest of her life. Juliana was resting on a white pillow pet covered with a white hospital blanket. Juliana was going to have to be readmitted to the hospital.

Juliana looked up, at me, and gave me a little wave hello. Her eyes were so sad while the nurse took more blood from her Hickman Line. Juliana said, "it could be worse." Her attitude, throughout her war against cancer, continues to blow my mind. The nurse had to stick Juliana, with another needle in her left arm. Tammy and Juliana gripped each other's right hand. The look on Juliana's face as she looked up at the nurse was so sad. She just wanted to be a happy and healthy teenager. Why couldn't that happen for our baby girl!?!?!

Juliana turned her head away, from her left arm, as they put in another needle. She cried out in pain. Less than an hour later she dozed off to sleep while we were still in one of the Johns Hopkins Pediatric Oncology Clinic exam rooms. A couple of hours later Juliana and Tammy were across the hall, on the same floor, where they spent over a month in the hospital. Juliana was going to have to stay, again, for a couple more days.

Later that evening Tammy wrote in Juliana's journal, "T Plus 33 – Today was terrible, awful day. I threw up twice then this morning I got a fever and had to go to the clinic. They drew cultures (including ANOTHER peripheral stick), gave me a Tylenol and some antibiotics. My fever went away and has not come back again BUT I still had to be readmitted (to the hospital) for at least two days to see if the cultures grow anything. I feel totally fine and I, absolutely, HATE being back in the hospital again after only being home (well, in the apartment) for 3 days."

June 2, 2016 brought more boredom at the hospital. Juliana got another bath which she really enjoyed. Later in the day Tammy wrote, in Juliana's journal, "T Plus 34 – I spent the day in the hospital again. The only good news is that I have not had a fever since yesterday in clinic and all my cultures are still negative. If I stay fever-free and the cultures stay negative I will be discharged late tomorrow afternoon. I REALLY hope I can go home tomorrow-I REALLY hate being inpatient at Hopkins especially when I'm NOT SICK! I, also, want to be able to celebrate Dad's $50^{th}$ birthday, on Saturday, at home!"

I was back home, for June $3^{rd}$, because I found out Juliana and Tammy were coming home for the weekend!! I walked outside, our house, waiting for Tammy and Juliana to come home for the first time in over forty days. I could hear the birds chirping as our car came down our driveway toward our house. To the right, of the driveway, was our basketball hoop where Juliana and the rest of the kids would shoot baskets so many times. The sound of the basketball hitting the driveway brought back so many memories.

Tammy pulled into our garage and I yelled with excitement. I yelled, "Awesome....they're home, they're home, they're home!!!" I could see Juliana raised her arms, sitting in the passenger seat, in celebration. The birds, that day, seemed to be chirping much louder. In my imagination I thought they were celebrating too (of course, I know that's not possible).

Tammy helped Juliana put on her backpack which had her TPN and pump inside. Juliana walked around the passenger door, gave me a huge smile and raised her arms (again) in celebration. She was wearing her "I'm not a giver-upper" shirt and a pink Nike baseball cap. She said, "40 days!" then Maddie heard her voice and let out a barrage of big barks. Maddie and Juliana were so excited to see each other. Juliana walked up the steps, leading into our house, and Maddie ran (full speed) into Juliana's legs. Juliana yelled, "Hi Baby!!!"

Maddie was beyond excited to see Juliana and Tammy. Juliana walked, into our kitchen, and yelled, "Hi everyone!" She was home! Maddie was running in circle she was so excited. Juliana sat, on the floor, in the kitchen and picked up Maddie onto her lap and gave her a big hug. She looked at Maddie and said, "Hey…did you miss us?" Maddie gave her a big kiss on her left cheek. Maddie let out a single bark and then another as she wiggled on Juliana's lap. Maddie missed her Mommy (Juliana). Maddie, then, ran over to Tammy to get some love from her as well. Juliana got up and gave Timothy a big hug and then a hug for Kristina.

Tammy was coaching Timothy and Kristina how important it was for them to wash their hands and not to eat and drink after Juliana because she was still recovering from the bone marrow transplant. Juliana turned right, facing the sink, and I yelled, "WELCOME HOME!" as she gave me a big hug. I said, "I'm so glad to see you!" Juliana walked into our family room, where Maddie was playing with one of her toys and Juliana said (to Maddie) "you are so adorable!" She knelt down and began playing with Maddie. Juliana said, "It feels good to be home."

Tim and Kristina came, into the family, room and sat down on the floor with Juliana and Maddie.

Juliana looked at Maddie and said, "I missed that little face...are you happy that I'm home?" Maddie was so special to Juliana. A little while later we celebrated Timothy's 15th adoption anniversary with a chocolate cake.

A few hours later Tammy wrote, in Juliana's journal, "T Plus 35 – All of my cultures were negative and I was fever-free this afternoon so I was finally discharged at 2:30pm. Mom and I went back to the apartment and unpacked from the hospital then repacked to go HOME! Mom, also, packed some brownies for Tim's Adoption Day party (2 days late). I was SO HAPPY to get home! Maddie went crazy when I walked in! We had Tim's party and I got to sleep in my own bed, for the first time, in 42 days! I wish we could stay home for good, but it's only for the weekend, then we go back to the apartment."

June 4th arrived, which was my 50th birthday. Each birthday, since Juliana first got cancer in 2007 was for Juliana to be healthy and be able to live a full life and live all her dreams. Tammy baked me a chocolate cake and all six of our kids would be at the house for a little birthday party.

Juliana and Maddie were cuddling and playing, together, as we waited for everyone to arrive. Juliana was so happy to be home. The bond, that Juliana and Maddie had, is difficult to explain. I could, really, tell Maddie missed Juliana as much as Juliana missed Maddie.

The time came, for my birthday party, on the back porch. My parents and all our kids were able to be there that day. Juliana was sharing, with my mom, how happy she was to be home and her being

off of some of the medications. Tammy, always, did her best to make birthdays and adoption anniversaries very special. As I sat down, at the picnic table, next to Juliana as all of them sang Happy Birthday to me my thoughts and hopes were on Juliana. As Juliana was singing our eyes met and she gave me a big smile. I motioned for Juliana to slide closer so she could help me blow out the candles. I said, "ready, set..." then Juliana and I blow out the candles. After we blew out the candles I gave her a big hug then kissed her on the top of her head.

Juliana handed me some birthday cards, from a few people, for me to open.

When I was done opening the cards Juliana handed me a blue bag with a Star Wars movie in it. That evening, Tammy wrote, in Juliana's journal "T Plus 36 – Today is Dad's $50^{th}$ Birthday and I turn 14 ½ today. We had a little party for Dad on the back porch. I ate a little pizza and cantaloupe at the party. We gave Dad a new Star Wars DVD for his birthday then we had a movie night and watched it. I really enjoyed being home today and relaxing with my family and my dog. I got to sleep in my bed again tonight. Tomorrow night Mom and I will be back at the apartment."

It was, now, June $5^{th}$, I Juliana was holding Maddie on her lap. She was missing her so much since she wouldn't see her for another five days. A little after 7pm Juliana and Tammy got ready to leave to go back to the apartment. Tammy hooked up Juliana's TPN. While she was doing it Juliana said, "I can't wait for the 4$^{th}$ of July…have some hamburgers on the grill…" She was feeling good but not happy about not being home for another five days. She said, "It's better here (at home) with Maddie."

Later in the evening Tammy wrote, in Juliana's journal, "T Plus 37 – I enjoyed another day at home today. I relaxed with Maddie and watched TV in the morning (I can't go to church yet). Then we had a cookout when everyone came home from church. I was very sad when we have to leave and come back to the apartment this evening. I am feeling a little better. I ate a little at the cook out and then I ate a whole nectarine at the apartment this evening. I'm, also, having less diarrhea now. I can't wait to get off of some of these medicines and to stop needing TPN! Tomorrow I have an early clinic appointment."

I got back, the Believe in Tomorrow, apartment around lunch time on June 6$^{th}$. Juliana and Tammy were watching a Star Wars movie. Later, Juliana played on her IPAD. I could tell she needed another blood transfusion as she was very tired. That night, Tammy wrote in Juliana's journal "T Plus 38 – I had an early clinic appointment this morning. My platelets were low (7) and I needed a transfusion but everything else was good. My chimerisin test showed that 100% of my bone marrow was Iryna's (they have her DNA and not mine). This is really good news and the reason we did the transplant. I am still feeling good and ate more today than yesterday. Miss Nancy (from the hospital clinic) is going to start decreasing my TPN later this week if I'm still eating and feeling good when we see her on Wednesday. We were from (the apartment), from the clinic, by noon and Mom and I hung out at the apartment all day. We are pretty bored."

Not too much happened on June 7th. The next day, June 8th, Tammy wrote in Juliana's journal, "T Plus 40 – Today we were at the clinic between 9am and 3pm. I needed a blood and platelet transfusion. My blood pressure was high when I got there so I had to have blood pressure medicine before they could start. Everything else was good. My ANC and white count is good…I just need my marrow to start making red blood cells and platelets! Since I am starting to eat, they are reducing my TPN (food in a tube) to only 10 hours a day which is awesome. I have to go back to the clinic on Friday at 8am."

On June 9th I stopped back by the apartment. Juliana was playing more games on her IPAD. The time, at the apartment, was pretty boring for Juliana and Tammy.

The next day, Juliana and Tammy were able to come back home for the weekend. Juliana walked in the house. Juliana said, "where's poochie?" Maddie was outside going to the bathroom. Juliana walked out the front door, saw Maddie and said, "Hi You." She picked her up and loved on her for a bit. Juliana said, "it's good to be back home." They sat down on one of our sliders on the front porch as Juliana enjoyed the beautiful day and being home again.

Just before dinner Tim did some magic tricks for Juliana. About an hour later Juliana was playing fetch with Maddie. Juliana loved Maddie so much. Later on Tammy wrote in Juliana's journal, "T Plus 42 – Today was a quick day in clinic. We had to be in by 8am but we were out by 11am. I needed another platelet transfusion – I can't wait until they graft so I don't need any more transfusions because three a week is TOO MANY! We went back to the apartment, ate lunch and packed to go home for the weekend. We had to stop at Game Stop, on the way, to pick up a new Kirby game for my DS. I was so GLAD to get home. We're going to stay until Monday morning!"

June 11$^{th}$ was the day to uncover Juliana's Make-A-Wish pool, in our back yard for the summer. Lindsay, Tim, Kristina, Tammy and I helped get the pool ready for the kids to swim in it when the water got warmer. It's a lot easier to cover and uncover the pool when there are people to help. Juliana sat on the front porch and watched. Once that was done Kristina and Lindsay helped Tammy plant some herbs in our garden. Juliana said, "The pool looks so nice. I want to go swimming in it." The kids were a big help that day. Matthew came home and played soccer, with Kristina, in the front yard.

It was, now, June 12$^{th}$. All our kids love to be outdoors. Juliana was on our slider swinging and said, "nothing much is happening…yay home!" If Juliana would not have been sick she would have been helping get the pool ready, helped Tammy plant herbs in the garden and play in the yard.

Cancer destroys so much of a child's life is so many ways.

Juliana walked over to the herb garden as Tammy showed where each of the herbs was planted. It was getting really windy but that didn't stop them from enjoying the smells of some of the herbs like mint and lavender. They were discussing all kinds of things about the herbs. The wind made it hard for the video camera to hear much of it. When they were finished Juliana held my hand as I helped her back to the house. We stopped and looked at the tomato plants alongside the house. Juliana LOVED tomatoes. She sat down as she was getting tired. She said, "I'm getting better. It's, definitely, getting easier. Before it was really hard to walk. When I was in the hospital, for the month and stuff and, of course, I wasn't really walking, I was in the bed all the time because I felt so bad so you're legs get all weak. You're not using the muscles. When you start to walk it's like getting brand new legs then you're walking up and down the steps and stuff…walking around the house more."

On June 13, 2016 Tammy wrote, in Juliana's journal, "T-Plus 45 – I needed platelets again today, in clinic, but Miss Nancy decided to try to let me go three days without a platelet transfusion to see how I do during the week. She thinks I may be starting to make some platelets. So, I don't have to go back-and-forth to the clinic until Friday morning! YAY!! Mom decided to just go home since we would have nothing to do at the apartment all week which made me VERY HAPPY! I'm, always, so bored at the apartment. I sure hope I can make it until Friday without needing another transfusion then we should only have to go to the hospital twice a week."

June 14$^{th}$ came and most of the kids were outside playing badminton. It was another beautiful day. I know Juliana was wishing she felt good enough to run and play. She let out a big sigh watching the other kids play in the front yard. She was cuddling with Maddie. She gave Maddie a hug and said, "such a good puppy and today is her adoption day (anniversary)" Juliana gave Maddie a kiss on the top of her head then on her left cheek and said, "four years" referring to how many years we had Maddie. It must have been so frustrating for Juliana not to be able to play badminton with her siblings. She loved to play that game.

Two days later, on June 16$^{th}$, and Juliana gave a quick update to her fans. She said, "This week we went to clinic Monday and we got platelets because they were low and we have not been to the hospital since. I'm home relaxing. Feeling pretty tired not like a (low) blood tired. We're going back (to the clinic) tomorrow and we'll update you then…not eating a lot at all…don't really know why…it just hurts for some reason." This was the beginning of a HORRIBLE..HORRIBLE Summer for Juliana!

The next day, just after Tammy and Juliana came back home from the clinic, Tammy updated me. Juliana was starting to make her own platelets. Juliana said, "WOO HOO!" She said, "I haven't needed a platelet transfusion in a LONG TIME!" She smiled so big and laughed. Tammy and the hospital thought Juliana's stomach was hurting because she had become lactose intolerant. Juliana has NEVER had that problem in the past. They hoped it was just temporary from the transplant.

That afternoon Rebecca, my sister Michele, her husband Thomas and toddler Thomas Ellis came by for a visit. They played some badminton, on the front lawn, while Juliana sat on the porch and watched them have fun. She stirred up the strength, for just a few minutes, to stand and pick up a badminton racket in case the birdie would come her way. You could, still, see the competition in her eyes. She was wearing a red shirt and black Capri pants that day. She served once and hit the birdie back over the net too. Juliana really wished she could get up and play with them too. The disappointment, in her face, ripped my heart out. Juliana was determined to get better and make cancer a distance, horrible, memory. A little later Tammy and my sister, Michele, held Juliana's hand as they went to look at the herb garden. Lindsay brought little Thomas Ellis to the garden to see too.

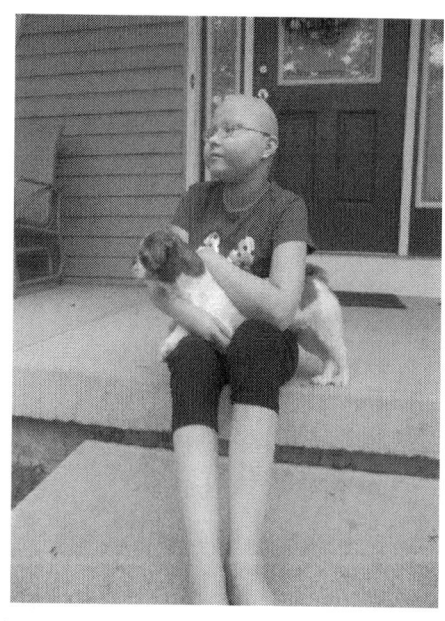

Juliana motioned for Tammy, after several minutes, to help her walk back up the hill toward our house but stopped to check on the tomato plants first.

Later, that day, Tammy wrote in Tammy's journal, "T-Plus 49 – My belly has been hurting when I eat and I've been having a lot of gas which has not been fun. Today, in clinic, Miss Mary Jo said she thinks it's temporary (I hope). It is not uncommon (she said) for this to happen after transplant so I'm not going to eat any dairy this weekend and see if it goes away. One really good thing happened---I did not need a platelet transfusion because I'm making my own platelets now!! My count was 13, but the platelets they gave me on Monday are long gone so these are mind (my goal is only 10) and my count should be slowly going up. Now, if I can just eat, get off TPN and start making red blood cells things would be great!"

A couple days later, on June 19th, Tammy and Juliana were out on a little walk, on the side of our house, to help Juliana get a little stronger. Juliana had to rest, in the grass, after several minutes. She needed another blood transfusion. Tim, Lindsay and Kristina were back, on the front lawn, playing badminton while the birds were chirping away. Tammy joined them a few minutes later.

It was, now, June 20$^{th}$, and Juliana was back home from the clinic. She had color in her face and had lots more energy. Juliana yelled "MADDIE!!" Maddie ran up to her and jumped in Juliana's lap. Tammy wrote, in Juliana's journal, "T Plus 52 – Today, I needed two units of blood – my hemoglobin was down to 6.7!! I know I needed blood because I was really tired but I couldn't believe it was that low! I, also, stopped TPN tonight and started getting fluids with electrolytes overnight. I, also, started taking megace (appetite stimulant) so I'll eat more (hopefully). I'm kind of nervous about stopping the TPN – I hope I can start eating enough."

June 21' 2016 arrived and the most of the kids, really, wanted to go swimming in our pool...Juliana too. They had so much fun. Lindsay said, when Juliana got in the pool, "My legs feel normal." I told Juliana, while she was in the pool, that swimming will help her get stronger. She said, "I don't feel like it's doing anything because I feel light." There was a lot of giggling and having fun while they were swimming. Juliana said, "OH WHAT FUN!" I asked her how it feels to be in the pool. She said, "It feels warm…nice." Moments later she said, "No more waves…mom is floating" as Tammy relaxed on top of the water. Juliana was running, in place, for several minutes while in the pool. She was determined to help herself get stronger.

On June 22$^{nd}$ Tammy wrote in Juliana's journal, "T Plus 54 – Today my platelet count was down to 5,000 so I had to get another transfusion. I haven't needed one for nine days and was disappointed because I didn't think I would need any more platelet transfusions. I, also, had diarrhea starting yesterday and a lab test showed some blood in it. Miss Nancy said it's probably because my platelets are low but we're keeping a close eye on it to make sure it stops. I sure hope so because I don't want to have any more procedures to check my GI tract! I start PT and OT after my next clinic visit on Friday." This was Tammy's last entry in Juliana's journal.

It was, now, June 24, 2016. Juliana amd Maddie continued to invest lots of time with each other. Tammy asked Juliana if she was interested in going on a little walk to a swing by the herb garden. Juliana agreed.

The next day I found them, in the woods, on a short walk. Juliana was doing great. Her steps were slow and solid as Tammy walked her hand. They stopped to rest a couple times. Juliana had been building up fluid again. Juliana had been so active and to see her having to take breaks on a short walk must have been, beyond, frustrating to her as she was only fourteen-and-a-half years old.

Fast forward to the end of June. She had been going back to the clinic every day that week. She was so tired and had no energy. Maddie stayed close by while Juliana rested on the sofa. I asked Tammy to give her fans an update, since they just got back home from the hospital, about Juliana on June 30$^{th}$. Tammy said, "They still haven't narrow it down to four things. We're really leaning toward one of them right now. They said it could be Adeno virus. They started at treatment in case it's that. It could be host versus graft disease but it doesn't, usually, present this way…they're not thinking it's probably that.

They found some EColi but it's not the type that usually doesn't cause any problems because it's the same type everyone has in their gut all the time anyway. They're leaning, right now, to it being a bleeding ulcer because, I reminded, them that

Juliana was treated for HPilori right before transplant and they think they didn't get it all during the first treatment because, a lot of times, it takes more than one course of treatment to get rid of HPelori or else it's a recurrence of it. Her bone marrow isn't able to make enough red blood cells and white blood cells to keep up with that like a normal person would. We've got an appointment tomorrow morning to see the Pediatric GI specialist at Hopkins in between our clinic visits for platelets and blood. Hopefully, they can confirm it and start some kind of treatment sooner rather than later…" Juliana was looking so sad.

Later that day Juliana was back on the front porch enjoying a nice day. The kid's friend, Aubrix, came by for a visit. Juliana was starting to really swell up again. The next four months were, mostly, HORROR for Juliana.

## Chapter 15

July 1' 2016 arrived and Juliana was back at the clinic. Tammy has, always, been on top of Juliana's medical care because she understands so much about science, medications and the human body. Juliana was watching videos on her IPAD. Juliana had the, amazing, ability not to get frustrated about the long wait at hospitals. She had been through this war against cancer, for so long, she had to become patient. It's a characteristic that I lack.

Juliana was getting platelets that day. We were trying to get her internal bleeding stopped too.

Her hemorrhaging, that month, was REALLY horrible.

The next day, Tammy and Juliana went for another short walk in our woods. They held hands and took their time. We, at the time, had no idea that their time for walks would come to a crashing and HORRIBLE end. They posed for a quick photo for me. When it was time to walk back to the house Maddie was not keeping up. Juliana said, "Stop being a slow poke." The connection, between Tammy and Juliana, was unbreakable. Juliana really wanted to be healthy and be a kid.

July 4$^{th}$ came and, as always, Tammy prepared a cookout for the family. Kristina and Tim were playing badminton. Juliana was on our swing, on the front porch, when I asked her how she was feeling. She said, "tired." Her extra fluids were starting to go down again. Tammy's mother, Jennifer, came over for the cookout. It started to rain so we brought the grill under our porch. Tammy was grilling hot dogs, hamburgers and chicken. All our kids were there, that day, for the July 4$^{th}$ celebration.

Juliana was holding Maddie and said, "she helps when I feel bad." The rain, finally, stopped so it was time to light the sparklers. In the past Juliana would be jumping and having such a good time playing with the sparklers. On this day, she sat on the front porch as we helped her light the sparklers. A couple hours later Tammy lit the ground-based fireworks for the kids to celebrate the holiday.

July 6$^{th}$ Juliana was back in the hospital. Her stomach was still bleeding. She was feeling really bad. Juliana changed into a hospital gown. They were going to look down into her stomach and take pictures of what was going on that was causing her to be hemorrhaging. After the procedure we met Juliana, in the recovery area, as she was waking up. Tammy said that the doctors thought Juliana had "host versus graft disease." According to medlineplus.gov that means "The new, transplanted cells regard the recipient's body as foreign. When this happens, the cells attack the recipient's body." Tammy was rubbing Juliana's head, as she was waking up, and said the doctors are going to try different medicine to try to stop it.

Juliana's throat was hurting, after the procedure, like happened last time. Tammy said, "We need to get your belly better as soon as possible." Tammy held Juliana's hand as was caressing it with her thumb. The hospital had gotten a new computer system called EPIC so the nurses were still learning how to use it to input patient data. My parents (John and Edna) came, to the hospital, to visit Juliana. Pam Hawkins, a very dear friend of many decades, stopped up to see Juliana and brought her a big balloon.

Two days later Juliana and Tammy came home. Maddie was waiting at the door when she heard the garage door open. Her tail was wagging and she started barking. I opened the door and she ran out to see Juliana. She was feeling pretty weak. Aubrix Bromley, a close friend of Lindsay, Kristina and Juliana came over for a visit. They were planning Animal Jam, online, with each other. "Girl time" was so precious to Juliana as cancer kept Juliana from having a "normal" group of friends.

Juliana was getting sicker.

On July 12, 2016 I asked Tammy to give Juliana's fans an update. Tammy said, "About a week earlier Juliana had an endoscopy. She was admitted because they thought it was Host versus Graft disease. The next day we found out that it was not Graft versus Host disease.

It was chemical damage to her stomach lining specifically steroid induced gastritis. It's good that it wasn't Host versus Graft but bad that her stomach lining is eroded and bleeding.

She's only 74 days out from transplant her new bone marrow is not able to make enough platelets and red blood cells right now to keep up with the bleeding. It's not clotting. She's still bleeding and having bloody diarrhea. They decided, this week, that they're going to give her platelets every day to try to get the bleeding stopped. Yesterday they gave her platelets and two units of blood because she was very anemic.

When they checked, afterward, to see how much the platelet count had gone up it had not gone up very much. Now, their concerned that she could, possibly, be starting to make antibodies against the platelets because she's had so many platelet transfusions. Her body may be killing the platelets that they are giving her. If that's the case...they might have to start giving her IVG which will stop some of the antibodies that she's making so that they aren't attacking the platelets that they're giving her. She'll, probably, need more blood by tomorrow. If we get the bleeding stopped it's going to take a good while for her stomach to heal...so she's going to have to go back on TPN." Juliana looked so sad sitting next to Tammy.

A bit of interesting information to put what was happening, by this point, into perspective. Between 2007, when Juliana first got cancer, and April 22, 2016 Juliana had received about 120 transfusions. Between April 23, 2016 and July 13, 2016 Juliana had received an additional 55 transfusions. Between July 14, 2016 and July 29, 2016 Juliana received another 22 transfusions.

While Juliana was playing with Maddie, on July 14, 2016, Tammy got an email update about Juliana transfusions. Before her last platelet transfusion her platelets were only 57. After her last platelet transfusion it was 133. Tammy said, "that's the highest they've been in I don't know how long."

The very next day, Juliana was back at the hospital. Juliana was getting readmitted to the hospital again. She was so sad and just wanted to be healthy. The nurse was very happy that a lot of the fluid since last time she was seen by that nurse (Katie). She received another platelet transfusion. Juliana said, "Stinks being here…bored." Later in the day Tammy and I took Juliana, in her wheelchair, for another walk around part of the hospital to get her out of her hospital room. Juliana has spent more time, in hospital, than most adults do in several lifetimes.

Finally, on July 17$^{th}$ Juliana and Tammy were able to go home. Juliana bought a toy, for Maddie, from the Hospital store. It was a stuffed toy that squeaked. Maddie loved it. Later that day we held a little birthday party for Matthew (one day early) as he was turning twenty one years old.

July 18, 2016 Tammy shares a summary of that day, "Check up, Labs & Platelet transfusions at Hopkins Clinic. Again explained what I thought had happened with NP who listened to me and added IV famotidine back into Juliana's fluids (it was discontinued when Juliana stopped TPN and changed to fluids back on June 16th and a few days later she started having bloody diarrhea—famotidine helps treat stomach ulcers and when it was stopped it allowed the prednisone she was taking to make horrible bleeding ulcers). I also told her I thought the sirolimus (an anti rejection drug she was taking to help prevent GVHD) was keeping her stomach from healing—I had read case studies where people with stomach ulcers had bleed to death while taking sirolimus and others whose ulcers wouldn't heal until the stopped taking it). She agreed it was possible and said the "team" would discuss it."

July 20th – Check up, Labs, Blood & Platelet transfusions at Hopkins Clinic. Met with Dr. Loeb to discuss stopping sirolimus—he agreed Julie should stop taking it.

July 22nd – Check up, Labs, Blood & Platelet transfusions at Hopkins Clinic followed by a Meckels scan.

On July 23rd our friend Jess, Jennifer and their son Chase came by, the house, for a visit. They went swimming with Tammy, Kristina, Tim and Juliana. Juliana was walking around, outside, without any of us supporting her. Juliana really wanted to go swimming again. Tammy helped her down to the pool. Juliana was determined to have what fun she could have being so weak and, still, bleeding internally. She, slowly, backed into the pool (when she was feeling good she would jump in). Privately, Tammy and I were so worried about Juliana and have been since 2007. Juliana wouldn't let Tammy help her off of the pool ladder into the water. She was very independent. After several minutes, Juliana stepped down into the water.

Later that evening Juliana vomited blood and it happened again on July 25th. On July 29$^{th}$ we found out Juliana had fluid around her heart.

## Chapter 16

On August 1st Juliana had a check up, Labs, Blood & Platelet transfusions at Hopkins Clinic. A couple days later, on August 3rd she was back at Johns Hopkins Hospital for Check up, Labs, Platelet transfusion and repeat echocardiogram (pericardial effusion stable). Later in the evening the kids were playing outside. Juliana said, "We're gonna have to fun!" Rebecca and Tim were tossing water balloons back and forth to see if they could catch them without popping them.

Juliana was sitting, on the porch, watching them. Rebecca through a water balloon and got Tim right in the face. He started laughing and Rebecca yelled, "I am so sorry!!" Juliana said, "That was AWESOME…that was funny!" Juliana stepped, off the porch, and walked over to the bucket where the water balloons were being held. She reached in and walked within a few feet of Tim and tossed a water balloon at him. Moments later Rebecca picked up a bucket of water, that the water balloons were in, and carried it toward Tim. Tim had taken off his glasses a few minutes before so they wouldn't get broken. He started to move away from Rebecca who was going to dump water in him. Juliana yelled, "STOP RUNNING. DON'T BE A COWARD!" Tim ran away from Rebecca. Later, Tim got Rebecca back and got her with a water balloon.

That evening Juliana helped Tammy make some cupcakes. Juliana wanted to be a chef with she became an adult. Over the years Juliana cooked several meals and helped Tammy bake cakes and Christmas cookies. A few days later Juliana was back in the kitchen helping Tammy make chocolate pies.

Juliana had more clinic appointments at the Johns Hopkins Pediatric Oncology Clinic on August 5$^{th}$ and 8$^{th}$.

August 6$^{th}$ came and we had a little birthday party for Tammy a few days before her birthday (August 9$^{th}$). I bought Tammy and ice cream cake from a local ice cream shop. Juliana sat on Tammy's right as we sang Happy Birthday to Tammy. All the kids came over along with my parents and Tammy's mom. It was the last time I was able to take a photograph of Tammy and, all, six of our kids.

On August 11th Juliana had an appointment with Pulmonary doctor followed by Force 3 (force3.com) Crab Feast to benefit The Children's Cancer Foundation (childrenscancerfoundation.org). While, at the fundraiser, we enjoyed eating crabs and shrimp (Juliana loved seafood). Once Tim was done eating he walked around and performed magic for several people. He amazed them all.

The next day, on August 12th Juliana had another check up, Labs and echocardiogram (still stable) at the Hopkins Clinic. The next evening, Juliana was back in her pool in our backyard. She was really having fun. She had more energy too and swam, the entire length of the pool, underwater. She said, "It's fun."

August 15th came and Juliana gave a quick update to all her fans. She said, "Today I have been feeling, really, active because counts are low. Pretty much, all I did today was watch TV. Still not eating a lot…didn't really eat anything today. We're going back (to the clinic) tomorrow for counts and, probably some blood and platelets so we'll be there all day."

The next day, August 16$^{th}$, Juliana had another check up & Labs at Hopkins Clinic.

August 17, 2016 Juliana visited the Utz Potato Factory with Emily Kolenda and her sisters and Mom (Kelly) then had lunch and went swimming in Julie's pool. (This was the last time Juliana ever swam in her pool). The girls had so much fun. Juliana loved to swim. Emily and Juliana became very close friends because they spent so much time in Sinai Hospital together. She took her time getting into the water, put on her goggles and started swimming. They enjoyed playing Marco Polo too.

There is something about the siblings of children with life threatening illnesses. Most of them acquire a great level of compassion and patience for other people. They are heroes too.

On August 18$^{th}$ we were invited by Believe in Tomorrow (believeintomorrow.org) to go watch the Baltimore Ravens Football Team training. It was a lot of fun. The Ravens players lined up, after practice, and signed autographs for all the kids who were invited that day. Coach John Harbaugh knelt down, in front of Juliana wheelchair, and talked with her for a few minutes as she signed a football that many of the other players signed for her.

The next day, August 19$^{th}$ Juliana had another check up, Labs and blood transfusion at Hopkins Clinic.

August 20$^{th}$ came and it was a big day. We went to her cousins' (Allie & Tristan) 21st birthday party. Tammy and I were privileged to be at the birth of Allie and Tristan and would babysit them a lot when they were babies. This was the last time Juliana ever went swimming—she actually swam all the way across the length of the pool underwater—with a pericardial effusion!! At one point, while she was in the pool, Juliana swam to the bottom of the pool. It was incredible to watch.

The next several days were full of more clinic appointments.

August 22nd – Check up, Labs and echocardiogram (still stable) at Hopkins Clinic and

On August 26th, Juliana had another check up, Labs and Blood transfusion at Hopkins Clinic. This day is very special to Tammy and me because it's Juliana's Adoption Anniversary. Later that day, like we do for each of our children's Adoption Anniversaries, we celebrate with a cake and singing "Happy Adoption Day to you!" This time Tammy baked a chocolate cake with cream cheese icing. YUM! Juliana was getting more and more hair. Tammy placed thirteen pink candles into the cake. Juliana practiced blowing out the candles before Tammy lit them. Juliana smiled as we sang to her. WOW!! She blew them out with one breath. Tammy said, "she did that to show everyone that nothing's wrong with her lungs..." Tammy said, to Juliana, "Good job!!" Later that evening Juliana was playing with Maddie. She looked at me and said, "I love her so much!"

August 29th – A few days later Juliana had another check up, Labs and Pentamidine infusion at Hopkins Clinic and on August 31st she had an eye doctor appointment.

In the month of August 2016 Juliana received, approximately, twelve transfusions.

Chapter 17

On August 26, 2016 Juliana was blowing out her Adoption Anniversary candles with no problem at all. September 2, 2016 she was in the hospital having a procedure to remove fluid that had accumulated around her heart. She was admitted to PICU (Pediatric Intensive Care Unit) at Johns Hopkins Hospital. Juliana was feeling terrible! She received two platelet transfusions. Her back was hurting but it seemed it may be from the radiation treatment she received on her ribs and back.

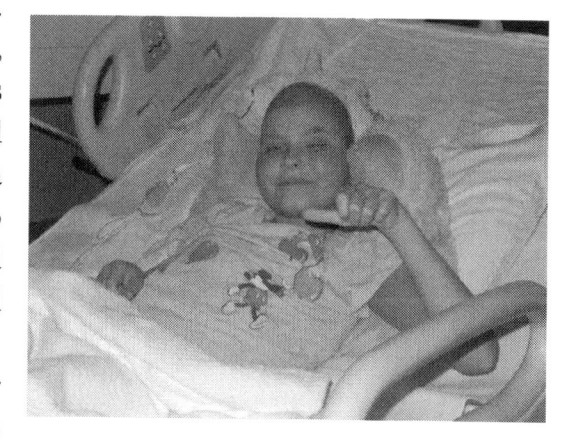

Juliana was wearing a pink shirt and looked so sad to be back in a hospital bed feeling awful. Juliana looked over to Tammy and asked if she had to have oxygen during the procedure to remove some fluid from around her heart. She hated getting oxygen. The nurse reassured Juliana what was going to happen. Juliana was scared. Juliana let out a sigh in, total, frustration. Tammy stood beside her and tried to ease her fears.

A few minutes later more hospital personnel came into Juliana PICU room to do the procedure right there...not in an operating room. Tammy and I stayed right there with Juliana trying to reduce as much of her stress as possible. The frustration on Juliana's face ripped our hearts out. She just wanted to be healthy. The hospital personnel hooked Juliana up to a monitor that could show them an image of Juliana's heart, on the sonogram, as they prepared to remove some fluid. Her heart was beating at 115 beats per minute and jumped to 120 beats per minute as they started working on her. It was 6:30pm as I looked on the screen showing her beating heart.

They were hurting Juliana as Tammy leaned over Julian's bed within inches of Juliana's face. Tammy and I were scared out of our minds. A heart doctor walked in to perform the procedure. There were, now, several hospital personnel standing around Juliana's bed. A nurse gave Juliana some "loopy juice" to help relax her to get some of the fluid off her heart. A nurse was asking Juliana questions about our family to distract her from what they were doing. At one point a nurse said, "You'll love it when you're older." Juliana let out another sigh in frustration. She was so sick and tired of hospitals.

Tammy reached over and held her hand. By now, the PICU room was getting busier. Tammy was caressing Juliana's hand. Juliana was so worried...so worried. She asked Tammy if they were going to put an oxygen mask on her as she had a bad experience, with those masks, in the past. As the "loopy juice" went in Juliana she looked over at me and said, "It feels weird." Juliana waved to me with her right hand. I said, "You're doing great baby." Juliana looked up at Tammy then closed her eyes as Tammy continued to caress her hand.

I was sharing, with a nurse in the room, how many of Juliana's fans (around the world) love her so much. Tammy and I were escorted out of Juliana's PICU room while they did the procedure. When we returned, about forty five minutes later, Juliana said her chest was hurting from the procedure. They put a drain in her chest so it was VERY painful. Juliana said, as she was trying to wake up, "My chest hurts." Juliana had her fingers, of her right hand, wrapped around Tammy's right thumb. Tammy reached her left hand up and caressed Juliana's head and tried to find out how high her pain was in order to get Juliana some more pain medication to ease some of the pain. Juliana said, "It feels weird when I breathe.' Juliana moaned in pain. Juliana said, "I'm trying."

An X-Ray technician, a little while later, came in to take an X-Ray while Juliana was still in bed. The technician pushed the metal casing behind Juliana's back and the yelled out in pain. She was hurting so bad. The technician said, "I know." Juliana said, "This is not comfy." The technician responded, "I know it's not comfy. If you can find a way to make one of these that's soft and comfortable you'll be very very rich so that's a good thing for you to work on." Juliana just nodded.

Tammy and I had to step, just, outside the PICU room as we watched the X-Ray being taken. Juliana's head was laying on one of her favorite Pillow Pets...the pink one (https://www.pillowpets.com/). The technician asked Juliana to "take in a big breath....hold your breath....good...now you can breathe normally." Finally, the X-Ray was done.

Moments later, Tammy was standing on the left side of Juliana's bed. Juliana was trying to explain who "loopy" she felt during the procedure. I said "there was a lot of people in here…there must have been ten people in here." She asked us, "Did we ever move (into the operating room)?" I said, "No." Tammy said, "You're still in the same bed that you started out in." Juliana asked, "Did they put something over my face?" I said, "Yes, there was a cloth that, kind-of, draped over you…not to blind you…it was just a piece of paper." Juliana said, "yea..why is that there (remembering pieces of what had happened during the procedure)."

Wayne Littleton, from Believe in Tomorrow (believeintomorrow.org), had arranged for us to stay at their condo in Ocean City Maryland starting on September 4$^{th}$ for several days. Juliana had been looking forward to this trip since her bone marrow transplant. Now, it was looking doubtful that she could be able to go on this amazing vacation. Wayne Littleton, Believe in Tomorrow and their many volunteers, has been so kind to our family for several years.

The next day, September 3rd, Juliana and Tammy were in PICU all day. They clamped the drain in the morning to see if more fluid, around

Juliana's heart, started accumulating again. Juliana's chest was still hurting from the chest tube sticking out of it. A nurse came into Juliana's PICU room to take some more blood for some tests. As I looked up at the monitor, in Juliana's PICU room, her heart rate was 141 and her blood pressure was 115/49. The monitor showed that her heart rate jumped to 160 at 5:10am and 177 at 8:37am and an alarm had gone off.

The next day, September 4th, Juliana was trying to pass the time and play on her IPAD. Kelly and Emily Kolenda came up to see Juliana while she remained in PICU. Remember, Emily Kolenda and Juliana had become very close friends because they spent so much time, getting treatment, at Sinai Hospital in Baltimore Maryland. Juliana was so happy to see Emily. John and Wanda Thompson, once again, were kind enough to care for Maddie, as we had planned on going to Ocean City. Juliana was concerned, because there was a bad storm at the ocean, and she didn't think she would be able to go on the beach. Tammy reassured her everything would be cleared up by then.

Later, the same team of people came back into Juliana's PICU room to unclamp the drain (in Juliana's chest) and decided it was safe to remove it and discharge Juliana so she could still go on vacation to Ocean City. Tammy held Juliana's left hand as the doctor worked on Juliana. The nurse was trying to get Juliana to talk about Ocean City to distract her from what was happening. The doctor trained more fluid, from the drain in Juliana's chest, as Juliana didn't want to look at him doing it. The doctor said, "it looks like Apple Cider." Juliana LOVED apple cider.

Tammy asked Juliana, "Remember, what did we say platelets always look like?" Juliana looked up at her and said, "Chicken noodle soup." Tammy said, "We have to find out why it keeps doing it." She was referring to, as the doctor continued to drain fluid from around Juliana's heart, why the fluid kept building up. The doctor injected some of the fluid that was around Juliana's heart into a specimen cup to be tested. He emptied that syringe and reattached it back to the drain in Juliana's chest. He began draining more fluid. Finally, the doctor was done. Juliana was free to leave the hospital.

Juliana showed a picture, from her IPAD, of the condo where we would be going to in Ocean City Maryland. We were, now, waiting to be discharged. The nurse hooked Juliana up to some morphine. Juliana began to cry because she was, VERY, afraid because the hospital staff was going to remove the drain in her chest. Two hospital personnel came into Juliana's PICU room to remove Juliana's chest tube. She was TERRIFIED!! A nurse laid Juliana back, a little, on her bed. Juliana cried, in terror, as they raised her shirt to remove the chest tube.

Our baby girl was about to be in agony!

Juliana was, now, crying!! They were hurting her. Tammy reached over to wipe away some of her tears. OMG…this was horrible for Juliana. One of the hospital personnel said, to Juliana, "You're getting yourself all nervous watching." They encouraged her to look at something else. Juliana's tears continued to flow. She started sobbing! It was HORRIBLE HORRIBLE HORRIBLE watching Juliana, in agony, and there was nothing we could do. WHY didn't they put her to sleep to take out the chest tube?!!?! They pulled out the chest tube and Juliana SCREAMED IN PAIN! She cried so hard. It was a NIGHTMARE!

Less than a half-hour later we were leaving the hospital. As we were walking to the elevator Juliana said, "It felt so weird." The next morning, after receiving clearance from Johns Hopkins Hospital, we were on our way to Ocean City Maryland. Tammy and I decided to drive separately

in the event she had to take Juliana to a hospital while I had the Tim, Kristina and Lindsay with me. I can't describe how much Juliana loved to fish and be at the ocean. The joy, that this gave her, is beyond my ability to describe to you.

We arrived at the Believe in Tomorrow (believeintomrrow.org) condo, that Wayne Littleton arranged for us, and Juliana wanted to fish right away. The condo has a pier, out back, so the kids could fish as much as they wanted to fish. Less than twenty four hours before she was screaming in pain as a chest tube was removed from her little body. Juliana, as Lindsay was untangling a line on one of the fishing roads for Juliana, was wearing her "I'm not a giver-upper" shirt and was wearing pink pants.

Lindsay and Juliana walked out on the pier and Lindsay casts the line into the water for Juliana. I could tell Juliana was in pain as she was walking, a little, hunched over. Juliana was only fourteen-and-a-half years old.

Juliana's drive and determination rival any adult that I've ever met. I walked out on the pier and asked Juliana, "You okay?" She said, "yup" and continued to fish.

Her focus was incredible. Kristina joined us on the pier for a little while. A neighbor, who lives next to the condo, offered us some minnows for bait. The neighbors, on both sides of the condo, were so kind to us. Juliana and Lindsay continued to fish as the wind was starting to pick up. Juliana was happy but not feeling very good. She never whined...she never complained.

Kristina came back out, from the condo, and helped Juliana put some bait on her line. Juliana went back, to the end of the pier, and cast her line into the water. Juliana was at her "happy place" with a fishing rod in her hands. Tim came out, onto the pier, with Kristina. Tim said, "How's it going Jul (one of our nicknames for Juliana)?" I think she said, "Pretty good." The sound of the water made it hard for me to hear her at that moment. All three continued to talk at the end of the pier. Tim brought out a fishing rod, out of the condo, and cast it into the water. Tim's patience with Juliana has been extraordinary. Moments later Juliana caught the first fish of our trip to Ocean City. Tim said it was a puffer fish. It was September 5, 2016. She was SO excited as Tim helped her hold it up so I could take a photo.

A few minutes later my cell phone started to ring. It was Chef Robert Irvine (chefirvine.com) and his wife Gail. Giant Food had arranged for Juliana to meet Chef Robert Irvine back in July 2015 when they found out that Juliana wanted to be a chef when she became an adult. Chef Irvine promised that he was going to stay in touch with Juliana. Up to that point, Chef Irvine had called and FaceTimed Juliana MANY times to encourage her and tell her to keep fighting to get well.

On this Facetime call Juliana told Robert and Gail where we were staying. Robert asked Juliana, "How you feeling?" Juliana said, "Good." Mind you, she was in serious pain but never complained about it. A couple of years earlier she said, "Whining is for babies."

Robert saw that Juliana was starting to get hair. He yelled, "You've got hair!!" Juliana said, "some." Robert joked, to Juliana, "You've got more hair that me." Gail said, "This is true." Robert said, "this is crazy...you doing okay?" Juliana said, "Yup." Robert said, "I was telling my audience, all last week, about you and we sent that little video to you and there's a show about a family and I brought you up in it and it's about to air so I will tell you. It was, kind of, cool because I talk about you quite a bit actually...I think more than the family on the show." Juliana chuckled. Robert said, "So, you're at the beach? Where are you?" Juliana said, "Yup, we're at Ocean City." I said, "on the Chesapeake Bay" to give Robert and Gail a more exact description where we were staying.

Gail (Robert Irvine's wife) said, "My sister used to go there all the time." Robert said, to Juliana, "Nice...nice." He walked about how he and Gail had just finished working out. He said, "I'm glad you're feeling better." Juliana said, "Me too" and she smiled into my cell phone on their Facetime chat. I said, "it was a rough few days in the hospital."

Robert said to Juliana, "I don't know anyone else who is stronger than you." Gail said, "I don't either and I work with a lot of strong people." Robert said to Juliana, "You're a tough little cookie." Gail agreed. Robert said, "All those people who whine when they get a headache…they're little whiners." Juliana laughed. Robert said to Juliana, "When they're all crying like little babies and then I bring up what you go through and they say "OH MY GOODNESS!" Juliana laughed. Robert continued, "It's a good awakening for them right?" Gail said, "Sometimes we forget."

Robert said to Juliana, "You caught a fish…which is awesome!" Juliana said, "YUP!" Gail asked if I took a picture. I told her that I would send it to her in a few minutes. It was a great call. We appreciate Robert and Gail so much!

After the Facetime call Lindsay, Kristina and Juliana were back on the pier. Tim was baiting a line to join them to try to catch some fish. Moments later Tim was attempting to help Juliana cast better. Moments later, I had placed wireless microphone on them so I would hear them better (looking back I am so glad it did to save those great memories). They fished for a little while when Juliana's back started hurting again. She went and sat down for a few minutes.

The next day we went to the beach. Juliana was walking slowly as we approached the beach. She was in pain but so happy to be at Ocean City Maryland. We set up some beach chairs and Juliana sat down for a few minutes. It was a beautiful and sunny day. Tammy put sun screen on Juliana before we left for the beach and as we arrived.

A few minutes later Juliana got up, with her camera in hand, and walked toward the ocean. She was taking photos of the water. There was a time when Juliana would have been running up and down the beach screaming with laughter. Today, however, she was walking slowly.

She was, slightly, hunched over from the pain in her back. Juliana approached the ocean and the water touched her feet. She tipped-toed through the water as Tammy and I stayed very close to Juliana. A couple minutes later Juliana was sitting in the beach chair next to Tammy. There is something about waves that is so relaxing. Tammy and Kristina went for a walk, on the beach, for a few minutes while I remained close to Juliana. Tim, Kristina and Lindsay were having a great time walking and playing in the ocean water. We could, all, tell Juliana was not feeling good but she was determined to have fun.

It must have been so frustrating for Juliana knowing that, so many times in past, she could run and play and go swimming in the ocean. Now, her abilities were so much less. She was so thankful to be at Ocean City Maryland. Juliana remained on the beach chair for some time. Lindsay came over and sat beside her as I stood near them both.

Ten minutes later, Juliana got up and walked toward the ocean. She was wearing purple shorts, a white and pink shirt and a pink baseball cap. Tim and I walked very close to Juliana as they chatted. Juliana said a seagull landed right next to Lindsay then flew away. Juliana's steps were slow but sure.

She walked closer to the ocean as the foam touched her feet. The connection, between Tim and Juliana, is so precious. The connection is unbreakable. After about five minutes Juliana walked back to the beach chair. This happened a few times. She would rest, on the beach chair, then she would walk a little on the beach. At one point I asked Juliana, "Are you okay?" She said, "YUP!" We stayed on the beach, for a couple hours, then went back to the Believe in Tomorrow, condo.

Juliana wanted to go fishing, again, when we arrived back at the condo. The wind was picking up and the water was getting choppy. Tim and Kristina joined Juliana on the pier to do some fishing also. Juliana's back was really hurting so I brought a chair for her to sit on while she was fishing. Tim was giving Juliana some more tips on fishing. Lindsay came out onto the peer to cast her line. Juliana was, still, so full of confidence and determination.

Juliana said, "This wind is very windy...very strong." Tim went to get more bait. Juliana said, "It's way too windy." Juliana was being silly even though she had to sit in a chair because of her pain. Tim put some more bait on Juliana's line and brought the fishing rod to her.

The waves began to splash a lot more so Juliana went and sat on the back deck of the condo.

Juliana recorded a short video message, while standing on the back porch of the condo, to the people who work with Believe in Tomorrow (believeintomorrow.org). She said, "Hi, it's Juliana Carver and last Friday I went to the hospital for an appointment and they said I had more fluid around my heart and we had to be inpatient for about three days. I was, really, bummed out because I really wanted to go HERE to Ocean City. They cleared everything up, we got the fluid taken (off) from around my heart and they took some test results and now we're just waiting for that. They were, like, you can go to the ocean and I'm so happy that Believe in Tomorrow could make this happen for us. It's only been two days. I'm having so much fun already. I caught a fish the first day. It's beautiful. Thank you, so much, Believe in Tomorrow for making this happen."

The sun began to set and Tim and Kristina continued to fish. The next day, September $7^{th}$, we were back at the beach. Lindsay and Kristina were in the ocean while Tim played in the sand. Tammy was spraying sunscreen on Juliana. Believe in Tomorrow had a beach wheel chair that we borrowed so Juliana would go up and down the beach without having to walk so far. Tammy walked out into the ocean as I stayed close to Juliana. Juliana sat in the beach chair for several minutes while Kristina and Lindsay were swimming in the ocean.

Moments later Juliana, and the other kids, walked toward the ocean. Juliana, only, stood there for a few minutes. I asked if she was in pain. She said, "No." The morphine was helping. I told her, "You look beautiful!" She said, "Naaa." I asked, "Are you okay?" She said, "Yup." Juliana never complained. She, slowly, walked back to the beach chair. Tammy, Tim and Kristina were enjoying the waves. Lindsay and Juliana were feeding the seagulls Cheez-Its.

A few minutes went by and Tim, Kristina, Lindsay and Tammy took Juliana for a ride in the beach wheel chair as she rode along the water. They were gone for about then minutes and wheeled Juliana back. Just a year or two earlier Tammy, Juliana and all of us would go on long walks on the beach. Now, Juliana couldn't enjoy those long walks.

As parents, it was ripping our hearts out. Juliana just wanted to be healthy. You could see the stretch marks, on Juliana, from all the fluid she gained after the bone marrow transplant. If you have healthy children feel lucky.

A couple hours later we were back at the, Believe in Tomorrow, condo. Tammy was rubbing pain medication on Juliana's back because it was hurting so much. We brought a chair back out to the end of the pier as Juliana wanted to fish. It was hurting Juliana to cast her line into the water so Tim cast it for her. Juliana was starting to feel pretty bad. We put a pillow behind her back since it was hurting. Kristina went to get some rags to hold a fish in case they caught something and then came back, to the end of the pier, to fish also. The sun was out and the wind was much calmer than the day before. Juliana's hair was coming in really well. At one point, while Tim, Kristina and Juliana were on the pier fishing Juliana said, "Come on fish...take my bait." A few minutes later, Juliana stood up and cast her own line, then sat back down.

Tim stayed right beside Juliana and continued to coach her on fishing. Something was on Juliana's line!! She reeled in another crab. She said, "it takes five minutes to reel in the dang thing." Tim helped her pull up the crab and recast the line for Juliana. I could, still, hear and see the high level of determination in Juliana. Nothing, not even cancer, was going to stop Juliana. Juliana was going to catch more fish. She was "not a giver-upper."

Almost two hours later, since we came back to the condo and some of the kids were fishing, Juliana went back into the condo. She, Kristina and Tammy were drawing some pictures for a blanket that Believe in Tomorrow was going to make for us.

The next day, Believe in Tomorrow arranged for us to go on a boat to go fishing with two amazing gentlemen who do the same for other families with sick children. We were out, in the Chesapeake Bay, for almost three hours. We slowed down close to Assateague Island to see the wild ponies. The kids had so much fun.

The next day, September 9, 2016, we took a short drive and played miniature golf. We wheeled Juliana around, in the wheelchair, and when it was her turn to play she would get up and take her turn. She was, again, wearing her "I'm not a giver-upper" shirt. A couple hours later we took a ride to Assateague Island to see if we would come across some of the wild ponies. At one point, we pulled into a little camp ground area and saw some ponies in the distance.

After a few minutes, we turned around and a wild pony had walked into the camp ground. Juliana saw it and grabbed her camera. Juliana squealed with surprise as the pony rolled around in the grass. She said, "OH THAT'S ADORABLE…OH THAT IS AWESOME…IT'S SO CLOSE…LOOK AT IT…NOW IT'S PRANCING…THAT IS AWESOME!!" As the pony walked away Juliana said, "Bye horsey."

We, also, found out on that day that the fluid around Juliana's heart was negative which meant there were no cancer cells in the fluid. Juliana said that was "AWESOME!" Later that evening we went out to dinner, courtesy of Believe in Tomorrow, and it was delicious. During the week Juliana's pain level went way up especially in her back. She had a prescription for morphine but, at times, that wasn't enough to stop the pain. The next day came and it was time to head back home.

It was, now, September 12$^{th}$. She had a Check up, Labs and echocardiogram at Hopkins Clinic. We found out that the biopsy of the fluid the drained from around her heart was negative for cancer and the echo showed the effusion was still gone, however, it now showed a pleural effusion (fluid around her right lung)! The next day she had another blood transfusion at Hopkins Clinic. Juliana had developed the amazing ability not to get frustrated over waiting and waiting for things to happen in hospitals. There were times it took a long time to get the blood for a transfusion. She just played on her IPAD, watched TV of played other games to pass the time.

On September 15$^{th}$ Juliana updated her fans. She said, "The other day we went back to the hospital and we got some blood so I'm feeling a little better from that and I'm still having the weird pain in my side and that's a little annoying. I think it's getting better. I'm eating much better than I was for some reason we don't know but that's good. Hopefully, next week we can get off the TPN…so excited about that and that's, pretty much, it and new (eye) glasses."

On September 19, 2016 Juliana had another check up and Labs. Juliana was admitted from clinic because they couldn't hear breath sounds in her right lung (the one with the effusion). Juliana was so sad. We were back in room nine…the same room we were in the day of Juliana's bone marrow transplant. A gift arrived while we were sitting in Juliana's hospital room. The gift was from Kristina Hartshorn. It was a stuffed, black and white, dog. It was so kind.

The disappointment, on Juliana's face, was so hard to witness. I cannot imagine her frustration that, still, she couldn't be a healthy teenager just like most kids. A surgery was to be performed to remove fluid from around Juliana's right lung. Juliana was wheeled down to surgery again. Tammy and I were trying not to get Juliana worrying but we were worried sick! Juliana never had an issue with fluid accumulating around her lung or heart. This was all new since the bone marrow transplant.

We waited, with Juliana, in the pre-op area like we had done so many times over the years. Juliana was quiet and played on her IPAD. Tammy helped her into a hospital gown. Juliana said she was "sleepy." She was so sad…so disappointed…sick and tired of being sick and tired. She said it hurts to yawn. Tammy put on a hospital gown to escort Juliana into the operating room. She said that she was "so tired of having all this stuff done…it's like every other month." She waved 'bye" to me as the hospital staff wheeled her out of the pre-op room heading to the operating room.

A while later, we found Juliana in the recovery area. Tammy was holding Juliana's left hand. Juliana was in pain. The nurse gave her some more pain medication. Juliana just wanted to be healthy. While in recovery there was another X-Ray taken. They left the drain in overnight. On September 20th, the drain was removed and Juliana was discharged from the hospital.

On September 21st Juliana looked good as she was playing with Maddie. She said, "She's AWESOME, (as she kissed the top of Maddie's head) she's the best Maddie dog ever….and she loves hamburgers…I'm eating again…no TPN…it feels good again not to be hurting after I take three bites. I'm ready for Thanksgiving now. (Maddie) is my best fluffy buddy."

The next day Juliana recorded a short video for all her fans. In the video she said, "Hi, I'm Juliana Carver and I wanted to thank all of you out there for praying for me and my family because I've been going through so much in the past nine years. We just got a transplant a while ago and we could not have made it this far without you so your prayers really help and mean a lot. Thank you so much for praying for me. It means a lot."

Several days later, on September 26, 2016 Juliana had another check up, Labs and pentamidine infusion in clinic. Juliana was once again admitted because she again had a pleural effusion in her right lung. The next day, September 27th, Juliana had surgery to place a Pleurx catheter (a drain that could be left in and drained at home for as long as necessary). Juliana was feeling really rough. She stayed in the hospital bed most of the time. I could hear her moan in her sleep. Her breathing was getting shallow and looked so sick. Every day Tammy would drain fluid from Juliana's right side into a transparent container.

On September 28, 2016, Mark Jenkins, a dear friend of mine, was in the area and stopped by to visit with Juliana. Juliana was sitting up and smiling and wanted to eat. Mark had come through several challenges, in his life, and was trying to encourage Juliana and shared some stories. Mark talked to Juliana about living in Texas.

Tammy shares, "Juliana had a PET scan, in the morning, because she was still having pain in her back (she was scheduled to have a six month post transplant PET at the end of October and it was moved up). We found out that afternoon that she had relapsed. In addition to her right lung pleura lighting up (meaning there was cancer in it), she had several new tumors, the most worrisome of which was one wrapped around the artery leading to her right kidney that was starting (as evidenced by her kidney function labwork) to cut off blood supply.

We discussed treatment options with Dr. Loeb and agreed to do radiation therapy to the tumor around the renal artery as soon as possible and then to try a new medication called Nivolumab that helped rev up the immune system (which would hopefully fight the cancer cells) for two rounds then rescan and if she showed no improvement switch to pazopanib. Julie was discharged from the hospital after they showed me how to drain her right lung using the new Pleurx. Juliana had cancer for the eighth time."

I remember when Dr. Loeb came into Juliana's hospital room to tell us Juliana had cancer for the $8^{th}$ time. I lost it. I started sobbing, uncontrollably, as Juliana had walked into the bathroom moments before…when she came out and got back into bed I went over to her and put my head on her lap. I was still crying, I said something like I am so sorry that I am crying. She said, "It's understandable." She was so much stronger than me…so much more. I was not a pillar of strength to Juliana at that moment.

WAIT A MINUTE!?!?!

1. We were told, months earlier, that the teenager who had a bone marrow transplant that her situation was "apples and oranges" compared to Juliana's situation. I discovered, much later, that the teenager had the exact same disease alveolar rhabdomyosarcoma.

2. After the bone marrow transplant Juliana was hemoragging due to a specific medication Johns Hopkins Hospital was giving Juliana. Tammy kept telling them they need to stop giving it because, she believed, that was causing the internal bleeding. Tammy's request fell on deaf ears for weeks. When they, finally, listened to Tammy and stopped that

particular medication the bleeding slowed down then stopped.

The next day, September 29, 2016, Juliana was adamant about keeping up with her school work. She worked on some science classes with Tammy and Kristina. Nothing was going to slow Juliana down even though she was so tired. After lunch, Aubrix Bromley, came by and sat with Juliana and played video games (Hay Day) watched TV and ate some ice cream then and they shared a blanket together on the sofa. It was one of the kindness acts of compassion I've seen in a child. Thank you Aubrix Bromley!

Chapter 18

Kristina turned eighteen years old, in late September 2016, and we planned a big eighteenth birthday party for her just like we did for Rebecca, Matthew, Timothy and Lindsay. October 1, 2016 was the date, set, for the party. Kristina was so excited. Almost all of our extended family plus many friends were at our house. Even though Juliana was not feeling good, afterwards, she told Tammy she had "such a good time."

The next day, most of the day, Juliana just stayed on the sofa. She was feeling horrible. Maddie would rest on the blanket that covered her up while she slept. Looking back, on the videos clips to write this book, something was very wrong with Juliana. Maddie didn't leave her side. Maddie would start to lick Juliana's hand. She said, in such a weak voice, "She's (Maddie) so good." Maddie and Juliana cuddled for the longest time. She said, "She's so soft and gentle" and gave Maddie a kiss. Juliana just wanted to be healthy. Juliana dozed off to sleep. She was feeling really bad.

October 3rd – Check up and Labs at Hopkins clinic. Also met with Dr. Terezakis to discuss radiation therapy.

October 4th – Radiation therapy simulation followed by blood and platelet transfusions in the clinic.

October 5th – Juliana had an echocardiogram and we found out the pericardial effusion was back. Even during the echocardiogram Juliana was in good spirits but so sick. The frustration, on her face, ripped our hearts out. Juliana and Tammy chatted while the technician was probing her chest to get images of her heart.

On October 6th, when we arrived, back at the Hopkins Clinic, Juliana got back up on the bed and waved to me with her left hand. She wasn't feeling good at all. Her hair was coming in so beautifully. She got another platelet transfusion. A little while later we took her down to the radiation area. Juliana, slowly, got out of her wheelchair to get up on the table to get radiation therapy to a tumor wrapped around the right renal artery. Juliana was in pain. There were about five radiation technicians in the room. They raised the table to get it to the right height for the radiation treatment. The technicians were so gentle with Juliana. Tammy and I stood inches away from Juliana while they got the alignment correct. We were terrified even though Juliana had so many radiation treatments in the past. We had to step out of the room in order for the radiation treatment to happen. They locked her in the room with a huge door that was several inches thick. I couldn't wait for the door to be opened so we can get to Juliana again.

Later that evening, after we got home, Juliana was feeling worse. She just rested, on the sofa, while Maddie rested on her lap.

Juliana was in the Johns Hopkins Pediatric Oncology Clinic every day that week. She was due to not have to go to the clinic on Friday October 7, 2016. We raced Juliana back to the Hopkins clinic on the morning of October 7, 2016. Juliana was gasping for air.

On or about October 4, 2016 Dr. David Loeb and Gilcrest Hospice personnel met with Tammy and I about introducing Hospice care, for Juliana, to help us at home with her care. In January 2018, after requesting it from my health insurance carrier, the actual paperwork reads (Gilcrest Kids) "Goals of care: continuing to treat cancer aggressively but making sure patient is free of pain and optimizing time at home by decreasing admissions and emergency room visits." In addition, the paperwork described Juliana's "Level of consciousness: lethargic." The paperwork, also, reads: "Mother (Tammy) states that patient has a fighting spirit and that the family will fight alongside her as long as she continues to want to do so." It, also, was noted (on the paperwork) "Discussed 24 hour on call line and goals of care."

Juliana had been in the Johns Hopkins Oncology Clinic, every day, from October 3-6, 2016. EVERYDAY!

On October 7, 2016, Tammy shares, "Juliana was not supposed to have to go to the hospital today but when I drained her right lung, I got over 500 ml of fluid off as opposed to the 50 ml every other day that I had been getting since the drain had been placed. I texted Colleen (Julie nurse) and told her—she said to bring her to clinic.

When we arrived at clinic, Julie was breathing room air, but Colleen notice she was "grunting" and took her to the back and put her on oxygen. Over the next couple of hours she continued to need more and more oxygen (they started her at "1" and gradually increased it to "5"). The PA (Physician Assistant) came in and told us she was admitting Julie to the PICU because she needed pressurized oxygen. When she got to the PICU, they put the pressurized oxygen on and it helped for a little while, but even with that her oxygen saturation was starting to drop—about that time Dr. Loeb came into her room and asked John and I to come talk to him.

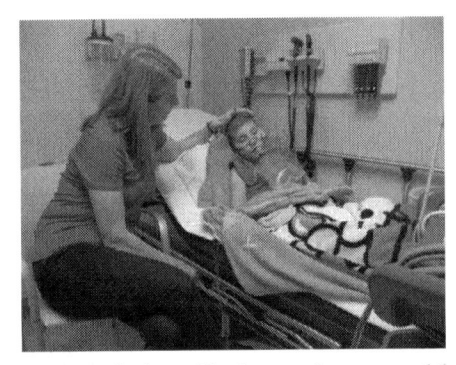

He told us that Juliana needed to be intubated and put on a ventilator immediately or she would die. He also told us that with the pericardial effusion she would probably go into cardiac arrest when they tried to place the breathing tube and that even if she survived that, he wasn't sure if she would make it or if she would ever be able to come off of the ventilator and breathe on her own. We had to make a quick decision—since Dr. Loeb thought there was a chance that the problem was a lung infection and she might recover, we told them to place the breathing tube.

HOLD ON! Juliana was at the Johns Hopkins Oncology Clinic for the prior four days, every day, and they missed a MSSA infection until it was so bad Juliana needed a breathing tune?!?!

Tammy shares, "Dr. Loeb then sent us back to Juliana's room to "tell her good-bye." When we got back to her room, Julie was struggling to breathe with both a pressurized mask and regular oxygen cannula on. I climbed onto her bed with her, gave her a hug and told her that the doctors and nurses were getting ready to do a procedure to help her breath easier (she could see everyone running around the room getting ready to intubate her), told her that I loved her and asked her to fight. John and I were escorted out of her room and taken to a waiting room. John called all of our kids and his parents and they all arrived at the hospital to wait with us. Emily and Kelly Kolenda also came. We waited what seemed like forever when finally they came in and told us Juliana had been successfully intubated, however, her heart had stopped for a full two minutes during the procedure.

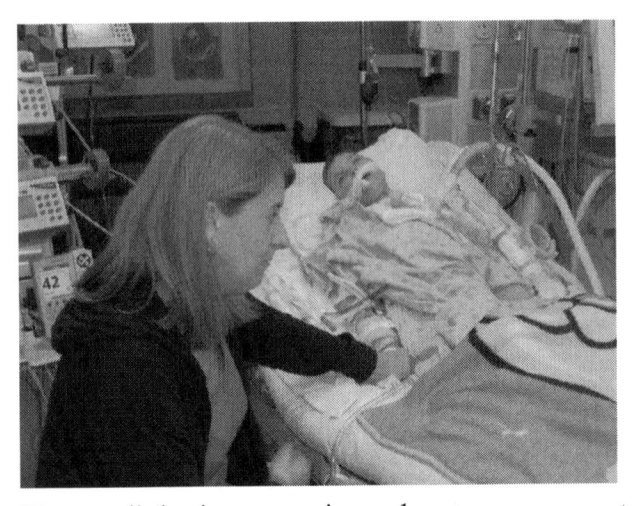

The cardiologist came in and got our consent to drain the pericardial effusion then went straight to her room to do that procedure (they do these types of procedures right in the PICU rooms at Johns Hopkins). It was several hours later before we were finally allowed to go back to her room. John and I took Emily with us to see her first—she gave her friend a big hug even though I know she must have been scared and shocked seeing her laying there on life support. All of her siblings and grandparents then took turns coming back to visit (they would only allow three people at a time back). Neither John or I slept that night."

We went from understanding Juliana was to start new cancer treatment on October 26, 2016 to, now, saying a final good bye to Juliana on October 7$^{th}$?!?!?! According to our Health Insurance Carrier paperwork the cancer treatment was, actually, scheduled to start on October 12, 2016 but Dr. Loeb that the treatment could cause more trouble with Juliana's lung. Why didn't Hopkins know about the infection before it got so bad?!?!

When Tammy and I saw Juliana, to say our final goodbye, Juliana looked really bad. The infection she got, while in the Johns Hopkins Clinic, was causing her not to be able to breathe. We told her we love her so much. Tammy was caressing her head and kissing her. I was caressing her too. Less than ten minutes later we were told they have to put in a breathing tube her right away. We had to leave her…Juliana opened her eyes and waved goodbye to us not knowing what was about to happen. Juliana was resting, her head, on one of her favorite pillow pets. The PICU room was, now, full of hospital personnel. My parents walked in the PICU room. Alarms starting going off in Juliana's PICU room but she was still able to talk to Tammy. Tammy told Juliana, "we have to make your lungs better" as she sat on Juliana's hospital bed.

Juliana nodded that she understood. Tammy was caressing Juliana's right hand and caressing her head. I came around to Juliana's side and kissed her head several times. Juliana asked Tammy (I could read Juliana's lips) "are they almost done?" She was asking about the other people in the PICU room. I asked the doctors, as I was sobbing, "Please try you best."

Tammy kissed Juliana on her left cheek again. Juliana asked Tammy to lower her bed a little bit and Juliana gave her a "thumbs up". Tammy and I leaned over Juliana and embraced her as much as we could without disturbing the oxygen mask that was on her face. OH MY GOD...the pain in Tammy's eyes...Tammy touched her forehead to Juliana's forehead and closed her eyes for a few seconds then kissed Juliana's forehead. Juliana waved to my parents who were in the PICU room with us. After my parents gave Juliana a kiss Juliana pulled her mask away from her face, for a second, and asked Tammy, "How is Aunt Michele?" Tammy, then, helped readjust Juliana's oxygen mask.

I had knelt down, beside Juliana's PICU bed, and was holding her right hand. I started sobbing uncontrollably. I looked at Juliana and said, "I love you sooo much." She looked at me, nodded, and grabbed my wrist as I was caressing her head. It was time for us to leave Juliana in the hands of the PICU personnel. We stood at the doorway, to her PICU room, as I said, "Bye baby.,,,bye I love you so much!" Juliana lifted her right hand and waved goodbye to Tammy and I.

I can't describe the agony Tammy and I were feeling. Our amazing fourtheen-year-old Juliana might die?!?! How can this happen?!?!?! IT WAS HORRIBLE!!! How could this happen with thousands of people, around the world, who had been praying for Juliana to beat cancer?!?!

I found out, on Juliana's medical records, that I asked for and were generated on November 28, 2016, that (quoting from her medical records) "Admitted to PICU with respiratory failure on 10/7. Blood culture from clinic on same day grew MSSA." This was input, into her records, by Shubin Widad Shahab MD, Phd.

MSSA stands for methicillin-susceptible Staphylococcus aureus. Staph is the shortened name for Staphylococcus (staf-uh-low-KAH-kus), a type of bacteria.

SINCE SHE WAS IN THE CLINIC, EVERYDAY, FROM OCTOBER 2-6 WHY WAS THIS NOT

DISCOVERED SOONER SO THAT IS GOT SO BAD???

Just before we were allowed back in to see Juliana we found out Juliana's heart stopped, which they warned us might happen, and CPR was done to get her heart going again. When we were allowed to go back in to the PICU room Juliana had a breathing tube in and a drain leading to her stomach. Juliana was tied to her bed so she could not pull out the breathing tube. We brought each of our other children to see Juliana. How could this be happening to our Juliana!?!? Juliana was not conscience at this time. Her heart rate was 112bpm and a machine was breathing for her.

Later, in the day, while Juliana was still had a breathing tube in, she said by just moving her lips, "I want to get better so I can go home." My mother taught me how to read lips fairly well as a child and I can still do it so I was able to read Juliana's lips. Juliana continued to be a fighter even in one of her sickest moments. She was "not a giver-upper."

The next day, Tammy leaned over Juliana's bed after the nurses gave her some medicine to get her to sleep, and said, to her, "We're working hard on getting you better so we can go home, okay?" We knew Juliana could hear us.

The next morning, Maryland First Lady Yumi Hogan came to Juliana's PICU room. Mrs. Hogan had met Juliana and most of our family at a Cool Kids Campaign (coolkidscampaign.org) event at the Maryland State House when Maryland Governor Larry Hogan was fighting cancer. Juliana was unconscious and not aware that Mrs. Hogan was in the room. Juliana was on, among other things, antibiotics to get rid of MSSA infection. This is what put her in this situation!! Mrs. Hogan commented on Juliana's beautiful skin and how

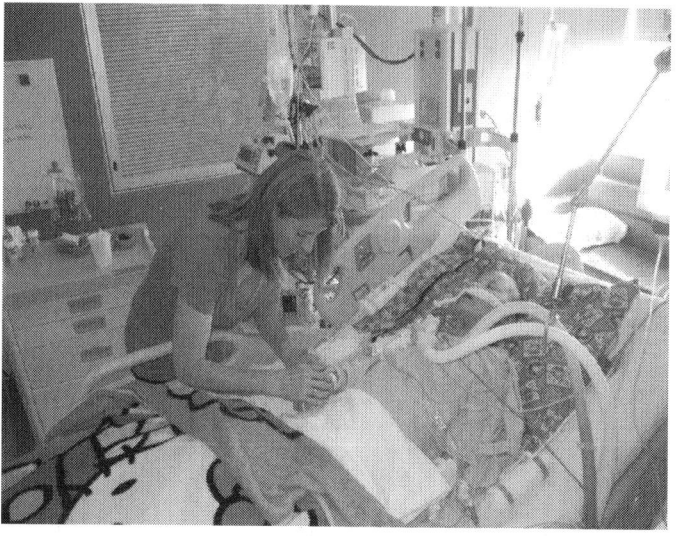

Juliana loves to swim from my "Angels for Juliana" posts on Facebook. She and Maryland Governor Hogan had been following Juliana's war against cancer. Moments later Tammy and Mrs. Hogan were at the end of Juliana's bed talking. Mrs. Hogan was caressing Tammy back as Tammy said, "She's going to get better…she's going to be okay." Tammy had tears in her eyes as she looked back at Mrs. Hogan.

Tammy and I stayed right by Juliana's side. Juliana knew we were in close by but was too groggy from the medication. We held her hand and comforted her as much as possible. Tammy leaned over Juliana and said, "You try to get better okay…you just rest. You're going to get that lung better. Okay" and leaned over and kissed her forehead and said, "I Love you….you're so brave…you're amazing. You know what I wrote on your white board? Juliana is amazing. That's the truth."

Most of what happened is not in this book as I am only sharing bits and pieces of the events in October 2016. Juliana was hooked up to so many hoses and wires.

The next day, October 9th, Juliana was still unconscious most of the time. My parents came back to PICU to visit with Juliana. At one point more doctors and nurses came in to check the status of Juliana. Tammy and I stayed very close to Juliana. We felt, absolutely, helpless. Why haven't all those prayers worked for Juliana? Why did Juliana have to get cancer EIGHT TIMES?!?!?!?!

Our friends Juan and April Waters, Derrick Claggett, John Litchfield and Arthur Hawkins came by to visit Juliana and us. The next day, Juliana was still in the same condition. Tammy and I continued to talk to Juliana, encourage her and caress her as much as possible. Juliana grabbed my hand, at one point, and was so frustrated that she couldn't speak. I was able to understand that she wanted something for her lips to moisten them. Both, Tammy and I, were trying to understand her. Juliana was SO frustrated by the breathing tube. There was nothing we could do except give Juliana's body time to get better.

The next day, October 10$^{th}$, our friend Wil Lerp came by to see Juliana. Wil lives in Texas. When the kids were small, when he lived in Maryland, he was their martial arts instructor. When Juliana was stricken with cancer, for the first time, we had to stop the classes. Juliana opened her eyes when she heard Wil's voice. Wil reached down and held her hand as tears filled his eyes. Juliana just wanted to be better so she could go home and play with Maddie. Wil loves our kids so much. Juliana wanted to talk to Wil, so bad, but was unable to speak.

Later, Juliana was going to try to write what she wanted to say. She couldn't do it. She was SO frustrated about not able to tell us what she wanted plus she was restrained and couldn't move her arms. A few hours later another ultrasound was done on Juliana while she was in her PICU room. As time progressed, that day, Juliana became a little more alert. NO ONE, in the PICU, was trained to drain the line in Juliana's right side so Tammy had to do it every day.

The following day Juliana was much more alert and trying to communicate more but she, still, has a breathing tube in her throat. The nurse did, however, free her from the restraints because Juliana promised not to pull out the breathing tube. By late morning Juliana was sitting up in bed, had her glasses on and watching TV but still not able to speak because of the breathing tube.

Tammy and I had not heard Juliana's voice for four days at that point. Juliana's hair was getting so nice and thick. Less than an hour later, Mary Bohlen (recently retired Social Worker from Sinai Hospital who helped us so much over the years) and Stephanie Entrup (also from Sinai Hospital) came up to Juliana's PICU room (at Johns Hopkins Hospital) to visit with Juliana. They brought Juliana a card and some gifts. Juliana's left arm was, now, strapped to a board because they had to put more tubes in her left arm. As Tammy talked to Mary Bohlen Stephanie caressed Juliana's head. Their kindness and compassion touched us to our core.

October 12, 2016 came and Juliana was awake more and watching TV between taking naps. She was able to change the channels, on the TV, with just a little help and dictate, with her fingers, which channel she wanted to watch. She just wanted to be healthy.

Again, I would like to thank the Cohen family for keeping Tim, Kristina and Maddie while Tammy and I were in PICU with Juliana.

Believe it or not, Juliana wanted to play "Hospital Bingo" later that day. Juliana was determined to win even having a breathing tube down her throat. She took another nap before "Hospital Bingo" started. Tammy and I took turns holding Juliana's hand and caressing her head. When the game started she sat up, in bed, and was determined to keep up with the game.

On October 13, 2016 Juliana was sitting up and watching more television between naps. The next day, Juliana slept most of the day.

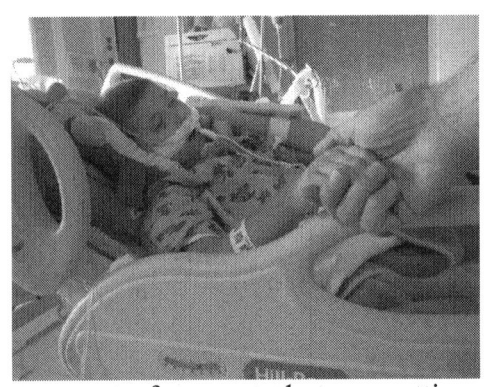

Tammy summarized the last few days, "October 8th to October 13th – Juliana remained in the PICU on the ventilator, but they were able to gradually decrease the amount of support she was getting each day. They found MSSA in the blood culture taken in clinic on the 7th and starting treating her for the infection. X-rays were done each morning--her left lung improved each day and I continued to drain her right lung with the Pleurx each day. Juliana was not sedated (as we originally thought she would be) and was very frustrated with not being able to communicate with us. The OT made up a board with pictures for her to point to of common things she might want and gave us an I-pad to use, but we often ended up playing a frustrating game of charades. After a couple days, I asked them to take the restraints off of Julie's arms (they put them on so she wouldn't pull the breathing tube out) and thankfully her nurse agreed because Julie (by shaking her head) agreed she understood not to pull out the tube. She then gave her the nurse call button and told her to push it if she needed something and she would come in right away (since she obviously couldn't speak). I told her if she wanted me at night (the sofa I slept on was behind her bed so we couldn't see each other) to just bang the call button on the side of her bed. It was a long week for all of us, but on Friday morning (seven days later), the doctor told us she was going to try extubating her (and if she couldn't breathe with the pressurized oxygen mask on they would have to intubate her again). They had several emergencies so she wasn't extubated until the early evening (much to Julie's frustration). I got permission to sit next her and hold her hand while they extubated and thankfully she was able to breathe fine with the pressurized oxygen."

On October 14th Tammy continued, daily, to drain Juliana's line in her chest as the PICU nurses were not trained to do it. Around lunch time, they took the breathing tube out of Juliana. We watched them do it. As the hospital personnel came around Juliana and untapped everything they asked Juliana to make a big cough then they pulled it out and put a full-face oxygen (over her nose and mouth) mask on her. It was AMAZING to hear Juliana's voice, again, because we had not heard it for several days.

Tammy and I reassured Juliana that she was getting better. I could see, on Juliana's X-Rays how the infection had cleared up…or so it seemed at the time. We tried to keep Juliana as comfortable as possible. We reassured her that she was doing a great job. Just after lunch time the nurses had Juliana sitting up in a chair for a few minutes. Watching your young child struggle, like this, is beyond description. Tammy and I would have traded places with Juliana in a second.

Sitting in the chair tired her out so the nurses helped her back in bed. Less than an hour later Emily Kolenda (Juliana's friend from Sinai Hospital) came back to visit Juliana. Emily has had some serious challenges for several years. Emily said, "You look a little bit better than you did last week." Emily is such a sweet-heart. When Emily left Juliana took another nap.

The next day came and Juliana had the full-face oxygen mask off and only had a nasal canula forcing air into her lungs. The air, going into her nose, was loud. This allowed Juliana to talk much better. Juliana looked up to me, as I videoed a message (from Juliana) to her fans and waved HI. Juliana was saying it's hard to talk because of the air blowing in her nose. I was holding her hand as I was listening to her sweet voice after so many days of not hearing it. I said, "You look great. It's so good to hear your voice, oh man, I've missed your voice so much."

A little later, while she was watching television, Juliana looked over at me and said, "It's so boring in here" then she blew me a kiss. A little later she dozed off for another nap.

October 16, 2016 arrived and Juliana was on less oxygen. She said, "it was much better than the other one." She was referring to the new canula in her nose. She was sitting up, wearing her glasses and watching more television. She was talking more and eager to go home. Juliana would hold hands while she napped. Tammy said, "I think that she's getting better." I said, "For Sure." Tammy told Juliana, "I think we will be home next weekend and not here…that's what I think."

A little later, in the day, I held her hand and sang to her, "you are my sunshine my little sunshine…you make me happy when skies are grey." It's a song that I have sung to Juliana for years. This time, she looked at me and said, "You're silly."

The next day, I asked Tammy to give an update for Juliana's fans. We videoed a message to share on Facebook's "Angels for Juliana." Juliana gave a thumbs up when Tammy was done. A little while later Juliana was eating some solid food. It was the first time she had eaten food since about October 6, 2016. She was eating french fries and chicken nuggets. She was looking so good. She was so happy to eat real food again. She, also, ate a few bites of a cookie. I told her, "You're doing great…I'm so proud of you…You're AWESOME!" Juliana said, "One more step to going home!"

On October 17th, Juliana and I did a LIVE video on Facebook's "Angels for Juliana". She was amazed how many people were watching the video. I don't think she understood, up to that point, how many people (around the world) love her so much. She was in a good mood. She said, "so many people….so many hearts…I love you too…my hair's a mess….I'm taking it one day at a time….thank you for your prayers…love you guys!"

October 18th came and Tammy continued to drain fluid from Juliana's side (every day) because the PICU nurses were not trained to do so. My parents came back to see Juliana. The nurses removed one more tube that day. Tammy pained Juliana's toe nails a pretty pick color. Juliana continued to get stronger and really wanted to go home. Juliana told the doctors what she needed more blood so they brought her more blood. Juliana knew her body very well. She asked me to bring more of her fan mail that was accumulating at our house. She was talking about her left arm that was strapped to a board. She said, "I'm locked and loaded….don't mess with me. I'm a tough cookie." I said, "You're AWESOME!" Even in her condition her sense of humor and desire to get better was not diminished one bit.

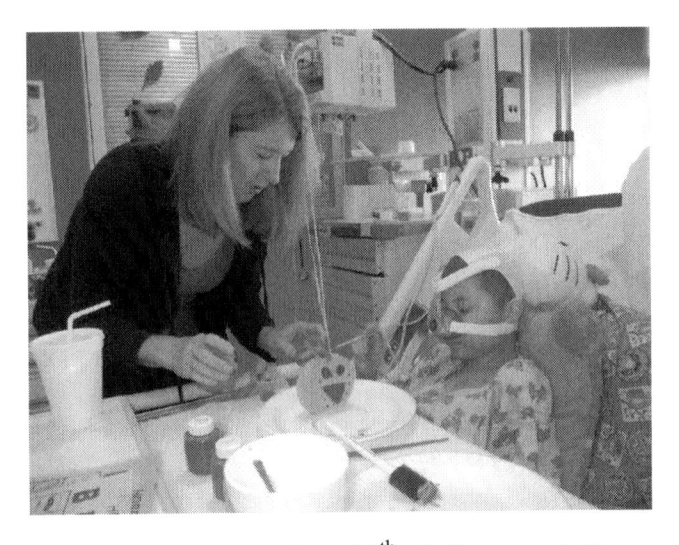

The next day, October 19$^{th}$, Juliana and Tammy were painting. Juliana had no oxygen mask or a nasal canula They left it off for an hour or two. Juliana was such a perfectionist, in everything, as when she made a mistake on painting she had to correct something before she could continue. Juliana just wanted to get better and go home. Juliana and Tammy were making plans for Halloween. Around lunch time it was "Hospital Bingo" time. Juliana was so focused on winning.

That night, as I was getting ready to head back home for the evening, Juliana asked me to stay and watch the television show "Survivor" with her. She, Tim, Kristina and our friend Dale Yingling loved watching that show. I pulled up a chair and sat beside her bed and watched it with her. She, and the other kids, would try to guess who would be voted off the show from week to week and who would win. This would be Juliana's last time to watch "Survivor."

October 20th arrived and guess who came back to see Juliana? Maryland First Lady Yumi Hogan. She brought Juliana a beautiful knit blanket. She sat right beside Juliana and talked. Mrs. Hogan is so nice. Juliana was, fully, conversational and happy, smiling and starting to feel better. Juliana told Mrs. Hogan that her hair (Juliana's hair) was getting thicker than my hair. Tammy told her that Juliana was scheduled to start new cancer treatment on October 26, 2016. Mrs. Hogan was telling Juliana that she was so strong and that so many people are praying for her to get better.

Juliana was showing Mrs. Hogan the pictures she drew the prior day. Mrs. Hogan said, "Everybody knows Juliana….she's so famous…everybody knows Juliana." Juliana smiled so big. Juliana said, "Almost everywhere we go we know someone or they recognize us. (They say) Are you Juliana?" Juliana told Mrs. Hogan that after we would do a LIVE Facebook post thousands of people would see it. It amazed Juliana how many people cared and love her so much.

I brought Juliana's hair brush, from home, for her a day or two earlier because her hair was starting to come in again. Just after lunch, she picked up her brush and started brushing her hair. She said, with a silliness in her voice, "Hello...the hair....the brush...it's getting so long so I have to brush it every morning so it doesn't look a mess. I want to look gooood for Maddie tomorrow."

Later in the day Tammy and Juliana played a game of scrabble and Juliana played on her IPAD. A couple of hours later Juliana asked me to go downstairs to get some cheesecake for her and Tammy. Juliana LOVED it. She wanted to celebrate her getting out of the hospital the next day. She talked about loving apple cider. She said it was "so good."

Tammy summarized the last few days – "October 15th to 20th – Julie remained in the PICU and gradually was able to use less pressure and oxygen until she was able to be on regular oxygen (which means she was finally able to eat) in the daytime and then she used CPAP at night. She continued to improve each day and plans were made to go home on oxygen and CPAP with oxygen and night plus a morphine PCA (pain pump).

On the 20th, she had a visit from Maryland's first lady, Yumi Hogan and was sitting talking to her. She asked for a grilled chicken salad from Subway for dinner and ate almost all of it then split a piece of cheesecake with me for dessert. She then stayed up late talking to her nurse that night.

During that day Dr. Loeb stopped by to see Juliana. He didn't enter her PICU room. Juliana was so excited to go home. We confirmed, with Dr. Loeb, that Juliana was scheduled to start new cancer treatment on October 26, 2016. His exact words were "That's the plan."

Later that night the pain team gave Juliana a BIG dose of pain medication. This made her so groggy that she could barely speak and keep her eyes open.

October 21st came and Miss Frostburg (Maryland) Victoria Graham, and her father, came by for a visit with Juliana. Victoria has had some medical challenges, herself, and wanted to try to cheer Juliana up.

Tammy writes, "October 21st – Juliana was very groggy when she woke up that morning (we were told because they had increased her dose of oral morphine), but plans to go home continued. We had to wait for the CPAP machine to be delivered so she was finally discharged around 4pm. I had to strap Juliana into her wheelchair because she was not strong enough to sit up, but we managed to get her home where she wanted to be."

The hospital still said Juliana was stable to go home. As she sat, in the wheelchair, outside her PICU room read to go home she could hardly speak. How could she be alert the day before, eating cheesecake with Tammy and talking about playing with Maddie to this….not even able to complete a sentence!??!!? A nurse escorted us to the car. This has NEVER happened all the time Juliana went to Johns Hopkins Hospital. Why was Juliana incoherent and, yet, the hospital and doctors said she was stable to go home? WHY!?!?!

On the ride home Juliana wasn't speaking and drifting in and out of consciousness. The nurses told us it was a result of the pain medication so Tammy and I believed them. When we got home, I carried Juliana from the car, to the sofa. I laid Juliana on the sofa and Maddie jumped on her lap being so excited to see Juliana after two weeks. Juliana tried to get excited about seeing Maddie but was in and out of consciousness. Again, we were told it was the pain medication. Juliana was NOT like this on October 20, 2016…not at all…she talked and talked and talked.

How…why…did Juliana go from excited and eager to go home on October 20, 2016 to, after they hospital hit her with heavy pain meds, to not being able to communicate?!?!?! Tammy called the nurse, after Juliana, did not improve from getting the pain meds and the nurse said the meds were still effecting her.

A little while after we got home I carried Juliana upstairs, to our bedroom, and placed her on a blow-up bed so Tammy and I could be close to her in order to help as much as we knew how to help. Maddie jumped up on the bed with Juliana and stayed there most of the day and evening.

Tammy called, many times, Gilcrest Kids HospiceCare (https://www.gilchristcares.org/services/hospice/do-i-need-hospice/gilchrist-kids/) who was set up to HELP US AT HOME while the cancer was "aggressively treated." The nurse never showed up even after us begging Gilcrest Kids to come help us because Juliana was failing fast and was too sick, for us, to move her. NO ONE SHOWED UP! This went on for two days.

October 23, 2016 and we continued to call for help, from Gilcrest Hospice, and no one came to help. Juliana was fading fast. That night, I knelt down, beside Juliana who was unconscious and BEGGED GOD, just like I had done so many times in the past, to help Juliana get better. I sobbed and sobbed asking God to, PLEASE HEAL JULIANA!!!!!

Our families came to visit Juliana that day as well including my brother, Chris, and his family who live in Florida.

October 24, 2016 I woke up knowing something was wrong. I looked to my right, two feet from where I was laying, and Juliana was gone. We had just been speaking to her less than two hours earlier. Our amazing fourteen year old Juliana was dead. How can this, possibly, happen?!? THOUSANDS of people were saying prayers for Juliana to get better. Our baby girl was gone…forever.

I texted Dr. Loeb, to tell him Juliana passed way, and I received no response, no call, no email, no nothing. Tammy called the Gilcrest Hospice people and told them Juliana had passed. The nurse, who was supposed to be helping us (at our house that weekend) said, "Are you sure?"

Are you f'ing kidding me?!?!?!?! When the nurse, finally, arrived at our house to confirm Juliana's death she had the balls to ask me if Johns Hopkins Hospital can have her body to get the tumors out and study them. I, almost, lost my mind.

Again, On October 20, 2016 Juliana was happy, talking and making jokes. Later that evening, she was given a high dose of pain meds. She never regained, full, consciousness. Juliana was released from PICU (due to an infection) on October 21, 2016. She was so incoherent Tammy had to strap her into the wheel chair so she wouldn't fall out. According to the Johns Hopkins Hospital doctor, Juliana was "stable" to leave the hospital and come back on October 26, 2016 for new cancer treatment. How can this be????

We were told by a doctor at Johns Hopkins Hospital, months earlier, that the teenager who died after getting a bone marrow transplant (who we met) didn't have the same disease as Juliana. The exact words were it was "apples and oranges" compared to what Juliana was fighting. We found out she did have the exact same disease. Johns Hopkins Hospital allowed Juliana to hemorrhage for WEEKS after transplant because a specific medication was burning holes into her stomach. Johns Hopkins Hospital had been seeing Juliana, every day, the first week in October 2016 and didn't catch the MSSA bacteria until October 7, 2016 and it was so bad Juliana had to have a breathing tube put in and stayed in PICU for two weeks! Johns Hopkins Hospital said Juliana was scheduled for new cancer treatment on October 26, 2016 and she was stable to go home on October 21, 2016.

NOW, Johns Hopkins Hospital wants our Juliana and cut her open...NO...NOT HAPPENING!!! I told the nurse she could leave our house.

Juliana was with us, for only, 12 years. 1 month. 29 days.

NOTES FROM JOHNS HOPKINS HOSPITAL RECORDS – "Admitted to PICU with respiratory failure on 10/7. Blood culture from clinic same day grew MSSA."

October 7, 2016 Dr. Kristen Nelson did CPR on Juliana after breathing tube was placed in Juliana.

October 20, 2016 – Attending physician – Changed pain meds to M/S cotin to 30 mg BID.

October 21, 2016 Dr. Chen said Juliana was okay/stable.

Dr. Schuette said, in a October 21, 2016 note, "Critically ill – requiring frequent evals. To treat respiratory failure.

October 21, 2016 – Pain team said – seems overly sedated with increased M/S Cotin – continue PCA and continue M/S Cotin.

Dr. Nathaniel Bohn, CRNP and Jennifer Schette, MD. discharged Juliana, from PICU, on October 21, 2016. He prescribed, Juliana 15 mg morphine (MS Cotin) 12 hour tablet.

https://www.hopkinsmedicine.org/kimmel_cancer_center/centers/pediatric_oncology/becoming_our_patient/programs/sarcoma_program.html

"Other hospitals offer bits and pieces of specialty care, but we bring every expert to the table," says sarcoma (former) program director David Loeb, M.D., Ph.D.

Chapter 19

It is impossible to describe (unless your child has died) what it's like to go to a grave yard and funeral home to make funeral arrangements for your child. We contacted Eline Funeral Home in Reisterstown Maryland, the morning of Juliana's death, to take care of the arrangements for us.

A couple days later we had the first of four viewings for Juliana. People from all over the region came to see Juliana. Her Oncologists from Sinai Hospital, in Baltimore Maryland came to pay their respects to Juliana. They are Dr. Jason Fixler, Dr. Joseph Wiley and Dr. Yoram Unguru. Many of Juliana's nurses, from Sinai Hospital, came to as well.

Mary Jo Holuba, who worked in the Johns Hopkins Oncology Clinic, came by as well. Mary Jo was listened to Tammy's concerns that acted on them immediately whereas other, at that hospital, ignored Tammy's concerns.

One evening, during the viewing, I was standing by Juliana's casket and Dr. David Loeb walked up to me along with his girlfriend. When I saw him I began to sob. He said, "It was the cancer." How can this be when we were told that Juliana was "stable" on October 21, 2016 and had an appointment, to come back to Johns Hopkins Hospital, on October 26, 2016 to start new cancer treatment?

On October 28, 2016 we had Juliana's funeral. I was told by several close friends that it would be too much for me to conduct the funeral. I felt, and still do, that no one else (besides Tammy and me) could express our feelings better than us.

The entire room, at the funeral home, was full plus people in standing in the back. There was another room, to the side, of where I was speaking that was half full of people. I started by sharing how we met Juliana (for context):

I said (in part), "Today, as Juliana's Dad I would like to share some thoughts that only a Dad could attempt to express on this horrible day.

Shortly after we adopted our fourth child, Timothy, we believed that we were done adopting. I had a hunch to hold a seminar to help other people adopt internationally like my wife, Tammy and I did, four times.

I advertised the seminar a lot. Our adoption attorney, Ron Stoddart from Nightlight Christian Adoptions flew in from California to help with the large crowd that I expected. Eight people showed up.

After the seminar Tammy and I were up in the Ron Stoddard's hotel room going through photos of children who needed to be adopted. We were NOT going to adopt again. We were just looking through the photo album.

We turned the page and this little girl, with crossed eyes, jumped off the page at my wife and I. Our son, Timothy, also had crossed eyes when we adopted him. Why would a photo of this little girl impact us in such a strange way when we were NOT adopting again.

All of a sudden my tears started to flow down my face. Tammy and I knew that little girl, who name was Irina, was to be our daughter.

Months later we flew to Minsk Belarus and adopted Irina who we renamed Juliana Irina. While there we found out she had a bio sister named Svetlana. You can read between the lines. With the amazing help of friends we flew back months later and brought Svetlana home to America who is now known as Kristina Svetlana.

Juliana was ALWAYS spunky, determined, a perfectionist in everything she did. Everything in Juliana's life was perfect until 2007 when we found out she had cancer in her right arm and metastasis to right axillary lymph nodes.

She suffered and struggled for months. She, almost, always had a smile on her face. She was only five years old.

She beat cancer until March 2011 when the cancer returned in her right leg and more lymph nodes. She beat cancer a 2nd time.

In June 2012 we found out that Juliana had cancer a 3rd time. This time it was in her chest . The tumor was compressing the vena cava and pressing on the aorta. She, also, had disease in her lymph nodes. We were told Juliana had no hope of survival.

One day, as we believed she was going to die (in 2012) I asked if she had three wishes what would they be. It was a little pause and she said:

Not to have cancer

A BILLION dollars…longer pause…

A Puppy.

With raising six kids you can imagine that we did not want another mouth to feed. Long story short…Juliana got her puppy and Maddie (her dog) is with us today.

She beat cancer, again, in RECORD TIME for the 3rd time. I remember when her oncologist called me and told me her scans were clear after only a few months of treatment.

In March 2014 the cancer returned in Juliana's right eye orbit. She beat cancer again for the for the 4th time.

All during these battles with cancer Juliana fought back with all she had in her little body.

On July 2015 the cancer returned for the 5th time. This time it was in more lymph nodes and in her left anterior upper chest. We were TERRIFIED again. She beat cancer for the 5th time.

In July 2015 we were told that Juliana might qualify for a bone marrow transplant. As adoptive parents there was no way we would be a match. I had to find Juliana and Kristina's birth mother (Kristina was not a match after getting tested). Within a couple of months the government of Belarus and our State Department worked together to help us locate Juliana's birth mother.

The birth mother, Irina (same name as Juliana's name in Belarus) agreed to be a bone marrow donor. It took months to finalize paperwork and fly Irina to America.

On December 30, 2015 the cancer attacked our baby girl again in the back but her 11th rib. Guess what? She beat cancer for the 6th time.

Juliana was scheduled to get her bone marrow transplant in February 2016. Irina, the birth mother, had her plane tickets, travel visa and luggage and was ready to fly to America.

On February 10, 2016, a few days before Irina was to fly to America we found out that the cancer was back for a 7th time which would eliminate Juliana's chance of getting the bone marrow transplant. The cancer was near her spine (T-9, T-10, and T-11)

Due to the extreme circumstance of finding Irina Johns Hopkins Hospital agreed to freeze some of Irina's bone marrow and when Juliana was cancer free again they would do the transplant.

On April 30, 2016 Juliana received a bone marrow transplant that SHE and WE hoped would CURE her of cancer FOREVER.

The effects of the transplant was brutal!

On September 27, 2016 the cancer returned for the 8th time. Juliana and I sobbed in each other's arms. The cancer was in the plura around her right lung, diaphragm and a small tumor in the left lung. It was pretty bad but we had hope because of some newer treatment options.

In October 2016 got an infection in her lungs, that she caught, which put her in Intensive Care for two weeks. The day before she was to leave and go home she was happy, eating salad and could not wait to see her dog. A few days later she was dead.

All during these battles (wars) with cancer Juliana tried to live as normal life as possible. She loved to swim, bake (she wanted to be a chef when she grew up), LOVED to fish because of the

CHALLENGE OF IT and play with her dog Maddie.

A few years ago "Give Kids the World" granted us a trip to Florida. One evening Juliana and our son Tim were fishing. Of course, I had my cameras in hand. Tim, an amazingly patient big brother, was helping Juliana fish. I said to Juliana that it was getting late and you could try to catch some fish the next day.

She turned her head, to the left, where I was standing and said, "I'm not a giver-upper." Moments later she caught a fish with Tim's help.

"I'm not a giver-upper." I'd like to "park" right there for a few minutes.

Juliana's will power, the prayers of many thousands of people, partnered with my amazing wife Tammy, the two were unstoppable. Tammy was with Juliana for EVERY needle, every scan, every bout of vomiting and diarrhea…months and months stuck in the hospital.

When Juliana was 5 and fighting cancer the first time she cried because Tammy was going go home for a few hours and come back later--instead of taking a break, Tammy stooped down, gave her a hug and made a promise to her that Tammy would never leave her in the hospital--a promise Tammy kept until the end.

They were a TEAM. Tammy told me that she and Juliana were "in it together."

There were so many times, when Juliana would be too sick to get out of bed or off the sofa so I would get close to her ear and sing:

"You are my sunshine…my little sunshine..you make me happy when skies are gray."

I can't count how many times I sang that to her including when she lay lifeless in our home.

Juliana, truly, gave me courage. Her very short life showed me what love and excellence and tenacity and patience looks like…she showed me that you can smile WHILE YOU'RE STRUGGLING!

Obviously, I am NO WHERE CLOSE to mastering that skill.

Juliana never understood her, global, influence, I don't think until her last days. One day, while she was in Intensive Care, we did a LIVE Video for her fans on Angels for Juliana. She was

AMAZED that over 50,000 people watched her sharing what was happening in her day.

One day, a few years back, I asked her why she didn't complain about fighting cancer so many times. She said, "whining is for babies." WOW! "whining is for babies." She, verbally, yanked me by my collar and challenged me (without even knowing she was challenging me) to not whine.

Juliana's siblings Rebecca, Matthew, Lindsay, Timothy and Kristina would spend countless days at the hospital while Juliana was getting treatment. They had to set their own lives aside for their little sister for several years. Tammy and I were trying our best to save Juliana's life AND parent 5 other kids. It was SO difficult!

Juliana was on a breathing tube for several days, in October 2016, and we could not hear her voice. She was trying so hard to communicate. One day, I read her lips as she told her mom…."I want to go home."

Her voice…I missed it so much. I was standing outside her PICU room, as Tammy held her hand and the hospital staff removed her breathing tube…I heard Juliana's voice again…the most precious sound that a Dad can describe..the sound of his child's voice.

On October 16, 2016 she told me, "I wish this would go away." She was talking about being sick again and fighting cancer for the 8th time. She was SO frustrated!

On October 17, 2016 I told Juliana "You're an amazing daughter." She responded, "you're an amazing Daddy."

That week she told someone else that Tammy and I were "Awesome." Juliana IS the awesome one. We were honored to be her parents.

On October 18, 2016, six days, before Juliana took her last breath I was sitting on her hospital bed in PICU chatting I asked her something like, "how are you handling all this?" She said, "Stay positive…don't think about the negative. When you think about the negative it just makes things worse."

"Stay positive…don't think about the negative. When you think about the negative it just makes things worse."

Back on August 31, 2016 Juliana told me, "If you think about the bummers it just bums you out more."

"If you think about the bummers it just bums you out more."

Today I am trying, DESPERTATELY, to follow Juliana's advice. She has touched the world in a way I would have never expected when I started sharing her story with the hopes that the tens of thousands of prayers would cure her from cancer.

Juliana was not afraid. Juliana should NOT have died. The Thursday, before her death, she was SO excited about going home the next day. She was eating salad and talking about wanting to see Maddie again. Juliana should not have died.

Juliana KNEW she was going to beat cancer for the 8th time.

I wrote, on October 8, 2016:

Pediatric cancer is:

- EVIL

- A Torturer

- A murderer

- Steals parent's attention from siblings of sick child.

- Thief of hopes and dreams of children with cancer.

- Destroyer of Joy

- A monster that turns smiles into tears and courage into fear.

- A series of diseases determined to kill.

- It separates husbands from wives and wives from husbands.

- It ASSASSINATES future inventors, musicians, artists, chefs, doctors, moms, dads, accountants etc.

- It leaves parents with a gaping HOLE in their heart...forever!

The people on this planet must demand cures be found. We are losing our future to diseases that CAN be cured!

NO CHILD SHOULD DIE of ANYTHING!

Reader's Digest, December, 1990.

CBS News anchor Dan Rather admits he was always fascinated by the sport of boxing, even though he was never good at it. "In boxing you're on your own; there's no place to hide," he says. "At the end of the match only one boxer has his hand up. That's it. He has no one to credit or to blame except himself." Rather, who boxed in high school, says his coach's greatest goal was to teach his boxers that they absolutely, positively, without question, had to be "get up" fighters. "If you're in a ring just once in your life--completely on your own--and you get knocked down but you get back up again, it's an never-to-be-forgotten experience. Your sense of achievement is distinct and unique. And sometimes the only thing making you get up is someone in your corner yelling…GET UP GET UP GET UP!"

Tammy and I surrounded Juliana with the "get up" mindset.

Raye Rhodes sent this to me:

"This is something my rabbi shared with me that may help be of comfort to you… On a tombstone there are three things besides the person's name… The day they were born, the day they died, and the dash in the middle. While we celebrate birthdays and recognize death through funerals, the real important part is neither of the dates, but the dash in the middle... It's celebrating each of those days in between, getting the most possible out of whatever dates we are afforded... It is THAT which identifies our life.

It may seem sad Julie is gone, and it is, but the important thing to remember is that JULIE understood exactly how important that "dash" truly was. You can tell from your own videos that she DID celebrate every day the best way she could. She DID understand the importance of living a full life... There is plenty she never got to do, but there is plenty MORE she did that many who have many more "days" did not get to do...

Many who did NOT understand the real thing to celebrate was all the days making up that dash. When you look at it... Julie's dash is much longer and larger than most people's... Not because there were more days, but because they were FULLER days.

Fuller because that's how Julie chose to see them. Nothing can "make her come back" but it's interesting... The fuller we leave our dash, it makes it ever more clear we are not "done" at the last date.

Our dash interacts with other dashes... Hers with yours, mine, and anyone else on Angels for Juliana. No... Her dash is still moving forward and will be for a VERY long time. Now it's our job to continue what Julie showed us all... That it's not about our day of birth or our day of death, but the days between it.

Juliana understood what my rabbi was saying... Now it's up to us to recall this lesson and keep going like Julie would have wanted... Because we are still growing our dash... And through us, she is still growing hers...

Wish your family the best."

Thank you:

July 2015 - Giant Food and Children's Cancer Foundation arranged for us to meet and have lunch with Chef Robert Irvine. Thank you Chef Robert Irvine for encouraging her so many times through FACE TIME CHATS.

First Lady Yumi Hogan of Maryland made several visits to see Juliana in the last year or two including two while Juliana was in INTENSVIE CARE...THANK YOU!

Friends and Family who visited with Juliana in the hospital.

Friends, like Pam, Derrick, Melissa and Kelly who just came and sat with Tammy in the hospital. HUGE THANK YOU!

My parents and Tammy's mom who did all they could to help our family.

Bonnie Cohen and family to helping us with Tim, Kristina and Maddie.

The Bromley family for a HUGE gift that make dramatic difference in our family.

I am sure I will leave many others out...

Juliana was happy. She did not allow cancer to steal her joy. She was sad and cried, at times, but always looked forward to getting back home from the hospital.

Juliana loved her family...very much...including her dog Maddie.

I have never watched a full episode of Survivor but last week Juliana asked me to stay at the hospital with her and watch Survivor. I sat beside her bed, watching her and the show…and wish WISH we could do it again.

Juliana :

The game Candy crush

The game Hay day

Her dog Maddie

She has a Get it done attitude

She could spot fake people

She Hated hospitals

She Never remembered being healthy

She loves Swimming

Her bond with Tammy is incredible

Julie's laugh…I miss it SO MUCH!

She would be annoyed when something was half done.

So…what can we all learn from Juliana's life???? I will leave out HOURS of details and memories.

Her will power would get her to go home from a long Hospital stay. Pushed herself to walk to the bathroom to prove to the doctor.

Loved to cook and bake with her mom.

Me watching her vomit from chemo as I cried seeing her suffer. She'd just pat my hand. She was consoling ME.

She missed so many years of being a kid because of cancer. She did NOT EVER REMEMBER BEING HEALTHY.

Always determined to keep up on her school work.

Other kids. Learn from Juliana's example. Make no excuses. Be kind. Be strong. Never give up. Always always do what's right.

Some wonder why so many photos and videos of Juliana. I never knew when it was going to be the last picture or video clip I would ever have of Juliana.

I will never be able to walk you down the aisle and give you away to the luckiest man on the planet. I will never be able to hold your babies.

Am I sad!? Beyond sad.

Am I enraged!? Beyond enraged.

Thank all the organizations (name them) who helped us over the years.

http://believeintomorrow.org/

http://caseycares.org/

http://coolkidscampaign.org/

http://www.childrensroadstorecovery.org/

http://wish.org/ Make a Wish – Juliana's pool

http://www.gktw.org/ - Give Kids the World – Disney World Trip

http://www.robertirvinefoundation.org/

stronghopefoundation

Dr Fixler Dr. Unguru and Dr. Wiley.

Nurses and Sinai and Hopkins.

Thank Juliana's family and fans 220 countries.

Emily – Juliana's hospital buddy.

Aubrix who just came to sit on the sofa with Juliana for hours because Juliana was too weak to run and play.

Tammy for being Juliana's full time nurse.

Thank Irina for coming to America to try to save Juliana. Thank the crowd."

Tammy spoke, next at Juliana's funeral and said, "I remember when we found out Julie had cancer back in February 2007 asking "Why God?" But I knew an orphan in Belarus would never have received treatment for a rare cancer at all—she would have died at age five--alone--in a sterile hospital with no one to hold her and love her. God gave her to us to love and to take care of, to get her treatment and to give her time to impact the world around her. Juliana accomplished more in her short 14 years than many people do in eighty years. She was an awesome daughter, sister and friend to us. She helped raise awareness and funding for cancer research. She helped encourage thousands of people with her positive attitude and incredible courage. She taught us to never lose hope and to never give up.

I told her last week as she was lying in PICU that I was so glad I was her Mom. Juliana and I were so very close--she brought an incredible amount of joy and love to my life and I'm going to miss her every single day for the rest of my life.

I Only Wanted You by Vicky Holder

They say memories are golden, well, maybe that is true.

I never wanted memories, I only wanted you.

A million times I cried.

If love alone could have saved you, you never would have died.

In life I loved you dearly, in death I love you still.

In my heart you hold a place no one else could fill.

If tears could build a stairway and heartache make a lane.

I'd walk the path to Heaven and bring you back again.

Our family chain is broken, and nothing seems the same.

But as God calls us back one by one, the chain will link again."

A little while later we drove to the cemetery. My father conducted the service at the cemetery. I couldn't do it. There are no words to describe what it's like seeing your daughter, in a casket, being lowered into the ground.

## Chapter 20

We waited and waited for Johns Hopkins Hospital to contact us because Juliana was scheduled to start new cancer treatment on October 26, 2016. We heard nothing from them. I emailed them in early November 2016 asking for Juliana's medical records. On November 16, 2016 at 10:26 AM Ms. Markia Dallas emailed me back and said my request was forwarded to Linda Carson in Medical Records. I, also, asked to have a meeting with the doctors that were treating Juliana. I was told to submit my questions before they agree to a meeting.

We asked to speak to the nurses who treated and discharged Juliana her last couple days in PICU (Mariah Miller – October 20 , Sara Penna – October 20, Katherine Conley – October 21) Page 1490 of medical records – Level of Consciousness – 11am – Lethargic 12pm Alert – 2pm Lethargic). Johns Hopkins Hospital denied us the opportunity to meet with Juliana's nurses.

Juliana had an appointment scheduled, on October 26, 2016 at 11:30am with Dr. David Loeb in the Pediatric Oncology Clinic to begin new cancer treatment.

## Some of Juliana Carver's Quotes

"I'm Not a Giver-Upper." (October 4, 2013)

"Whining is for Babies." (October 2013)

"Hi. I'm Juliana Carver and I've been through some stuff. I really don't know some people out there…if you're having a good time you can get through it. If I can get through it then you can and I know you can." (August 30, 2012)

"I know some of you are going through some struggles and I've been going through some struggles for a few years now. I just want to tell you that you can do it no matter what." (July 1, 2014)

"You gotta find another way around your problem" (June 2015)

"Don't complain about something you can fix. If you can fit it then fix it." (July 2015)

"You gotta do what you gotta do to make it work." (July 2015)

"You should never give up because you can fight it no matter what…it's a crazy journey…expect the unexpected." (December 3, 2015)

"I'm locked and loaded....don't mess with me. I'm a tough cookie." (October 18, 2016)

"Stay positive. Don't think about the negative. When you think about the negative it just makes things worse." (October 2016)

**Juliana's Medical History in Detail up to her Bone Marrow Transplant in 2016.**
Chronology:
12/4/01    Born in Minsk, Belarus (weighed 2220 grams, height 47 cm)
4/29/01    Placed in Baby House #1 (from hospital)
8/26/03    Adopted at the age of 20 months – Per orphanage no history of any    major illnesses or injuries.
9/03    Diagnosed with Strabismus
12/03    Surgery to correct Strabismus
2/07    Diagnosed with Alveolar Rhabdomyosarcoma-Stage 3, Group 3 (with 2q35 (PAX3); 13q14(FOX01) translocation). Tumor    was in right forearm with metastasis to right axillary lymph nodes.
2/07 to 1/08    Received 14 rounds of chemotherapy which included 7 rounds of Vincristine, Dactinomycin and Cyclophosphamide alternating with 7 rounds of Vincristine and Irinotecan. She was treated on a    phase III COG clinical trial (ARST0531).
4/07 to 5/07    Received 28 radiation therapy treatments to right forearm and right axilla. (total dose of 5040 cGy)
3/11    First Rhabdomyosarcoma Relapse to right thigh with metastasis to    right inguinal lymph    nodes.

3/11 to 1/12   Received 12 rounds of chemotherapy which included
    Cyclophosphamide, Vinorelbine and Temsirolimus. She was
    treated on a phase II COG clinical trial (ARST0921).
1/12 to 2/12   Received 25 radiation therapy treatments to right thigh and right
    inguinal lymph nodes. (total dose of 4140 cGy)
6/12    Second Rhabdomyosarcoma Relapse to mediastinum and
    retroperitoneal lymph nodes.
6/12 to 5/13   Received 12 rounds of Ifosfamide, Carboplatin and Etoposide.
6/13 to 8/13   Received 50 radiation therapy treatments—25 to retroperitoneal
    nodes followed by 25 to mediastimun nodes. (45 Gy to each area in 25 fractions)
7/13 to 9/13   Began maintenance chemotherapy while still getting chest
    radiation—daily oral Cyclosphosphamide.
9/13 to 11/13  Continued daily oral chemotherapy and added IV Vinorelbine (she
    had two treatments in Sept. and one in October—both were
    stopped due to neutropenia)
11/13 to 1/14  Continued daily oral Cyclophosphamide and began bi-weekly
    Vinorelbine at a reduced strength (60%).

1/14 to 3/14   Continued daily oral Cyclophosphamide and bi-weekly Vinorelbine
    at a 75% strength.
3/14   Third Rhabdomyosarcoma Relapse to right orbit
3/14   Near complete surgical resection of right orbital tumor
4/14   Received one round of chemotherapy—Cyclophosphamide,
    Vinorelbine and Temsirolimus.
4/14 to 6/14   Received 25 radiation therapy treatments (IMRT) to right orbit.
4/14 to 5/14   Continued to receive weekly IV Temsirolimus while getting radiation
    therapy.
5/20/14 to 6/10/14   Gave oral cyclophosphamide.
6/17/14 to 7/1/14   Gave oral etoposide and oral cyclophosphamide
7/2/14   Admitted for cellulitis of right upper arm. Stopped all oral
    chemo.
7/8/14 to 9/2/14   Gave every other day oral etoposide.
7/24/14   Began sub-Q mistletoe (three days/week)
9/3/14 to 11/10/14   Daily oral cyclophosphamide for one week followed by every
    other day oral etoposide for the next week then repeat

11/11/14 to 11/25/14 Received weekly IV temsirolimus along with daily oral cyclophosphamide

11/25/14 to 3/10/15  Daily oral cyclophosphamide for one week followed by every other day oral etoposide for the next week then repeat

3/11/15 to 4/1/15  Received weekly IV temsirolimus along with daily oral cyclophosphamide for one week followed by every other day oral etoposide for the next week then repeat

4/1/15 to 7/12/15  Daily oral cyclophosphamide for one week followed by every other day oral etoposide for the next week then repeat

7/12/15  Fourth Rhabdomyosarcoma Relapse to mediastinum and retroperitoneum lymph nodes, right cardiophrenic angle and left anterior upper chest

7/20/15 to 10/30/15  Chemotherapy – Vincristine, Irinotecan and Temozolomide – Received 5 rounds before getting severe stomach pain that required hospitalization for pain management, fluids and TPN

11/30/15 to 1/15/16  Chemotherapy – Topotecan and Cyclophosphamide

12/30/15  Fifth Rhabdomyosarcoma Relapse to right, rear 11th rib

1/22/16 to 2/5/16      Received 11 radiation therapy treatments (electrons) to
         right, rear 11th rib tumor
2/10/16                 Sixth Rhabdomyosarcoma Relapse—new 3cm tumor near
         T9, T10 and T11
2/16/16 to 3/18/16    Chemotherapy – Vincristine, Irinotecan and
         Temozolomide—2 rounds
2/22/16 to present    Receiving TPN
3/29/16               Diagnosed with H. Pylori

**Surgeries**:
12/03           Strabismus correction
2/07            Biopsy of right forearm and right axilla; bone marrow biopsy
2/07            Port placed
2/08            Lung Biopsy
2/08            Port removed
3/11            Biopsy of right thigh and bone marrow
3/11            Port placed
3/12            Port removed
6/12            Hickman placed; bone marrow biopsy
6/13            Hickman removed and port placed
3/14            Biopsy and debulking of tumor in right orbit
9/14            Port replaced (due to fracture in the catheter) and right eyelid lift
8/15            Bone marrow biopsy

1/16          Biopsy of right 11th rib
2/16          Bone marrow biopsy
3/16          Endoscopy w/biopsies
4/16          Bone marrow biopsy


**Blood/Platelet Transfusions**:
4/07 to 1/08      5 packed red blood cell transfusions
5/11 to 11/11      5 packed red blood cell transfusions
6/12 to 11/13      36 packed red blood cell blood transfusions and 35 platelet transfusions
3/14 to 7/15      7 packed red blood cell transfusions and 4 platelet transfusions
8/15 to present 13 packed red blood cell transfusion and 15 platelet transfusions

Hospital Admissions:
3/12 to 3/13/07     Chemotherapy
10/2 to 10/6/07     Neutropenic Fever
2/8 to 2/9/08       Lung Biopsy
4/4 to 4/5/11        Chemotherapy
4/25 to 4/26/11     Chemotherapy
5/16 to 5/17/11     Chemotherapy
6/6 to 6/7/11        Chemotherapy
6/27 to 6/28/11     Chemotherapy

7/18 to 7/19/11          Chemotherapy
8/8 to 8/9/11          Chemotherapy
8/29 to 8/30/11          Chemotherapy
9/19 to 9/20/11          Chemotherapy
10/10 to 10/11/11          Chemotherapy
11/1 to 11/2/11          Chemotherapy
11/21 to 11/22/11          Chemotherapy
6/4 to 6/13/12 Blood thinners, Scans, Hickman placed, Chemotherapy
6/19 to 6/25/12          Neutropenic Fever
7/2 to 7/6/12          Chemotherapy
7/23 to 7/27/12          Chemotherapy
8/13 to 8/17/12          Chemotherapy
9/10 to 9/14/12          Chemotherapy
10/8 to 10/12/12          Chemotherapy
11/5 to 11/9/12          Chemotherapy
12/3 to 12/7/12          Chemotherapy
1/7 to 1/11/13 Chemotherapy
2/18 to 2/22/13          Chemotherapy
4/1 to 4/5/13          Chemotherapy
4/16 to 4/18/13          Neutropenic Fever
5/6 to 5/10/13 Chemotherapy
3/17 to 3/19/14          Scans, biopsy and debulking of tumor in right eye orbit
7/2 to 7/3/14          Cellulitis (right upper arm)
7/12 to 7/13/15          Began steroids and pain management—4th relapse
7/27 to 8/4/15 Neutropenic Fever & Diarrhea
11/5 to 11/11/15          Vomiting/Stomah pain/Unable to eat (due to irinotecan)

2/19 to 2/26/16    Chemotherapy/Stomach pain/Unable to eat (due to
   irinotecan)/Went home on TPN


**Scans**:
2/07      CT & MRI of right arm, full body PET/CT, bone scan
6/07      CT & MRI of right arm, full body PET/CT
10/07     CT & MRI of right arm, full body PET/CT
2/08      MRI of right arm, full body PET/CT, bone scan
5/08      full body PET/CT, CT of right arm and chest
8/08      CT of right arm and chest
11/08     full body PET/CT, CT of right arm and chest
2/09      CT of right arm and chest
6/09      CT of right arm and chest
9/09      MRI of right arm and chest CT
1/10      MRI of right arm and chest CT
5/10      MRI of right arm and chest CT
9/10      MRI of right arm and chest CT
1/11      MRI of right arm and chest x-ray
3/11      MRI of right leg, full body PET/CT, CT of brain, chest, abdomen, pelvis and right leg, bone scan

5/11              MRI of right thigh, full body PET/CT
6/11              MRI of right thigh, full body PET/CT
8/11              MRI of right thigh, full body PET/CT
10/11             MRI of right thigh, full body PET/CT
12/11             MRI of right thigh and pelvis, CT of pelvis, full body PET/CT
3/12              MRI of right thigh and right forearm, chest x-ray
6/12              MRI of right thigh and pelvis, chest x-ray, CT of chest, abdomen, pelvis, full body PET/CT scan, bone scan
7/12              full body PET/CT
11/12             CT of chest and abdomen
1/13              MRI of left leg
6/13              full body PET/CT
12/13             CT of chest and abdomen
3/17/14           MRI of right eye orbit
3/20/14           full body PET/CT
6/27/14           Abdominal Ultrasound
6/28/14           Chest x-ray
9/22/14           Chest x-ray
6/25/15           MRI of right hip
7/12/15           MRI of spine
7/17/15           full body PET/CT
9/3/15            full body PET/CT
9/3/15            CT of chest, abdomen and pelvis
12/30/15          PET/CT (head to knees)

2/10/16      PET/CT (head to knees)
3/15/16      Abdominal Ultrasound
3/29/16      PET/CT (head to knees)
(The rest of the records, after April 1, 2016, I have chosen to not include on this list as I have discussed it in the book)

Juliana's Grave Marker


Please follow Juliana's memory on Facebook's

"Angels for Juliana" and

https://www.youtube.com/user/johnwcarver

Thank you,

John W. Carver, III

Juliana's Dad

john@johnwcarver.com

Printed in Great Britain
by Amazon